D0607499

GREAT ART AND ARTISTS OF THE WORLD

ORIGINS OF WESTERN ART

ITALIAN ART TO 1850

FLEMISH AND DUTCH ART

GERMAN AND SPANISH ART TO 1900

FRENCH ART FROM 1350 TO 1850

BRITISH AND NORTH AMERICAN ART TO 1900

IMPRESSIONISTS AND POST-IMPRESSIONISTS

MODERN ART

CHINESE AND JAPANESE ART

HOW TO LOOK AT ART

The most important aspect of any work of art is its impact on the viewer. How can the viewer judge whether a piece of art is good or bad; how can he assess its aesthetic value?

HOW TO LOOK AT ART answers these questions by examining first some of the positive qualities to be seen in a work of art, such as subject matter, technique, intention of the artist, and feeling and emotion.

An excellent guide to a more thorough understanding of art, this volume contains numerous black and white illustrations as well as more than eighty in full color. A glossary and extensive index is also included.

See back jacket flap for list of other volumes in this series.

HOW TO LOOK AT ART

EDITORIAL COMMITTEE

Sir Herbert Read
Visiting Lecturer at Wesleyan University, Middletown, Conn.; Former Professor of Poetry, Harvard University; Former Lecturer in Fine Arts, Washington University; President of the Society for Education in Art and of the Institute of Contemporary Arts.

Dr. Peter Murray
Witt Librarian, Courtauld Institute of Art, London; Lecturer in History of Art at Birkbeck College, University of London.

Mrs. Linda Murray
Extra-Mural Lecturer in History of Art for the University of London.

Professor Mario Monteverdi
Professor of History of Art, Liceo Classico Manzoni, Milan.

Mr. Alan Bowness
Lecturer in History of Art, Courtauld Institute of Art, London.

INTERNATIONAL ADVISORY BOARD

Professor A. M. Hammacher
Former Director, Rijksmuseum Kröller-Müller, Otterlo, Holland.

Dr. R. H. Hubbard
Chief Curator, National Gallery of Canada, Ottawa.

M. Michel Laclotte
Principal Inspector of Provincial Museums, France.

Professor Carl Nordenfalk
Head of Department of Painting and Sculpture, Nationalmuseum, Stockholm.

Dr. Hans Konrad Roethel
Director, Städtische Galerie und Lenbachgalerie, Munich.

Dr. Xavier de Salas
Deputy Director, Museo del Prado, Madrid.

Professor Mario Salmi
President for Medieval and Modern Art, Council for Antiquities and Fine Art, Rome.

Professor Everard M. Upjohn
Professor of Fine Art and Archaeology, Columbia University, New York.

RESEARCH EDITORS

Jenifer Barnes
Paul Drury Byrne
Elizabeth Claridge
Clare Collins
Jean Fraser
David Fuller
J. A. Gaya Nuño
P. H. Hefting
Rosemary Joekes
Margaret Jones
Marguerite Kay
Raymond Kaye
G. E. Law
Mary Anne Norbury
Carol Nordlinger
Janey O'Riordan
Hazel Paget
Shirley Parfitt

DESIGN

George Adams
Frank Harrington
Anthony Truscott
Sandra Sphika

EXECUTIVE EDITOR

Joy Law

GREAT ART AND ARTISTS OF THE WORLD

HOW TO LOOK AT ART

By Bernard Myers

Lecturer, Royal College of Art, London

WITH GLOSSARY AND GENERAL INDEX

FRANKLIN WATTS, INC.
A Division of Grolier Incorporated
575 LEXINGTON AVENUE, NEW YORK 10022

72098 28

NOTE TO THE READER

This volume, the final volume of the series, ranges over the whole field of art from primitive times to the present day, and is intended to provide the reader with a basis for a critical approach to the appreciation and evaluation of all art.

This volume also contains an illustrated Glossary, explaining all the basic technical terms used throughout the series, and a General Index covering all ten volumes.

A list of basic reference books for further reading appears on page 8.

With the exception of this volume, and of the volumes entitled *Origins of Western Art* and *Chinese and Japanese Art*, which are more general in their scope and treatment, each of the books in the set is arranged in accordance with the following basic plan:

First, a historical Introduction sets out the main lines of development within the period covered, with special reference to the major artists and the major works of art. This is followed by an illustrated Biographical section outlining the life and work of every major artist and important minor artist. Next follow sections of Color Plates, Drawings, and Sculpture. A final section, entitled Influences and Developments, rounds off the volume by drawing together the main ideas and characteristics of schools and styles, and by exploring the internal and external influences that have made their impact on the development of the arts during the period concerned.

Throughout the series the location of every work of art is included in its caption. Every effort has been made to include also the size, medium, and date of each work represented in the plates. The reader will appreciate that the precise dating of some works of art is the subject of scholarly controversy; however, no dates have been included here unless they have the authority of qualified experts and art historians.

NOTE.—The terminal dates in the titles of some of the volumes are inevitably approximate. One volume will sometimes overlap with another. Some artists mentioned under French Art, for example, are also represented under the Impressionists, and the Post-Impressionists merge imperceptibly with the Moderns. In the ever-continuous process of Art it is difficult to contain schools or periods within precise boundaries.

701
MAY

Library of Congress Catalog Card Number: 65-10272
Copyright (©) 1965 by Grolier Incorporated
Also published 1965 by Grolier Incorporated under the title of *The Book of Art*

Designed and produced by George Rainbird Ltd., London
PRINTED IN ITALY by Amilcare Pizzi S.p.A., Milan

Contents

132481

LIST OF COLOR PLATES

ACKNOWLEDGMENTS

The publishers and producers wish to express their gratitude to all the museums, art galleries, collectors, photographers, and agencies who have courteously assisted them in obtaining the material for the illustrations reproduced in this volume. They would especially like to thank the following:

A.C.L., Brussels
A.D.A.G.P., Paris
Alte Pinakothek, Munich
Ampliaciones y Reproducciones Mas, Barcelona
Anni Albers, New Haven, Conn.
The Art Institute, Chicago
The Baltimore Museum of Art, Baltimore, Md.
Herbert Bayer, Aspen, Colorado
Bayerische Staatsgemäldesammlungen, Munich
Comte Bégouen, Montesquieu-Avantès, Ariège, France
Bibliothèque des Arts Décoratifs, Paris
Bildarchiv Foto Marburg, Marburg/Lahn, Germany
Joachim Blauel, Munich
The British Film Institute, London
The Trustees of the British Museum, London
Brompton Studio, London
Ets. J. E. Bulloz, Paris
Gallerie Louis Carré, Paris
The Cleveland Museum of Art, Cleveland, Ohio
Colorphoto Hans Hinz, s. w. b., Basel
The Container Corporation of America, Chicago
A. C. Cooper Ltd., London
The Courtauld Institute Galleries, London
Durand-Ruel et Cie, Paris
Professor Harold E. Edgerton, Cambridge, Mass.
Daniel Frasnay, Paris
Robert Fraser Gallery Ltd., London
Fratelli Alinari, S. A. (I.D.E.A.), Florence
Gemäldegalerie, Vienna
Gemeentemuseum, The Hague
Gimpel Fils Ltd., London
Goethehaus, Frankfurt-am-Main
The Hanover Gallery Ltd., London
Heal and Son Ltd., London
Barbara Hepworth, c.b.e., St. Ives, Cornwall, England
The Hermitage, Leningrad
Peter Heywood, Southwell, England
Anthony Hill, London
Joseph H. Hirshhorn Collection, New York
The Historical Monuments Commission of Southern Rhodesia, Bulawayo
Gerald Howson, London
Kasmin Ltd., London
F. L. Kenett, f.i.b.p., London
Dr. Alfred Krech, Krefeld, Germany
Kunsthaus, Zurich
Kunsthistorisches Museum, Vienna
Kunstmuseum, Basel
Kunstmuseum, Düsseldorf
Galerie Louise Leiris, Paris
The London Museum, London
The Mansell Collection, London
Marlborough Fine Art Ltd., London
Georges Mathieu, Paris
Mauritshuis, The Hague
The Metropolitan Museum of Art, New York
Meyer Erwin, Vienna
Sibyl Moholy-Nagy, New York
Musée Fernand Léger, Biot, France
The Museum of Modern Art, New York
The Trustees of The National Gallery, London
The National Galleries of Scotland, Edinburgh
The Natural History Museum, London
The National Museum, Athens
Öffentliche Kunstsammlung, Basel
The Philadelphia Museum of Art, Philadelphia, Pa.
The Phillips Collection, Washington, D. C.
Peter Phillips, London
Photographie Giraudon, Paris
Pitkin Pictorial Ltd., London
Eric Pollitzer, New York
The Prado, Madrid
The Radio Times Hulton Picture Library, London
Rijksmuseum Kröller-Müller, Otterlo, Holland
Rolls-Royce Ltd., London
Walter Rosenblum, New York
Rowntree and Co., Ltd., York, England
The Royal Academy of Arts, London
The Royal Collection, London, by gracious permission of Her Majesty the Queen
The Royal College of Surgeons, London
Royal Holloway College, Egham, Surrey, England
The Royal Library, Windsor, by gracious permission of Her Majesty the Queen
Scala, Istituto Fotografico Editoriale, Florence
The Science Museum (Crown Copyright), London
Société Française des Laboratoires Abbott, Montreuil-sous-Bois, France
S.P.A.D.E.M., Paris
Staatsgalerie, Stuttgart
Statens Museum for Kunst, Copenhagen
Stedelijk Museum, Amsterdam
The Sunday Times, London
The Trustees of The Tate Gallery, London
O. Vaering, Oslo
Verlag Arthur Niggli, Teufen, Switzerland
The Victoria and Albert Museum (Crown Copyright), London
The Trustees of the Wallace Collection, London
The Warburg Institute, London

ABBREVIATIONS

et al.	and elsewhere
in.	inches
St.	Saint (English and German)
S.	Santo, Santa (Italian and Spanish)
Acad.	Academy
Accad.	Accademia
B-A.	Beaux-Arts
Bibl. Nat.	Bibliothèque Nationale
B.M.	British Museum, London
Cath.	Cathedral
Coll.	Collection
Gal.	Galerie
Gall.	Gallery
Gemäldegal.	Gemäldegalerie
Gemeentemus.	Gemeentemuseum
Inst.	Institute
Kunsthist.	Kunsthistorisches
Landesbibl.	Landesbibliothek
Mus.	Musée, Museen, Museo, Museum
Nat.	National, Nationale
Naz.	Nazionale
N.G.	National Gallery
Nationalbibl.	Nationalbibliothek
Öffentl. Kunstsamm.	Öffentliche Kunstsammlung
Pin.	Pinakothek
Rijksmus.	Rijksmuseum
Staatl.	Staatliche
Staatsgal.	Staatsgalerie
Staatsgemälde-samm.	Staatsgemäldesammlung
Tate	Tate Gallery, London
V. and A.	Victoria and Albert Museum, London

Introduction

If we have some knowledge of the development of art through the ages, and of the problems—aesthetic, philosophical, technical, and social—that artists have tried to solve in their various ways, we can look at the products of their work with deeper understanding. The main purpose of this book is therefore to present an informal history of the arts of painting and sculpture in a roughly chronological treatment, taking into account changing attitudes over the centuries towards the technical aspects of form, style, realism, color, perspective, and light.

But when all is said and written about the historical context of a work of art, there remains the most important aspect of all: its aesthetic and emotional impact on the viewer.

How can we attempt to judge a work of art, to assess its aesthetic value? How, in fact, do we distinguish between good and bad art? In learning how to look at art, this is the most difficult of all questions to answer. There is no precise answer, and probably no answer that would be right for all individuals or for all ages.

We might start in a simple and obvious way by examining some of the positive qualities that may be perceived in a work of art.

Subject-matter

First, what does the painting or sculpture represent? Its subject may be factual, or an analogy drawn from everyday experience of the visual world, or a refined, idealized version of that world, or a statement about the impersonal world of geometry, or a picture of the spiritual world, the innermost mind of the artist.

"Great" subject-matter does not automatically ensure the creation of a "great" work of art, any more than a beautiful picture depends upon "beautiful" subject-matter. The notion that this is actually so regularly occurs from time to time, encouraged by a well-intentioned censorship of visual art by some body or authority that may decide what sort of art is required to uplift the people. Plato in his ideal republic wanted artists to conform to noble themes and impersonal form; in the 18th and 19th centuries the Academies of France and England laid down strict requirements for history paintings on noble themes; and today bodies as far apart as the Russian government and the Rome Prize committees still insist on ennobling themes.

The intention is simple: by contemplating noble themes the artist will be inspired to corresponding heights. Unfortunately for the well-intentioned, the mind, even the artist's, does not work in this simple and literal way. A painting of a still-life by Chardin (p. 64) may well be more inspired and inspiring than acres of official painting or stirring battle scenes by academy painters. Floral ironwork on a pair of ornamental gates of the 19th century may contain more of the true spirit of sculpture than a bronze statesman in mock-Roman senatorial dress.

Technique

Many of the great masters were superb draftsmen, or colorists, or observers of light and shade, or masters of geometry and composition. But these skills are only the means of making a work of art; they must arise out of the work, but they cannot be the cause of it. Alone they do not guarantee quality in a work of art.

Alfred Stevens (1817-75) was one of the great draftsmen of his day. He sought to emulate the masters of the High Renaissance, but when we compare his drawings with those he took as his standards we see that they fall short in an essential way. His was an entirely self-conscious imitation of outward form or language, without understanding of idea or meaning. Michelangelo's drawing arose out of the desire to set down ideas in the most powerful way; Stevens merely tried to go one better than Michelangelo in technique, to "clean him up" and so produce perfect drawings free from hesitations and alterations (p. 90 A, B).

William Blake (p. 15 A), too, tried to emulate Michelangelo. If this had been his only aim he would have to be accounted a failure. But Blake wanted to draw like Michelangelo in order to express certain strongly held ideas. He never did draw like Michelangelo, but his efforts led him tc find a means of expression that was at one with his ideas, and as a consequence he produced minor masterpieces. Paradoxically, an awkward drawing by Blake is of finer quality as a work of art than a brilliant drawing by Stevens. Draftsmanship alone is not sufficient to produce a work of art.

Compared with the work of Titian or Renoir, who were both master colorists, Michelangelo's Sistine Chapel paintings are almost monochromatic. Color of itself does not make a masterpiece, nor does lack of it deny one.

Vigorous brushwork by Tintoretto or Goya (pp. 69 and 50) was marvelously allied to the illusion of three-dimensional form, but other painters, such as Vermeer or Stubbs (pp. 62 and 65) or, in the 20th century, geometrical painters such as Mondrian or Herbin (pp. 128 and 189), deliberately tried to suppress their brushwork in accordance with their philosophy of painting. In Epstein's portrait busts his free handling of material is essential to his form, but some other sculptors, such as Barbara Hepworth (p. 21 G), require a mathematically precise finish. Fluency in handling material does not produce great work of itself.

We can admire the geometrical precision of composition of Piero della Francesca, Stubbs, or Mondrian, but we equally admire the amorphous staining of a canvas by Turner or the tangle of dribbled lines of Jackson Pollock (pp. 148 and 198). *The Virgin of the Rocks* by Leonardo (p. 140) is compositionally built up on a triangular theme as stable as an engineer's girder bridge; Degas' *The Absinthe Drinker* (p. 39 F) derives its strength from an off-center focus of interest pulling strongly toward the top right-hand corner.

The Mannerist painters and sculptors of the 16th century thought they could make masterpieces by analyzing the work of Leonardo, Michelangelo, and Raphael, taking the best characteristics of each and synthesizing them into a whole to produce perfect works of art. The work they produced as a result was by no means negligible as good painting and sculpture in its own right, as an account of an age, and as an early statement of Baroque philosophy. But Mannerist art was a failure in the light of its avowed intention, and individually the artists fell far short of the masters they tried to emulate.

Each period tries to formulate its own rules for making works of art. These rules may be enormously helpful in the production of good sound painting and sculpture, from Roman portraits to Cubist paintings, and work of sound caliber is always much in demand. Rules are, however, constantly being broken by more restless artists, and sometimes finer work is produced as a result of their non-conformity.

We would not today accept the rules laid down by Sir George Beaumont in the late 18th and early 19th centuries as a yardstick by which to judge great landscape painting. Yet at the time he was considered to be both an incontrovertible authority on the subject and the greatest landscape painter of his day—and this in the age of Constable and Turner.

It must then be asked whether qualitative judgments can be made about works of art at all. Of course, anyone who likes looking at pictures and sculpture has his own ideas of good and bad art. This is primarily an emotional judgment. "I don't know anything about art, but I do know what I like." Yet no one would rely on such a judgment in business, in civil or criminal law, in buying a house or a car, in ordering a new suit or in cooking a meal; our judgments in these matters, where the consequences must be lived with, have to be based on more than the emotion of a moment. It is only in the field of the arts that we feel we can indulge freely in opinions based on nothing more certain than our prejudices.

The artist's intention

One of the most important factors in judging a work of art must surely be an understanding of the artist's intention. The value of the work depends first on the quality of his intention, and secondly on the success of the technical realization of that intention. It would be foolish and pointless, for example, to compare the achievement of a modest painter like Chardin with that of so dissimilar an artist as Rembrandt, whose inner compulsion had an intensity that is extremely rare. Again, it is unreasonable to compare a personal giant like Rembrandt with a great public figure like Michelangelo or to argue about the relative values of their achievements. They both express profound truths in their particular ways.

Unthinking comparison and emulation, the bugbears of the arts in the 19th century, still lead people today to try to judge modern painting by what they believe to be the standards of the Italian Renaissance. Conversely the reaction that condemns the whole of the work of the past is equally unreasonable.

Our appreciation of the artist's intention depends on our ability to sort out the fake, the imitative, the second-rate, and the second-hand. The essence of criticism is the asking of questions, and once we start asking such questions we must go on. Books can tell us something of artists' lives and times, something of technique, something of composition, and it is certainly helpful to be made aware of these things. But the best way to widen our knowledge of art is to look at many more pictures.

Time and experience are great separators of true art from false. In the art of our own age the passage of time may be too short, but here the critic can come to our aid. He can use his knowledge of the recent history of painting and his specialized research to put new work into proper perspective, point out influences and reactions, and discuss the qualities of technical achievement.

Yet the attitude of critics and experts can change very quickly in the space of a few years. Jackson Pollock's work was first seen mainly as a symptom of reaction against conventional paintings and methods of making them. His dribbled and splashed tangled skeins of paint were seen by critics, students, and public as an act of rebellion against the use of brush and palette. He became associated with every kind of free or automatic technique. In order to emulate his technical innovation, "action" painters bombarded their canvases or trod on them. Students took the liberation to mean a crude kind of freedom, and used color in a new and haphazard manner.

The essence of Pollock's work in fact lies in an extension of the formal means of painting and a highly sophisticated use of color. His technique, the actual dribbling of the paint on the canvas, was so striking that the real point was overlooked; it was thought that the same effect could be achieved by any other means provided the technique was free, indirect, and cultivated the accidental. Now a more sober estimate of Pollock's work can be made. The battle for acceptance is over, and the critics can relax and re-assess. Pollock's painting can be seen to grow quite logically out of Classical Cubism and takes its place naturally in the recent history of painting.

Feeling and emotion

Ruskin said that there can be no art without understanding. If this is so, if criticism and appreciation must be based on knowledge and experience, can there be any place at all for instinctive feeling and emotion?

Some people are drawn much more toward the visual arts than to others; not just to one kind or another but to all drawing, painting, and sculpture. Such people want to find out about these things for what is in the first place an emotional reason. They enjoy looking at them. Generally this emotional involvement is very strong. Many people find that the visual arts are an essential part of their way of life. They may start with a preference for only one kind of picture or one school of sculpture; if they want to know more about or see more of what they like, then they find themselves drawn into contact with many other kinds of work and automatically their interests widen. It is this emotion, the driving force that makes people want to look at art, that is the source of the energy that enables them to do so.

There will always be people with strong ideas about the superiority of Greek to Roman sculpture, or vice versa, people who prefer color to *chiaroscuro*, who find Raphael too cold for their taste, or who consider Braque a better Classical Cubist than Picasso, and who will give good reasons to justify their preference.

This ultimate personal preference is a good thing, not a bad thing. It means that the works themselves and not theories about them have the last word. We are lucky that there is no agreed set of rules either for judging or for producing works of art. We must be thankful that there is such a wide variety in the visual arts, always increasing and always changing.

SOME BOOKS FOR FURTHER READING

Heinrich Wöfflin, *Principles of Art History*, London, 1932.

James J. Sweeney, *Fantastic Dada and Surrealist Art*, New York, 1936.

Eric Newton, *European Painting and Sculpture*, London, 1941.

Kenneth Clark, *Landscape into Art*, London, 1949; *The Nude*, London, 1956; *Looking at Pictures*, New York and London, 1960.

Jacob Burckhardt, *Civilization of the Renaissance in Italy*, New York and London, 1952.

Bernard Berenson, *Seeing and Knowing*, London, 1953.

Richard Neutra, *Survival through Design*, New York, 1954.

Francis Henry Taylor, *Fifty Centuries of Art*, New York, 1954.

André Malraux, *The Voices of Silence*, New York and London, 1954.

Herbert Read, *The Meaning of Art*, London, 1956; *A Concise History of Modern Painting*, New York and London, 1959; *Art Now*, London, 1960.

E. G. Gombrich, *The Story of Art*, New York and London, 1958; *Art and Illusion*, New York and London, 1961.

Charles McCurdy (editor), *Modern Art*, New York, 1958.

Germain Bazin, *A Concise History of Art*, London, 1958.

Laszlo Moholy-Nagy, *Vision and Motion in Design*, Chicago, 1958.

John Golding, *Cubism: A History and an Analysis, 1907-1914*, New York and London, 1959.

Trewin Copplestone, *Modern Art Movements*, London, 1962.

H. W. and D. J. Janson, *A History of Art*, New York and London, 1962.

R. H. Wilenski, *Modern French Painters*, New York and London, 1963.

CHAPTER 1

Art Is Found Everywhere

WHAT is an artist? Above all else, he is a man who does something—man the "doer." Until just over a century ago—a very short time in the history of thinking man—"science" meant knowledge or theory, and "art" was putting that knowledge into practice. Science was applied to all theory, even to that of a sport, like boxing. It is true that this was a kind of slang, but the important thing is that everybody agreed as to what the word meant. The work "art" was used to mean anything that was made. Workmen were described as *art*isans. Engineers called themselves artists when speaking about the practice of their work. *Art*ifacts were manufactured goods. The work manufacture really means "handwork" even though it is now universally used to describe things made with machines. We today often talk about the art of cooking or tailoring, still using the word in its original sense.

This is not intended to be a quibbling argument to persuade people to go back to using words like art in an old-fashioned way. Language is a living thing, and is changing in meaning all the time with each generation. But it is important that we remind ourselves that the word art was not always used with a capital A to describe rather awe-inspiring pictures and sculptures which are kept in museums—a world into which we step that seems to be withdrawn from everyday life. This atmosphere of "different-ness" can be discouraging. It can make art seem to be something reserved for those who have the time and facilities to make these things a special study, something for the scholar rather than the ordinary person. So it is important occasionally to remind ourselves that things in museums are there by the accident of time rather than the artist's intention, and that while we use the word art to describe pictures and statues, man the artist is not limited just to this sort of expression but to some extent or other is everywhere in society.

This book is about the arts in the everyday use of the word, that is to say music, poetry, painting, and sculpture. All these things have a function. The function of a chair is obvious. We sit on it. The act of sitting sums up the use of all chairs. One word also covers all the "fine" arts in a sense. The word is *communication.* The artist has ideas, as we all have, and to tell us about them he writes them down, sings them, draws them, paints and carves them, and gets other people to act them. Sometimes he can do this single-handed, and with no other materials than a sheet or two of paper and a pen or pencil. Sometimes a team of artists is needed to produce a work of art. This might be a large building, or even a town, or a moving picture.

Fine art is not a luxury, but a necessity. It sounds very sensible and down-to-earth to say food, shelter, security must all come first, and then art if you like. But the architect who designs modern buildings really believes that he can make man a better social being by improving the physical conditions under which he lives, and this means visually as well as mechanically. Artists, painters, and poets have endlessly preached upon man's behavior. Even art that apparently has no immediate message, art made spontaneously out of *joie de vivre*, will lift up the spectator or listener with it, take him out of himself as we say, give him temporary release from trouble and worry so that he can tackle, rested and refreshed, the complicated problems of everyday life with new energy.

The subject of this book will be limited to one kind of art, that which we see, or more specifically, that which we look at. This slight but important distinction must be made right away, for seeing is not quite the same thing as looking. To look at something carefully requires both time and concentration. A more familiar analogy may be drawn from the world of sound. We can hear someone talking, or the sound of music, without listening to what is being said or played. By concentration we can sort out what one person is saying against a whole background of noise which we can hear but to which we do not listen.

If we are fond of music of any kind, simple and popular or complex and formal, we say that we *learn* such and such a tune. We hear the piece several times and each time we listen to it, the piece becomes more familiar and understandable.

We expect music to be like this but tend to take *seeing* things for granted. Somehow we do not expect to have to learn to look at pictures and statues. We take them in at a glance, and dismiss them if we do not immediately receive their message. Most people learn how to read and write at quite an early age, and such powers are taken for granted among adults. They forget the effort in looking and learning that literacy cost them. When they read a difficult book it is the ideas that require deep understanding, not the alphabetical symbols themselves.

There is an adult language of vision as well as of writing and speech, a language which most of us neglect in favor of literacy. Only a relatively few people, mostly connected in some way professionally with the visual arts, go on to develop and exercise this concentrated way of looking at things (A), with the result that the layman often complains that the visual artist and his critics and scholars are no longer in touch with everyday life. He feels cut off from much of painting and sculpture, and so he is.

The remedy is not an easy one. There is no substitute for actually looking at pictures, and the time and opportunities to do so are not easy to come by.

Books can help, but interpreting pictures by means of words can be very difficult for both writer and reader, and reproductions can never be a substitute for the real thing. After all, the work of art must always have the last word. Painters choose to paint rather than write, and no amount of written description and analysis of the simplest picture can become a complete substitute for it. Often ideas expressed in the visual arts defy translation into another form.

Nevertheless, there are certain facts about artists, the way they work, the materials they use, and how they live, that can be written about and that can help us to see more clearly these works, which must always in the end have the last say themselves.

(A) THOMAS ROWLANDSON Drawing from Life at the Royal Academy (engraving), 1811

CHAPTER 2

The Artist in a Primitive Society

MAN could draw before he could write. We have no record of how man spoke 20,000 years ago, but we do know how he communicated certain ideas by means of drawing. What the ideas were can only be conjectured; we can only try to interpret these drawings with our 20th-century minds. We may be certain of one thing, that these drawings were made for a purpose. They were not paintings made for their own sake, not even for simply decorating cave walls. Somehow or other, at a time when sustaining everyday life must have been a hard battle against every kind of natural hazard, man found it necessary to draw, paint, and carve.

The few paintings that have survived to this day, hermetically sealed in caves in Spain or France (p. 41), are probably a tiny fraction of the paleolithic output. These caves were very likely meeting-halls, or, when the Ice Age came, communal dwellings after the manner of the Dyak one-house villages. Paleolithic men probably lived also in simple shelters similar to those of the Australian bushman, or against overhanging rock faces, as did the African bushman. As in Australia and Africa, a great number of these external rock faces and camp sites would have been painted, but have since weathered away.

The cave-painter used colored earths bound by animal fat, fish oil, or milky plant juices, or perhaps milk itself. He scratched his outlines into the rock, and put on the color with a pad, with his hands, with a brush, and it even looks as if he sprayed on paint through a blowpipe with his mouth. The artist often took advantage of natural stains and three-dimensional variations in the stone surface to help his modeling of form. Often these shapes must have been the starting point of the painting itself, suggesting a picture to him in the same way that Leonardo da Vinci describes when he advises would-be painters to study marks and stains in walls and ceilings to extend their imaginative powers by finding likenesses there.

The accidental discovery of the first known cave-paintings at Altamira in Spain caused a great stir, not only as a remarkably lucky find that added to man's knowledge of himself, but also because they were found at a time when a belief in progress was a matter of faith. Generally, the 19th-century historian held the view that the history of mankind was rather like the history of an individual man, growing from simple childlike beginnings to final grown-up maturity. Although believing that the best was yet to come, the Victorians still thought that man had reached a fair way towards his goal, and that the 19th century was a significant stage in the improvement of the human race. The art historian's parallel view was that painting, drawing, and sculpture had grown from simple primitive abstract patterning towards greater technical skill and realism, and that these together had now reached a higher peak than ever before. If these cave-paintings, astonishing in their naturalism, really were as old as certain enthusiastic archeologists claimed, then this naive picture of progress was destroyed, for the discoverers said that these paintings were much older than all known fragments of non-figurative geometric patterns. To accept the authenticity of these cave-paintings was to deny what much of 19th-century ideas stood for. They were held to be contemporary with early civilization, or they were denounced as forgeries and fakes. Their defenders and propagandists were attacked and accused of publicity-seeking sensationalism. In time common sense prevailed. A little thought convinced people that a hoax on this scale was extremely unlikely. Other caves were explored and similar remains were found. Bushman's art in Africa (p. 42), which had been known for some time, was suddenly taken seriously. The battle was finally ended by the discovery of new and exact methods of dating to end all doubt.

The Abbé Henri Breuil, who did so much to make European cave pictures known and who was their first defender, lived to see himself vindicated in his old age. Today no one questions their antiquity, at least to the pre-dating of all other monuments of man. The question remains as to how man could, under such conditions and at such a remote age, produce paintings of such beauty, vision, and with such technical skill, and then die to leave an apparent gap of thousands of years before producing the next known simple abstract pattern work, such as on neolithic pottery.

One conjectural answer, which seems sensible, is that these men painted realistically because they were incapable of abstraction. The most familiar form of abstraction to us all is to be able to read and write the letters MAN instead of having to draw a picture of a man. The result of using abstract symbols for MAN is that we can also think of man in an abstract way, not only of a man in particular but of mankind and all its relationships. Behind this ability to communicate with each other by means of symbols lies a long and slow evolutionary process of thought.

Primitive man, the hunter and food-finder, must have lived from day to day, almost from one meal to the next. His necessary knowledge was related to hunting skills. The control of his weapons lay in his own hands, but the only control he could have over the quarry he hunted was by luring it. This depended on a great measure of luck; skill in luring is intangible and akin to magic. The breeding and replacement of game too was outside his control. Certainly a great deal of cave painting is about hunting, about luring game by imitation, and also the act of painting in itself was a ritual, an act of concentration, exercising some sort of power of control over game by depicting it. The relationship of an effigy to power over its subject has persisted in witchcraft and superstition to this day; most religions still use physical symbols or statues to aid concentration in prayer.

So the caves may be thought of in part at least as chapels, and the painter himself as a forerunner of prophets and priests. The early hunter depended on the sharpness of his sight for survival. His vision was photographic and could freeze the image of an animal in motion. There is something of the best of the cartoon film drawing about cave-painting: they are both concerned with this split-second rendering of movement, the former as one frame of a sequence, the latter as a thing it itself (A). The cartoonist builds up his subject artificially from a knowledge of movement and anatomy. The cave artist did not paint his pictures from theoretical knowledge but rather by drawing round the image imprinted in his mind from direct observation. Thus these paintings remind us of instantaneous photographs of animals in motion (B).

This ability to project a mental image onto a surface, to see it as if it was there and then copy it, has been investigated by psychologists and named by them *eidetic* vision. It occurs among those whose capacity for learning abstract techniques, such as reading and writing, is for some reason retarded. As a child has put it, "I think a thought and then draw round it."

Because early man's powers of abstraction were

(A) WALT DISNEY Still from the cartoon film "Bambi" (detail) 1942 *(Copyright Walt Disney Production)*

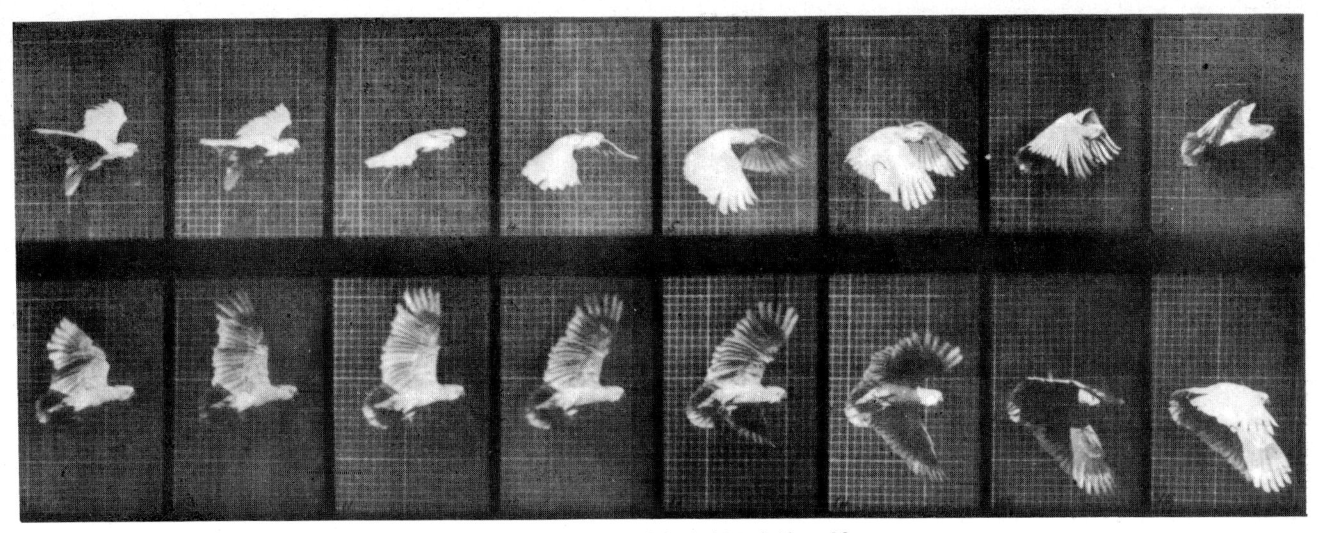

(B) Sequence of instantaneous photographs of parrot flying *Photo: Edweard Muybridge, 1887*

limited it does not, of course, follow that he was at all backward or childish in the modern sense. He depended upon acutely sharp physical senses, and immediate reactions to them, for his survival, and a capacity for abstraction tends to raise a barrier between the mind and the senses to a certain extent. Together with a high intensity of vision and visual memory, early man would have developed a fine sense of mimicry for purposes of communication with his fellow beings that might be the beginning of imitating action by gesture and noises by words.

The painting from the Cave of Les Trois Frères (p. 43) tells us a great deal about these hunters besides the fact that they drew and painted. The figure of a man is dressed as an antlered animal with the beast's head worn as a mask. It can be interpreted in a number of ways, all equally valid. The figure may be a mimic decoy in the hunting field, a technique still practiced by bushmen of Africa and Australia. It may be a mimic in a ritual dance, a ceremonial enactment of a hunt, either as thanksgiving and celebration, or in preparation for the chase. Or it may be yet another form of mimicry, but this time not the sorcerer but his victim, a sacrificial figure dressed as quarry, and slain. These men danced thus and imitated, and made costumes from sewn skins. The paintings are spectacular, but no less impressive was the technological achievement of boring a hole in the thicker end of a fish bone, to make the first sewing needles, without which man would not have survived the Ice Age.

These paintings were probably carried out by professionals. Presumably young acolytes who showed a talent for picture making were chosen to be trained. This is suggested by the evidence of repeated copies. Often pictures are superimposed. Sometimes they appear to be deliberate visual puns, with a change from one beast to another in the same drawing.

Often the underlying painting was obliterated and another painted on top; the obliterative ground has decayed or become translucent with time, while the more powerful stains have survived.

In addition to the cave paintings, a quantity of beautifully engraved tools and weapons have survived (C). These are mostly of bone and antler, sometimes of stone. There are fundamental differences between these engraved drawings and the wall paintings. To begin with, the wall painter was free to work where he liked and to whatever size he cared to choose within reason. The tool maker had to make his tool first. Then, if it was a good tool, it was worth decorating. This decoration may have had both a mystical significance, and also a more functional purpose, that of signing and identifying

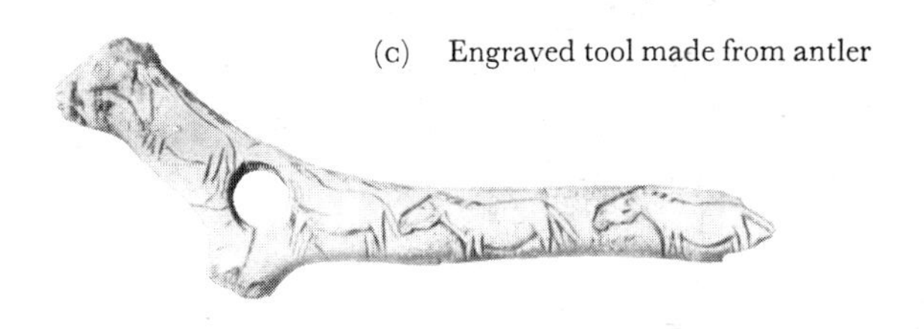

(C) Engraved tool made from antler

the tool as a mark of ownership. The engraver was a toolmaker first and artist second. His engraving was limited by the physical extent of the surface he was working on. Distortions and simplifications arise through these limitations.

As society changed from one of hunters and food gatherers to nomadic herdsmen and food planters, a different kind of knowledge was needed. Man needed to count, to measure time, to have an idea of quantity. The priest developed from painter to poet. At first, essential information would have been handed down in the form of chants and rhymes, using rhythms, alliteration, and, possibly, rhyme as an aid to memory, much as we say "A red sky at night is the shepherd's delight"—still chanted by children who have never seen a hill covered with sheep. The Homeric epics and much of the Old Testament are of this order.

Words became more important than pictures, and they were the beginning of abstract ideas. The visual arts became the sole province of the toolmaker, and would always be dominated by his primary craft, which might be sword and shield making, pottery, or weaving. This might explain the gap between the highly realistic cave painting and the first crude geometric patterns on early pottery, as naturalism came to an end and decoration gradually became symbolic pattern making (A).

These earliest patterns tell us something of the dramatic change in man's way of life. The paintings are about man and animals. The patterns are about man and the land. A zigzag line might be a simple representation of mountains or sea, finger-made stripes a rainbow.

Primitive societies still exist today, or have existed within living memory, that tell us something of early man. There are hunting and food finding peoples ranging from the Eskimos of the north to the desert dwellers of South Central Africa and Central Australia, and the Indians of North America. Although their visual arts vary as much from one continent to the other as do the lives they lead, they are all concerned with one thing, the gamble of the hunt, and all are great mimics and dancers and produce marvelous images of the animals they hunt.

(A) Example of Neolithic pottery *London, B. M.*

The settled agriculturalists of Africa, the ocean-going peoples of the South Pacific, both developed an abstract pattern making culture in which decoration was full of meaning for those who could read it, stories of tribal history, timetables, and maps.

Modern society everywhere is dominated by such abstract signs and symbols, from religious symbols to road signs, from medieval heraldry to the trade mark, national flag, and automobile radiator badge.

CHAPTER 3

The Artist as Philosopher

A PHILOSOPHER is an explorer in the realms of ideas. A great deal of the history of philosophy has been the search for simple unchanging fundamental laws in an apparently everchanging world. These ideas are all the result of practical observation and experience. Something just happens. A tree is struck by lightning: we explain it in terms of a god hurling a thunderbolt, or as an electrical discharge. Someone is taken ill: he is described as being invaded by evil spirits, or by virus organisms. How we describe these phenomena depends upon the extent of our experience and the gradual accumulation of knowledge (A).

In the beginning all such phenomena were described in terms of everyday experience. We use the word *cosmos* as name for the universal order of things; microcosm for the universe on a tiny microscopic scale, and macrocosm for the universe on an astronomical scale. The word *cosmos*, or *kosmos*, was originally a craft word. It is the same word as "comb" and was used to describe both the action of combing—carding—wool, or combing one's hair. When we comb wool before spinning it into thread, or comb our hair, we straighten out tangled skeins. We set them in order. Homer calls the marshal of the Greek armies in the Iliad the *Kosmetore*—he who sets in order. We still comb our hair, and women still use *cosme*tics to set their faces in order.

Today the word *cosmos* has an abstract meaning—*the* order generally—and philosophy has become an abstracted study of definitions. But originally philosophy was very much a part of everyday life, at least as far as the average educated man was concerned, and not the specialized study of a minority. Philosophers borrowed freely from popular everyday life for their images.

In the early settled civilizations of Egypt and the Middle East, the artist was the direct servant of philosophy, and religion and philosophy were one and the same. Men divided the idea of God into a number of personages each with a special duty. These personages were described in terms of everyday experience; they often had the bodies of men, and the heads of various birds or animals to symbolize their special roles, like the use of actors' masks (B). The original portrayal of the messenger of God is a terrifying affair quite different from our own humanist idea. He has the head of a man symbolizing wisdom and the power of speech, the body of a bull for strength and tenacity, and the wings of an eagle for speed. Such was the angel that spoke to Abraham, and the throne of Solomon was supported by seraphs like these.

(A) WILLIAM BLAKE Satan Smiting Job with Sore Boils, about 1825 *London, Tate*

(B) Egyptian god Horus: from an Egyptian tomb (after Dominique Denon)

(A) Assyrian human-headed winged bull with attendant, about 700 B. C.
London, B. M.

The human headed figure from Nineveh (7th century B.C.) is carved in the round. From either the front or side the figure is complete in a natural way, but from the three-quarters view it has five legs (A). This apparent "mistake" is similar to certain other peculiarities in relief sculpture and painting in the Middle East and Egypt. If we look at a typical Egyptian two-dimensional picture of a man we see what are to us contradictions in form: the head is in profile, but the eye is seen head-on; he seems to be perpetually looking over his shoulder, for his upper body is seen from the front. His arms and legs however are turned through a complete right-angle once more and seen sideways on, like his head. His waist band and linen kilt conveniently help the artist to disguise this twist in the form (p. 44).

At one time this was explained in terms of naive vision. The Egyptians were said to have drawn the various parts of the body as most commonly seen—characteristic views they were called—and then to have assembled them in the right order, but without attempting to relate them properly to each other, because they were unable to see in three dimensions. This explanation is completely contradicted by their sculpture in the round, where these relationships are absolutely controlled. Absolute is indeed the word, for these relationships are never allowed to vary. The figure sits staring in front of him, or stands at attention, or with one arm and one leg advanced, never turning body or head.

It is in this form of sculpture that we find the clue to our five-legged creature and flattened-out man. The sculptor took a block of wood or stone and squared it up into a rectangular solid. On each side he drew what an architect or engineer would call a set of views of the figure, plans and elevations. This was done by drawing up a squared grid like a map, and setting out all the parts of the body according to a set of ideal dimensions laid down in the artist's rule book. The surplus material was then gradually chipped away and the elevations joined up. The rough work was done by apprentices and assistants, the final polished finish being given by the master. It was this technique that automatically gave us the five-legged winged bull. When the artist worked in two dimensions and not three, he still had to use the rule book as his guide and not natural observation. He was the servant of an idea and not of his own self-expression; in fact he would not have known what the latter phrase meant. Consequently, his work was a combination of these working drawings for making a man. We might consider them as the blueprint for a man, anatomically correct in every detail, but in an exploded view, not shown three-dimensionally. The space shown in Egyptian wall paintings and reliefs is *idea*lized in the same way.

(B) Egyptian of high rank, attended by his wife, fowling in the marshes. From a tomb at Thebes, about 1500 B.C. *London, B.M.*

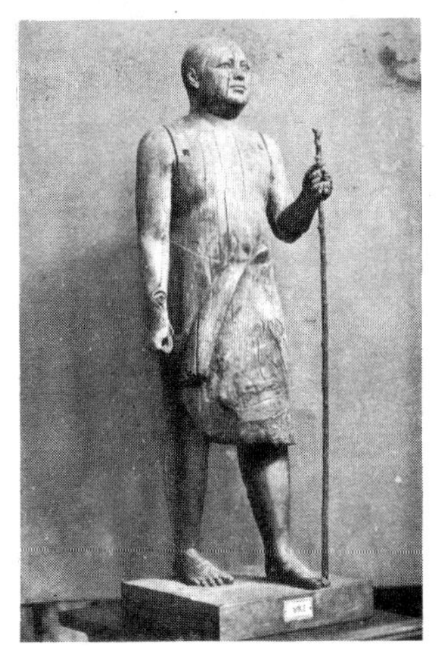

(c) Portrait of Kaaper, about 2500 B.C. *Cairo, Mus.*

(D) Greek archaic Kouros (youth) *Athens, Nat. Mus.*

(E) Greek archaic Kore (maiden) *Athens, Acropolis Mus.*

(F) Old Drunken Woman, copy of Greek sculpture *Rome, Capitoline Mus.*

The apparent size of objects is not governed by position and distance: people and things are graded in size according to their importance, rank in the social scale, or even in the creation generally.

Thus a man may be bigger than a tree, or the house he lives in. The king is equal to the gods, his wife and daughters may be half and one quarter his height respectively. Priests are next in size, while peasants are smallest of all when in the company of a superior. All are governed by the same rules of depiction, which never vary no matter what scene is being shown (B).

Egyptian portraits are not characterless but expressionless. We can recognize individual beings, who are sometimes drawn with great sympathy and dignity (C). The Egyptian artist was concerned with eternal values, stable enduring rules, not transient things of the moment. These rules persisted for 6,000 years without change, as regular as the annual flooding of the Nile that gave Egyptian civilization a surplus of food and physical security.

The early Greek settlers took both their sculptural techniques and their form from the more highly developed Egyptians. Their Kouroi, figures of young men, stand with hands by their sides and one leg advanced, and are severely frontal. They are not quite so expressionless as the contemporary Egyptian statues, an enigmatic smile is hinted at in their faces, but are at first far less recognizably realistic. They still have a timeless other-world quality (D, E). But the Greeks did not live under such socially secure conditions as the Egyptians and this insecurity made them restless both in mind and body. On one hand they made great advances in techniques of thinking which were applied in the sciences, in medicine, and in politics, on the other they founded a dispersed colonial empire, which started to split up almost as soon as it was founded.

Under the far from ideal conditions of a highly competitive everyday world, the Greek politicians failed to live up to the ideals of the Greek philosophers and teachers who had had such practical success in the world of medicine and science. As the empire grew rapidly, the gap between ideals and expediency grew, and philosophy, once synonymous with religion, morality, and the business of life generally, became an abstract specialized branch of study in which thinking men would withdraw into a world of their own. Here pure reason could be argued, free from any modifications or contamination.

Instead of being a graphic illustration drawn from life, the word *cosmos* became an abstract noun. In Plato's time (427-347 B.C.) philosophers thought the real world to be so inferior to that of the thinker that they denounced all who worked with their hands as *banaus*—banal or commonplace. This epithet of contempt applied equally to the skilled craftsman as it did to the manual laborer. Consequently the artist had turned from the ideal, timeless world to the realistic portrayal of the emotions, often of a sensational kind (F). No longer respected by the intellectuals, he turned to virtuosity of technique and sought popular approval. The pure philosophers accused him

(A) The five Platonic solids
London, Science Mus.
(Crown Copyright)

(B) ALBRECHT DÜRER
Melencolia, 1514
(engraving)

A B

of immorality and blasphemy, claiming that incredulous people were seduced by these popular works of art which aroused unreal feelings; that is to say feelings not resulting from personal, but second-hand and debased experience.

It is exactly the argument used today by those who claim that certain forms of entertainment, which depend on sensationalism of one sort or another, encourage irresponsibility, and also by those who attack spectator sports on the grounds that we become watchers instead of players.

The purest philosophers would allow archaic or Egyptian sculpture if absolutely necessary, but preferred to contemplate pure form. Man is at the mercy of feelings, they said, using *aesthetics* (feelings) as a derogatory word. Feelings must be conquered by the intellect, or man abases himself to the level of the lowest animal.

All form to Plato was based on the pure form of cubes, cylinders, cones, spheres, and other regular geometrical solids (A). In the actual world all these forms were modified by expediency, and as a result were impure and blemished.

Since that time, in one form or another, philosophers and artists have sought to express the world in these terms. Of all languages, the mathematician's is the most accurate, whether dealing with equations, figures, or geometry. In their search for fundamental rules, based on first principles and independent of the varying conditions of everyday life, men have sought to define the world in mathematical terms, seeing the Creator as a perfect mathematician-philosopher. It is with a feeling of relief that men of thought turn from the turbulence and uncertainty of the world about them to the contemplation of ideas which seem more durable. For example, the highest peak of Greek philosophy was reached at the time when Greece was destroying itself in a ferocious civil war that brought its culture to an end.

This feeling of disillusion is summed up at a much later date by Albrecht Dürer (1471-1528). The German engraver portrays the figure of Melencolia brooding on time and death. She is surrounded by the Platonic symbols of compasses and dividers and geometrical solids as well as the ladder and nails of the Crucifixion. On the wall is a table of numbers which are formed into a square, and which are related in a way that was thought to have mystical or magical significance (B).

The language of mathematics has often seemed to be the only one available to philosophers that allows no ambiguity of meaning and by which ideas about the nature of the universe could be exactly expressed.

Music is an art form that can be easily measured mathematically in terms of proportion. Painting and architecture also depend upon proportion, and it is thought from time to time that visual beauty can be ultimately analyzed by mathematical means. In particular some numerical series have been thought to be more beautiful than others. One such was called the ideal proportion or Golden Mean. It is a ratio, a series of terms in which every part is related to those before and after in a way that determines its relationship to the whole. Its algebraic equation is written as:

$$\frac{a}{b} = \frac{b}{a + b}$$

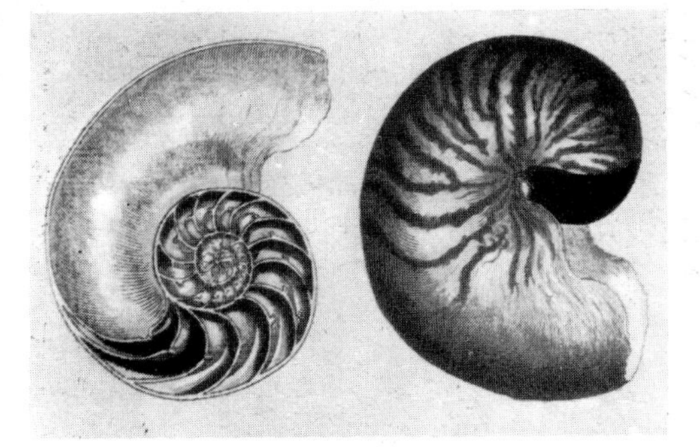

(C) *Nautilus* shell showing cross-section

(D) Sunflower center: from A. H. Church, "On the Relation of Phyllotaxis to Mechanical Laws" (Williams and Norgate, London, 1901)

It seems to have been known by the Egyptians and certainly by the Greeks. It was used by medieval architects and rediscovered in the Renaissance. It occurs in many forms of organic growth in nature, in sea shells, in the arrangement of plant leaves and flower petals, and in the form of animals and men (C, D).

At once let it be said that it is not necessary to understand it in order to look at pictures. All that one need remember is that there have always been painters, sculptors, and architects, who have used such rules in the same way that they have used brushes or chisels—as tools to help them in their work (E).

It is a certain way of relating all the parts to the whole, and was used for this purpose by many painters. Piero della Francesca divided up the floor plan as well as the plane surface of his picture of *The Flagellation* (p. 45), using the Golden Mean (F). The painting has a curiously calm and static quality, not only due to Piero's use of geometry, but also to his avoidance of any light and cast shadow in his painting. The modeling of his form is like that of a bas-relief, and severely limited to showing the roundness of individual forms. The poses are frozen and each figure is outlined by the finest hairline. This severe treatment contrasts strongly with the violence of the

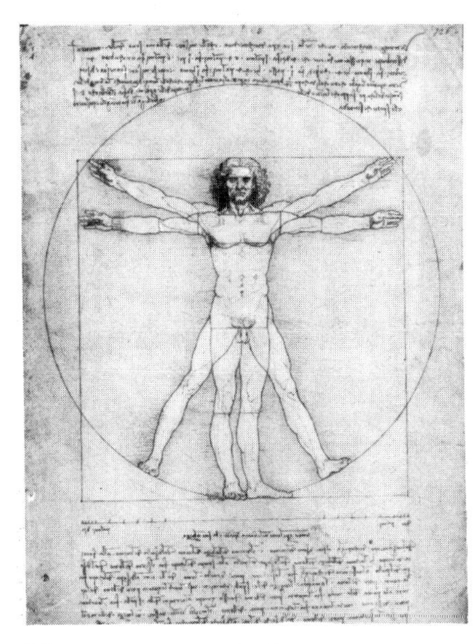

(E) LEONARDO DA VINCI
Vitruvian Drawing of Man, about 1485
Venice, Accad.

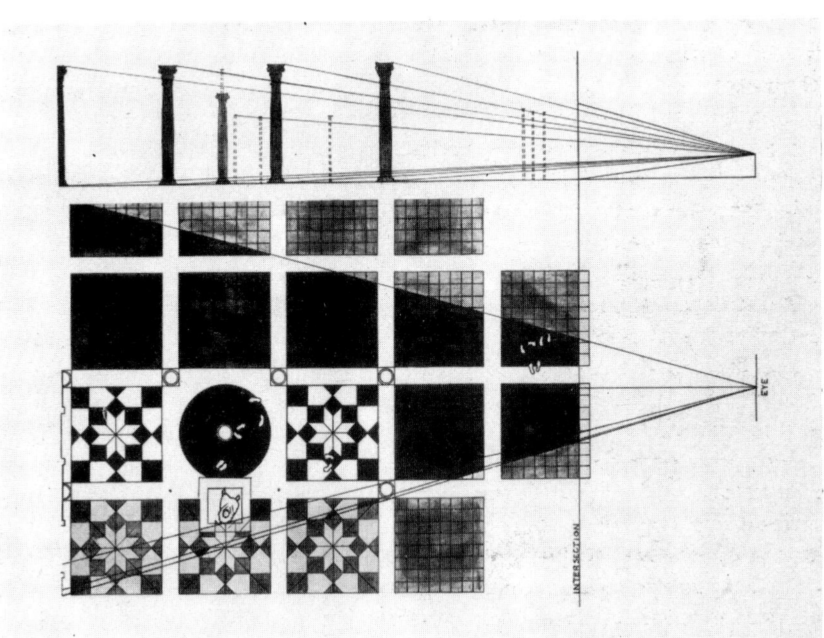

(F) B. A. R. CARTER Floor plan and elevation of *The Flagellation* by Piero della Francesca (p. 45)
By courtesy of The Warburg Inst., London

(A) VILLARD DE HONNECOURT Page from Notebooks, about 1240
Paris, École des B-A., Bibl.

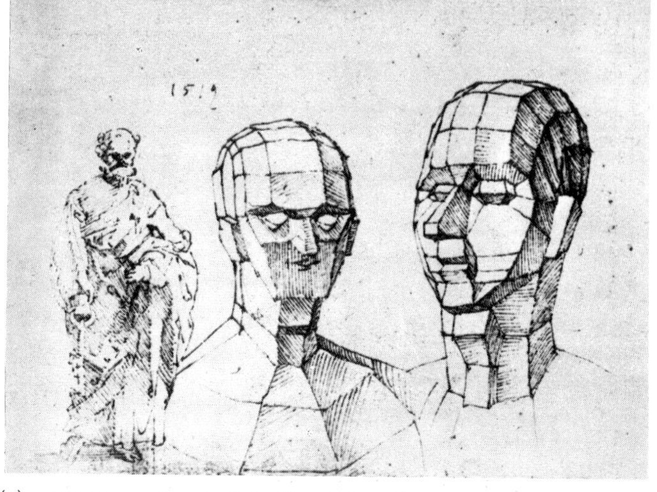

(B) ALBRECHT DÜRER Cubed head: from "The Dresden Sketchbook," about 1513 *Dresden, Sächsische Landesbibl.*

subject. There is no immediate appeal to the emotions, but only to reason. Piero's world is one where all problems can be solved by rational thought, where there must be an optimum solution waiting to be discovered to solve any problem.

Most of the great Renaissance masters used this system of composition. It is more surprising to find it used by the English sporting painter George Stubbs. In his work geometry regulates the position of every detail of the composition. It provides hidden depths to his apparent everyday view of the English countryside. His anatomy studies are also regulated by this proportional system.

(C) JUAN GRIS Breakfast, 1915
Paris, Mus. d'Art Moderne

Painters have not only used geometry as a method of composition, but have described form itself in this way. Early examples appear in the medieval notebooks of Villard de Honnecourt (A). Later Dürer not only drew figures to linear systems of proportion but constructed them cubically in the round (B). Schön, his follower, Piero, Uccello, and other painters worked in this way. Later, in the 19th century, Cézanne gave his still-life and figure paintings this monumental quality, by treating form as a series of spheres, cubes, cylinders, and hard-edged planes. His language of form was adopted by the Cubists, who sought to reconstruct nature in their paintings and sculpture, in an ideal manner removed from the accidents of the actual world. Georges Braque, Pablo Picasso, and Juan Gris (C) took simple objects of everyday life, glasses, bottles, pipes, newspapers, perhaps a bowl of fruit, or a guitar, and transformed them into a modern equivalent of the sharp clear world of the early Egyptian, complete with the superimposition of several views at once. Fernand Léger turned the human form into something hard and monumental, as if made of stone or

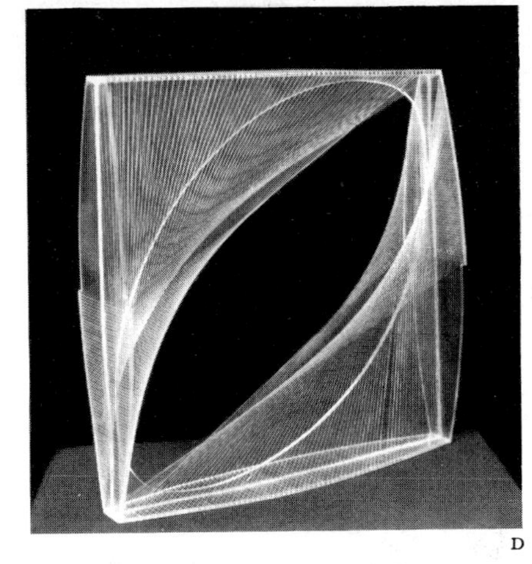

D

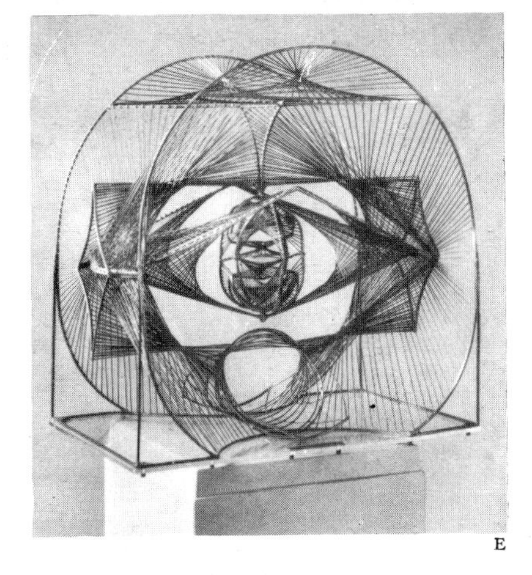

E

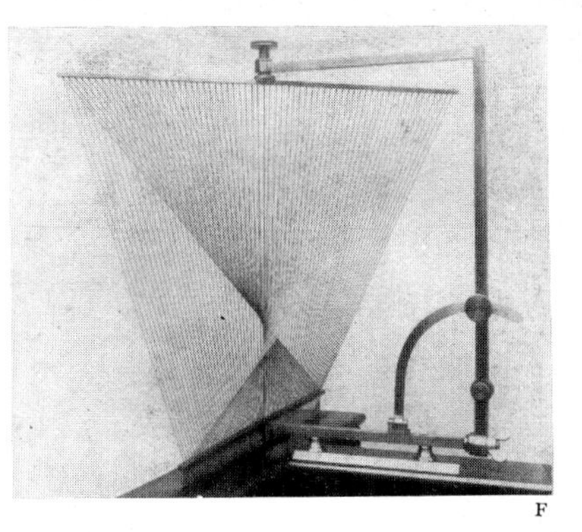

F

G

H

I

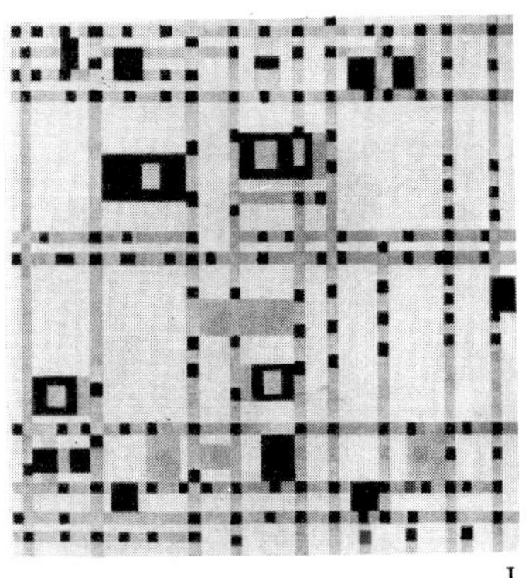

J

(D) NAUM GABO
Linear Construction, 1942-43
London, Tate

(E) ANTOINE PEVSNER Maquette for a Monument Symbolizing the Liberation of the Spirit, 1952
London, Tate

(F) Mathematical model
London, Science Mus., Lent by Professor Henrici

(G) BARBARA HEPWORTH
Small Form Resting, 1945
Lincoln, University of Nebraska Art Gall.

(H) Mathematical model
London, Science Mus. (Crown Copyright)

(I) THEO VAN DOESBURG
Counter-composition, 1924
Amsterdam, Stedelijk Mus.

(J) PIET MONDRIAN
Broadway Boogie-Woogie, 1942-43
New York, Mus. of Modern Art

metal (p. 127). Amédée Ozenfant foresaw a whole world built of the new, clean form in his *Esprit Nouveau* paintings of the 1920's (p. 46).

In their search for pure form painters and sculptors abandoned the subject altogether. The works of Jean Arp, Naum Gabo, Antoine Pevsner, and Barbara Hepworth often look like models of mathematical equations. The members of the *De Stijl* movement, Theo van Doesburg, Bart van der Leck, and Piet Mondrian, concerned themselves entirely with the geometry of proportion of a flat plane. They were much concerned with reformist movements generally, using their paintings to preach a new clean, clear, ideal, and logical world, where all is reason, much as the modern architect believes that by improving peoples' environment you improve people themselves (D-J).

CHAPTER 4

The Artist as Critic and Moralist

All art is exaggeration. The artist is always putting forward his own personal point of view on all subjects, whether it be his idea of what a landscape, a person, a still-life group, or an abstract ideal looks like. As a social man he has often put forward his ideas about society as well. In fact certain writers on art, such as John Ruskin, have based a whole theory of art on the reaction of man to society, and this point of view is still held to the exclusion of all others in communist countries.

Certainly pictorial form can be a very powerful weapon. The reception of the message is immediate, it crosses barriers of language and literacy, and can show us the world in heightened form. It can persuade us to believe in things that do not actually exist, such as people with animals' heads, or show us all the hidden stages of vice and cruelty.

Generally, this form of art is critical by nature towards man and society. In this way the artist carries on the tradition of the *jongleur* or jester. We must remember that the jester took his name from "geste" or deed; he was both public conscience and remembrancer to his noble employer.

Wit was one of his weapons and helped him to maintain his privilege, but his job as a comedian was secondary to that of commentator. Satire, that powerful weapon, leads us to the origin of the artist as critic, for the name comes from the Greek satyr plays. These comedies with a highly critical content were acted out by players who wore grotesque masks and whose costumes deliberately depicted characters with some sort of physical deformity (A, B).

The mad and physically deformed were both held not to be entirely responsible for their actions. Conversely critics could shelter behind such a shield, and the privileged "fool" and white-faced snub-nosed clown were given licence. The long tradition includes the players of the *Commedia dell'Arte*, who were regularly banned for their outspokenness, Shakespeare's railing clown Thersites in "Troilus and Cressida," and Punch of the Punch and Judy show.

(A) Greek vase: Scene from a comedy, 4th century B.C. *London, B. M.*

(B) DIOSCORIDES OF SAMOS Mendicant and Musicians, about 100 B.C. (mosaic) *Naples, Mus. Naz.*

The medieval artists and masons who put grotesque figures into the margins of prayer books, or carved them on sacred buildings, were following the tradition. These are not devils and gargoyles, but clown-like rustic figures who put out their tongues, stick out their backsides, and thumb their noses at the authority of the Church on earth as if to remind the prelates that although the cathedral spires reach up to heaven, the foundations are still very much of the earth (C, D, E).

This often extremely vulgar spirit of criticism was characteristic of Europe north of the Alps, where there was always some measure of opposition to the temporal authority of the pope and Church, as distinct from spiritual authority. The antagonism grew to a head towards the end of the Middle Ages, and the attempt to free local and national churches from central control helped to bring about the Reformation. At once the Reformers, led by Luther, used picture-propaganda. What had been individual and playful comments on the part of unknown craftsmen, became direct attacks on papal

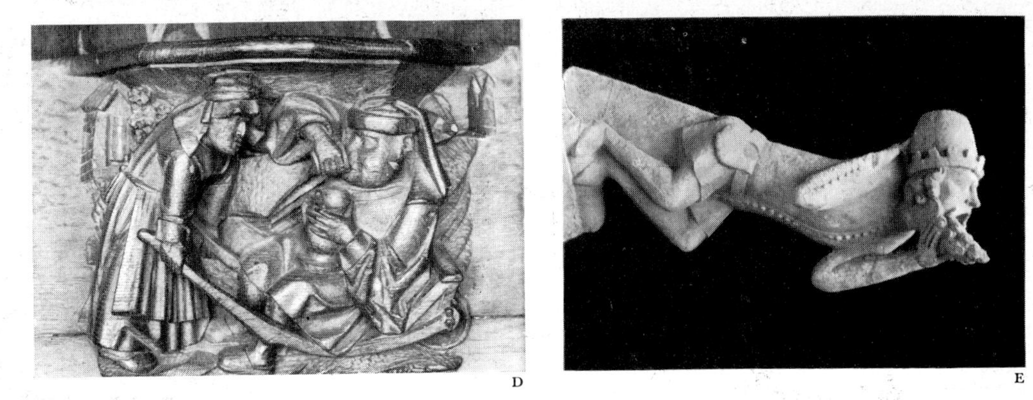

(C) Page from the Luttrell Psalter (detail) early 14th century *London, B. M.* (D) Misericord carving, 15th century (E) Waterspout, 13th century *Troyes, France, St. Urbain*

authority and papal morals, in the form of woodcut broadsheets. A great number of the woodcuts that Luther commissioned from Lucas Cranach are obscenely unprintable.

At a different level altogether is the Reformation propaganda of Mathis Grünewald, whose *Crucifixion* in the Isenheim Altarpiece expresses his feelings of man's inhumanity witnessed by him in the religious civil wars in Germany. Grünewald himself was a reformist insurgent. Disillusioned by the atrocities on both sides, he gave himself up to the authorities, narrowly escaped being hanged, and retired into obscurity (F).

Pieter Bruegel continued to blend the medieval spirit with the new pictorial techniques. He took for his subjects simple proverbs such as the Blind leading the Blind, and also made bitter comments on the religious war in the Low Countries (G). His *Adoration of the Kings* (p. 47) shows the Child surrounded by grotesque figures carrying worldly symbols of wealth and power. Joseph is portrayed as a greedy peasant calculating the value of the expensive presents.

Even the proverbs have a revolutionary content. Painters of the northern schools were at great pains to assert their independence from the Grand Manner of Italian painting, and deliberately countered the themes taken from classical mythology and scenes from everyday life that also pointed a moral story. A whole school of Dutch anecdotal painting sprang up in this way, of whom Jan Steen is perhaps one of the best examples (p. 48).

The English painter William Hogarth took this tradition and used it to preach a new public morality (p. 49). Hogarth was violently anti-classical, and the walls of the noble interiors in which some of his scenes are set are hung with wicked parodies of "great art." Hogarth painted pictures in series that tell a story like the successive chapters of a book. Each one follows logically from the other and is concerned with the logical consequences of certain actions.

His constant theme is the way in which the common faults of seduction, greed, expediency, and plain foolishness can lead to violence, horror, and high tragedy. The

(F) MATHIS GRÜNEWALD The Crucifixion: from the Isenheim Altarpiece, about 1505-15 *Colmar, France, Unterlinden Mus.*

(G) PIETER BRUEGEL the ELDER The Blind Leading the Blind, 1568 *Naples, Gall. Naz.*

(A) WILLIAM HOLMAN HUNT
The Awakening Conscience, 1854
London, coll. Sir Colin Anderson

(B) WILLIAM HOLMAN HUNT
The Hireling Shepherd, 1851
Manchester, City Art Gall.

(C) AUGUSTUS EGG
Past and Present (I), 1858
London, Tate

(D) SIR LUKE FILDES
Applicants for Admission to a Casual Ward, 1874
Egham, England, Royal Holloway College

A B

C

D

pictures are like scenes from a stage play in their story telling, but in composition they are very skillfully organized. Close-knit detail and pictorial incidents combine to underline the main plot and provide secondary plots of their own. At the same time all this wealth of detail is always subordinated to the whole.

Hogarth not only highly organized his pictures, but treated his market in the same way. The paintings were really to serve only as models for engravings, and when they had served their turn they were drawn for in lotteries. The best French engravers were sought to keep all the quality of the originals, and to ensure that the mass-produced prints were not merely inferior copies.

In spite of a few political engravings lampooning the abuse of power by the state and Church, Hogarth was not concerned with a revolutionary attack upon a social system. His moralizing series of pictures emphasize every man's own personal responsibility for his actions, the consequences of which are often unforeseeable. He preached to an English middle class that was becoming the most powerful and prosperous section of the community. Such personal freedom backed by financial independence was unknown in Europe save in the Low Countries.

Hogarth himself claimed to be not a caricaturist but a realist. In this he would be echoed by his 19th-century successors. During this century the new middle class reached the peak of its power and the taste for moralizing painting remained, but with this difference. The patrons did not care to be criticized themselves and demanded only pictures showing the awful results of any kind of departure from their own particular standards of life. In their prosperity they needed constant reassurance and comfort. In Holman Hunt's *The Awakening Conscience* a well-to-do man's mistress is suddenly reminded of her innocent childhood by the sheet of music on the piano (A). Contemporary critics found that the newness and vulgarity of the furnishings, the shiny varnish of a stucco love nest in St. John's Wood, a new London suburb with a reputation for such things, all reflected the awful depth to which the creature had sunk. *The Hireling Shepherd*, by the same artist, is full of overdone symbolism, and a series of three pictures concerning the dreadful fate of an unfaithful wife, *Past and Present* by Augustus Egg, amply demonstrates Hogarth's virile attacks degenerating into 19th-century sentimentality (B, C).

When painters did attempt serious comment in their work, they came up against the natural difficulty of what to do with such pictures. The drawing room reigned supreme, and clearly there was a limit to the grimness which patrons were prepared to put on their walls. Sir Luke Fildes's *Casual Ward*, a large painting of London's poor and homeless queueing up for a night's shelter at the casual ward of a workhouse, has in its deep sulphurous tones much of the atmosphere and realism of Gustave Doré or Honoré Daumier. It was a great success at the Academy, and as an engraving in the illustrated paper, "The Graphic" (D).

Morality and sentimentality had become synonymous and were even called downright hypocrisy. When, at the turn of the 19th century to the 20th, painters tried to free themselves from conventions which had become meaningless, this content of painting was the first to go. Indeed, painters had by then been freed from this task by political cartoonists, from whom came most of the critical comment on the violence of the first world war and the new power politics. The main exception was the series of etchings and drawings that culminated in the large painting *Guernica* by Pablo Picasso (E).

The occasion was the open declaration of war upon civilians by bombardment. This large painting, partly realist, partly surrealist, is ambiguous and open to various interpretations as to its detail, but its main meaning is obviously a condemnation of modern war and the suffering imposed indiscriminately upon the innocent.

The painting is directly in the tradition of Francisco Goya, to whose work there are numerous and obvious references. Goya stands as a giant among the great artist moralizers; his indignation was born of patriotism in the first place, but spiritual disillusion and physical affliction combined to isolate him from his friends and compatriots, by whom he was often misunderstood. He broadened his attack into a general condemnation of mass inhumanity to man.

The Executions of May 3, 1808 (F), an indictment of French reprisals invoked by the uprising of the population of Madrid against the French occupation, is

(E) PABLO PICASSO
Guernica, 1936
New York, Mus. of Modern Art
Extended loan by artist

(F) FRANCISCO GOYA
The Executions of May 3, 1808
Madrid, Prado

A

B

C

D

(A) FRANCISCO GOYA
The Stage-Coach Robbery (detail) 1787
Madrid, coll. Duke of Montellano

(B) FRANCISCO GOYA Bury them and be Silent: from The Disasters of War, 1810-13

(C) FRANCISCO GOYA
You will not Escape: from The Caprices, 1796-98

(D) JAMES GILLRAY Scientific Researches! - New Discoveries in Pneumaticks! or Experimental Lecture on Powers of Air. Royal Institution, 1802

paralleled by another of a firing squad of Spanish brigand/guerillas massacring the passengers dragged from a stage coach (A). French atrocities were rivaled by those of the Spanish patriots, and Goya does not excuse them. In the etchings of *The Disasters of War* he portrays both (B). Another series of etchings, *Los Caprichos — The Caprices*—is a broad attack on every kind of folly, cruelty, and superstition, and a plea for reason and truth (C). *The Disasters* were banned, while *The Caprices* series was never published in Goya's own lifetime. Goya portrayed on one hand the imbecility of dueling among men of "honor," and on the other painted a horrifying picture of two peasants fighting to the death with cudgels while sinking in a quicksand (p. 50).

Goya's paintings and etchings exist as masterpieces in their own right, apart from their message. His message, like that of Hogarth, or Bruegel, or Grünewald, was universal and timeless.

On the contrary and very much of its day, is the art of political caricature. This really came into its own in about Goya's own time, in the late 18th century. Political caricature needed a means of mass-production, widespread literacy, and a general interest in politics. These conditions were provided by two revolutions: one was peaceful, social, and technical—the Industrial Revolution; the other was short, sharp, and bloody—the French Revolution. The latter was too far-reaching to be regarded as a merely national affair, and if any thought of it as such, Napoleon's new nationalism and the French Empire soon dispelled any such opinion. Napoleon's "liberation" policy involved all Europe and a great deal of the rest of the world in war. Conscription and income tax ensured the concern of everyone, not merely the professional soldiers and statesmen. Political caricaturists sprang up on both sides to meet the demand for news, and to act as an outlet for national and political feelings. Their work was engraved, often in a hurry. The drawing is rushed and crude, but the urgency gives added bite to the message.

The most brilliant and prolific satirist of the period was James Gillray (1757-1815). His main targets were the protagonists, William Pitt and Napoleon (p. 51), but he often turned from war to sharpen his etching needle on social habits and customs. One such is his satire on the fashion of attending scientific lectures at the Royal Institution (D).

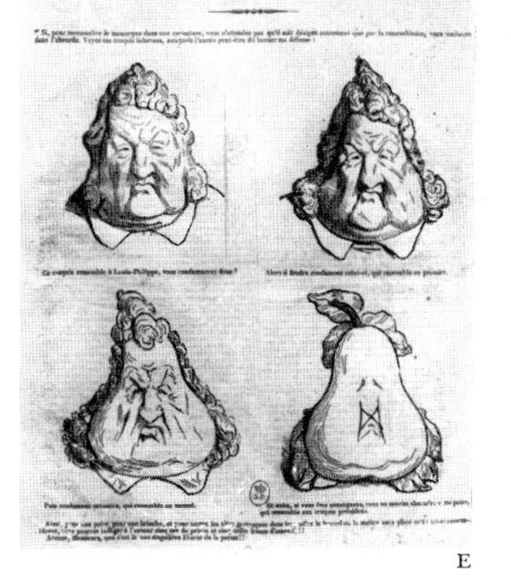

LES POIRES,

Vendues pour payer les 6,000 fr. d'amende du journal le *Charivari.*

E

F

G

H

(E) CHARLES PHILIPON
Les Poires: from "Charivari," 1834

(F) GRANDVILLE The Shadows: from "La Caricature," 1830
London, B. M.

(G) THOMAS HEINE The Liberty of Science: from "Simplicissimus" 1900 *London, B. M.*

(H) GEORG GROSZ
Christ with Gasmask, 1926
New York, coll. Erich Cohn

The popularity of prints was followed by an increasing public for daily newspapers and periodicals. Charles Philipon of Paris founded his "Charivari" in 1830, first as a weekly and then as a daily comic paper. These papers were the ancestors of today's "Punch," "New Yorker," "Simplicissimus," and all other satirical papers. Philipon himself achieved notoriety by his famous visual pun of Louis Philippe turning into a pear—French slang for a fathead (E). More important was his patronage and encouragement of the best of French caricaturists—Paul Gavarni, Grandville (F), and Honoré Daumier. Daumier, a fine painter, wore himself out producing a lithographed cartoon drawing almost every day of his working life, more than 4,000 of them, for Philipon's papers. In doing so he achieved an absolute synthesis between his drawing and the medium.

In Germany, Thomas Heine in "Simplicissimus" attacked Prussian domination of German culture (G) with an intensity that foreshadowed the work of Georg Grosz (p. 52), who in the 20th century first attacked the Kaiser's war-party and then the Nazis, with a series of drawings that made full use of all the modern movement techniques, including surrealism and collage. His drawing of Christ crucified in gas mask and boots was condemned as blasphemous. The drawing had its origin in Grünewald's altarpiece, and underlines the constant regeneration that takes place in all the arts (H).

Much is forgiven a great artist because he is such. He can claim a privileged position, something like that of the court fool. But here also lies a weakness, for he will be "forgiven" his unacceptable content on account of his powers as a draftsman or for some other great quality in his work. He will find himself collected and admired even by those he sought to attack.

On the other hand, satire pure and simple must die with its target. Eventually burning political issues become material for history books and a terse, laconic political cartoon of yesterday may need a lengthy and scholarly foot-note to explain it. What still makes it worth looking at is the quality of drawing.

Moral problems remain, for these are fundamental to human nature, and born afresh with each generation. So it is with works of art concerned with these issues; and with the work of a Bruegel, Hogarth, or Goya, not only is the form still as powerful as ever, but the message itself remains true and relevant to all times.

CHAPTER 5

The Painter as Dreamer and Prophet

"THE sleep of reason breeds monsters." Goya's motto to his *Caprices* suite of etchings reminds us that only too often our dreams take a sinister, left-handed turn (A). It is in the dark that our fears become dominant, and in sleep that the imagination runs riot. It has always been easier for poets and painters to draw a convincing picture of the torments of Hell, rather than the delights of Heaven. Milton's Satan and Marlowe's Faustus are heroic in their torment, of solid understandable flesh and blood. Dante dreamed of the aged Ulysses setting out on his last voyage of discovery, the one that took him beyond Gibraltar and the Pillars of Hercules, the gateway of the known classical world, and led him to drown in the whirlpool of damnation. He, an old man who should have known better, says Dante, ought to have stayed at home and looked after his family and his people, and lived virtuously to a ripe old age. Instead, he finished in Hell, damned together with all others who gave false counsel. Led astray and leading astray, our sympathies are with the restless, insatiably curious old hero who forsook the quiet life, which even Dante cannot help making sound extraordinarily dull.

The prophets of the ancient world were men with consciences large enough for the whole community, and their anxiety for the fate of mankind led them to draw verbal pictures of the terrible end awaiting wrongdoers, far more than the rewards for good living.

(C) Greek vase painting: The Sirens and Odysseus *London, B. M.*

The visual artist is given the power to bring these dreams to life, to give them the illusion of three-dimensional solidity and physical substance. He can turn the wildest imaginings into concrete form.

The dreams of the ancient world, where philosophy and religion were an inseparable part of everyday life, were universal dreams. The Egyptian "Book of the Dead," the imagined journey of the soul to the next world through an elaborate system of trials and tests, became so convincing that the original pictorial symbols of the soul's new life after death gradually grew into a literal reality, and the book became a bureaucratic guide book, a list of rules and regulations whose non-observance could lead to disaster (B).

(A) FRANCISCO GOYA The Sleep of Reason Breeds Monsters: from the Caprices, 1796-98

(B) The Weighing of Souls: from "The Book of the Dead" about 1250 B.C. *London, B.M.*

The dream world of the Greeks, less rigid than that of the Egyptians, was still strictly hieratic, that is to say, the symbols were laid down according to a well understood traditional formula. The harpies, furies, and chimeras, the monsters that beset Theseus, Hercules, and Oedipus, are still compounded of men and animals with a strong literal association, the bull for savagery and strength, the carrion-eating vulture for horror, the stinging fly for torment (C).

The great classical age came to an end, and myths and dreams became more personal. Just as Rome had replaced Egypt and Greece, so the Roman Empire itself dissolved. The conquerors and inheritors were either barbarian and pagan, in which case philosophy was replaced by superstition, or they were Christian and it was replaced by theology. For the time being the universal language of philosophy was forgotten.

Christian prophecy is personal and intimate, as seen in the dream of Revelation experienced by St. John on Patmos. This remained a poet's privilege. From early Christian times, strict rules were laid down governing the representation of God and His three manifestations and His saints. Heaven was beyond imagination and only portrayed by symbols of eternal peace. The only field in which the artist was allowed a free imagination was in the portrayal of scenes of torment and punishment in Hell. Here the more horrific and literal he could make his scenes, the more they would exercise a cautionary influence on the sinner.

Dante's great vision of Heaven and Hell marked a new attitude toward the acceptance of an individual and personal interpretation of doctrine, as a valid contribution towards understanding. The visual arts did not attain the same degree of liberty until the Renaissance when, with the new attitude toward man as an individual, the whole of painting became more personal, and the dream picture came really into its own.

In particular, idiosyncrasy became more marked in northern Europe, where Roman influence was always much less than in the south, and where people were less accustomed to disciplines both in thought and action. When a northern painter such as Pieter Bruegel wanted to portray *The Tower of Babel*, he took what was familiar to him and worked on it in his imagination, with far less reference to classical models (D). Lucas Cranach's picture of *Lot and his Daughters* (p. 53) has an extraordinary vision of the destruction of Sodom and Gomorrah in the background, with thunderbolts from heaven looking remarkably like rockets, bombarding the cities which are consumed in fire like that of a blast furnace. Dürer not only took the Revelation as a starting point for destructive fantasy, but had an extraordinary dream, in which he saw a city consumed by fire beneath a giant mushroom pillar of cloud (p. 54). On awakening he drew it as if he had really seen it happen. Dürer's dream is an isolated phenomenon in his own work, but, on the other hand, the visions of flood, fire, and earthquake by Leonardo da Vinci are based on his observations. Although works of the imagination, they are rooted in a firm knowledge of the behavior of winds, fire, and water, and have an unforgettable authentic realism (E).

(D) PIETER BRUEGEL the ELDER The Tower of Babel, about 1563
Vienna, Kunsthist. Mus.

(E) LEONARDO DA VINCI Floods and Whirlwinds, about 1514
Windsor, Royal Library

(A) PIETER BRUEGEL the ELDER Mad Margaret's Visit to Hell 1562 *Antwerp, Mus. Mayer van den Bergh*

As extraordinary in their way are the paintings of Hieronymus Bosch. His mind conceived images far beyond those of present science fiction; often his forms seem to have been created in a mad scientist's laboratory. He was fascinated by the portrayal of transparency. *The Garden of Delights* (p. 55) is a sinister pleasure ground, depicting strange pavilions built of armored and spined shell-fish claws, carapaces, and antennae, or giant fruit and seed husks from exotic plants. The forms appear to have been studied under a microscope and the human inhabitants have been accordingly reduced, although this change of scale is far from constant. Garden birds can dwarf men, or appear in natural relationship to them side by side.

His visions of Hell are like an industrial town by night during an air raid. On closer inspection this town is inhabited by very unconventional devils, if there be such. They are not mere monsters based on obvious combinations of natural repugnance, such as the more grotesque and savage animals and reptiles, but are made more sinister by being musical instruments come to life, by having a jug for a head or body, instead of a grotesque dragon's mask. Men have houses for bodies with others looking out of windows inside them.

Bosch stands almost alone. The only painter to approach his fantastic imagination as an equal was Pieter Bruegel, who occasionally enjoyed letting his mind run riot in drawings or paintings, such as *Mad Margaret's Visit to Hell*, but he never allowed his visions to become an obsession (A).

The symbolism of Bosch and Bruegel is firmly rooted in medieval thought, in witchcraft, and alchemy. But in the 16th century, when they were active, the revival of classical philosophy was well under way, and on this revival were founded the new and logical sciences. Growing rationalism still needed the irrational to turn to, but the caprice became the current form. We may refer to the strange scenes of Inquisitorial torture by Alessandro Magnasco, with his mannered technique, a debased, decadent abuse of El Greco (B). Monsu Desiderio painted strange scenes of martyrdom, which are dwarfed by fantastic architectural settings; violent explosions occur in cathedrals of nightmare proportions. Giuseppe Arcimboldi painted strange heads compounded of fruit and fish, or even landscapes (C). There is a strong smell of morbidity here, morbidity born of disillusion. Dante's Ulysses followed the path of knowledge, and it led him to damnation. The same fate befell Faust, whose story was later to fascinate both Marlowe and Goethe.

When painters such as Leonardo da Vinci and Michelangelo carried out anatomical research in the pursuit of truth, they were brought into intimate contact with death and corruption. These unforgettable experiences colored the rest of their lives with pessimism. So it was even in the new sciences of physics and chemistry. The more that men discovered about the physical world, the less they discovered that they really knew. They attempted by reason to find stable laws governing the universe, but reason seemed to lead them to places where everything dissolved into space.

Nowhere is this constant process more apparent than in the uneasy transition from the 18th to the 19th century. The simple rules for conduct of all kinds were dissolving. Although man was finding freedom, he was

(B) ALESSANDRO MAGNASCO Inquisition Scene *Vienna, Kunsthist. Mus.*

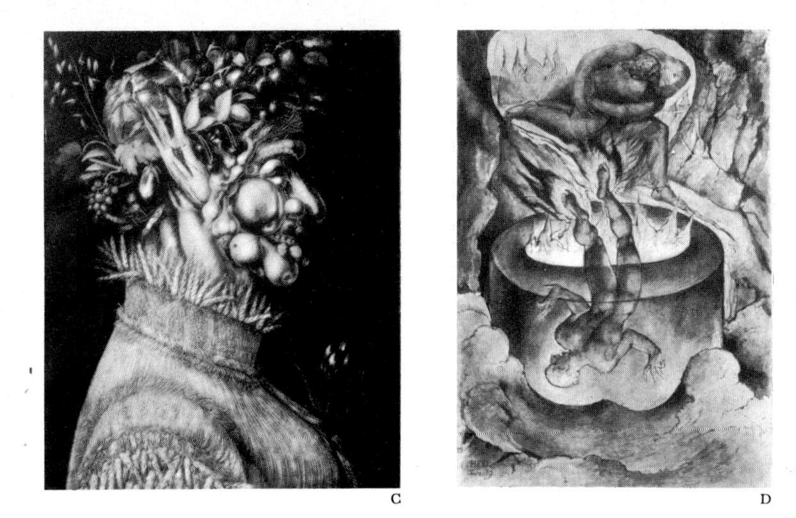

(C) GIUSEPPE ARCIMBOLDI Summer, 1563
Vienna, Kunsthist. Mus.

(D) WILLIAM BLAKE The Simoniac Pope, 1824-27
London, Tate

having a terrifying responsibility thrust upon him with it, and it was sometimes too strong for him to bear. Faust, the alchemist and philosopher, whose chief crime was to abandon faith for reason, becomes a scientist, Frankenstein. In Mary Shelley's novel Frankenstein used physical science, not magic, to create life which became an uncontrollable force that destroyed him. William Blake saw Isaac Newton in this role. Most of Blake's prophetic poems are long and involved, but every so often he states a fundamental truth with dramatic clarity. They—the Newtonian scientists—try to measure infinity by hours and seconds, whereas, according to Blake, it exists outside our measured time. The forces that scientists had discovered brought the dark Satanic mills into being, instead of the New Jerusalem that they had promised. Blake turned to Dante as his poetic model, and to Michelangelo for his form (D). He illustrated Dante and Milton, and wrote his own prophetic poems. Because his work ran counter to the thought of his time, he was held to be mad, but within a small circle of disciples his ideas were a powerful influence.

The way that leads beyond reason had been forced open by Blake and Goya, and they were followed by an extraordinary flood of eccentric personalities who deliberately cultivated the dark side of the mind.

Henry Fuseli, a Swiss painter who settled in England, and almost unaccountably became a respectable member of the Royal Academy, exploited Blake's images and style without understanding his deep philosophy. Compared to those of Goya, his nightmares are jack-o' lantern pumpkins for Halloween. His content is not of humanity and the human condition, but Gothic horrors and ghost stories by the fireside. He made the profound comment that one of the most unexpected regions of art is dreams, and set out to explore it himself (E).

His Bottom and Titania (F) are companions to the figures in Richard Dadd's *The Fairy Feller's Master-stroke* (p. 56). Dadd killed his father in an uncontrollable fit of rage, and spent the rest of his life in Bedlam, where he continued drawing and painting.

John Martin, one of an eccentric family of brothers, combined the dream world with a feverish interest in scientific development. He drew up plans for elevated railways, a dock scheme for London, a Thames barrage and sewage scheme, and used geological and archeological discoveries to create his enormous canvases of sea dragons fighting, the Deluge, or Belshazzar's feast.

HENRY FUSELI (E) Nightmare, 1782 *Frankfurt-am-Main, Goethehaus* (F) Bottom and Titania *Zurich, Kunsthaus.*

(A) JOHN MARTIN The Great Day of His Wrath, about 1853 *London, Tate*

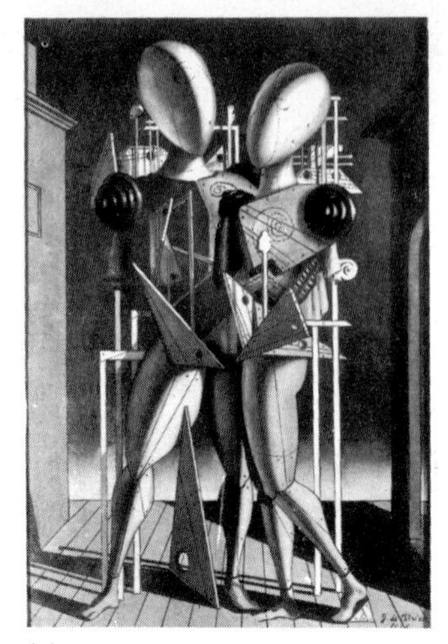

(B) GIORGIO DE' CHIRICO Metaphysics of Man and Woman, 1916 *Chicago, Cummings Coll.*

Disasters are presented on an heroic scale. The earth itself cracks open, and whole cities vanish into crevasses, or are buried under falling mountains. Lightning plays from cloudscapes apparently stretching into limitless distances (A).

There is a strong parallel to be drawn between the dream painters of the first half of the 19th century, and those of the 20th century. The latter too were born of disillusion. Instead of scientific progress leading to a new world of plenty, based entirely on reason, it apparently and unaccountably led to the catastrophe of two world wars, coupled with revolution and counter-revolution. The revolutions, which were welcomed at first by many thinking people, brought about their own particular disillusion born of revolutionary methods. Painters turned away from the solid world of modern abstract and constructivist work, that is to say, painting that was strongly geared to the idea of progress. They retreated into the personal world of the unconscious mind and its dreams. If reason has failed, then let us turn to the irrational, they said.

The main difference between the surrealist painters and all their previous forerunners was that by their time the mind itself had been subjected to scientific analysis. Freud and his followers had investigated the symbolic language of dreams and images and put them into categories. The strange symbols of Hieronymus Bosch, derived from the workings of his conscious and subconscious mind, were now available as ready-made material listed between the covers of books.

The disquieting images of Giorgio de' Chirico, already formed before World War I, are composed of strange figures made up of geometrical instruments and dressmaker's dummies, with broken statuary, giant *petit beurre* biscuits, bananas, or railway trains in lonely squares, whose scale is emphasized by perspective lines (B). These lines especially were to invade the whole field of commercial art. The movement became international: Paul Klee, Switzerland; Max Ernst, Germany; Man Ray, America; Salvador Dali and Joan Mirò, Spain; René Magritte, Belgium; Marcel Duchamp, Yves Tanguy and Marc Chagall, France (C-G).

Paul Klee was the most personal and poetic of the new movement, portraying a complete dream world on the scale of medieval miniatures. His work is careful, intense, and fragile; it has a childlike, not childish quality, and when disturbing or sinister it is tempered by a strong vein of irony (pp. 57 and 58).

Salvador Dali is the most obviously Freudian of the surrealists, drawing heavily upon the textbooks of psycho-analysis. His imagery and presentation are so heavily literal that at times his work verges on the banal (D). At first glance similar to Dali, but far more personal and intense, is Max Ernst. He uses the juxtaposition of commonplace and familiar objects in strange surroundings. These have the effect of recreating in our waking

C

D

(C) MARCEL DUCHAMP
The Bride Stripped Bare by her Bachelors, Even (The Large Glass) 1915-23
Philadelphia, Pa., Mus. of Art
The Louise and Walter Arensberg Coll.

(D) SALVADOR DALI
Autumn Cannibalism, 1937
London, Tate

minds those disturbing dreams that have a beginning based on everyday experience, and then suddenly turn into a situation where things are not what they seem.

Miró has evolved his own personal language (E), depending on flat shapes and brilliant colors. Tanguy takes us into a strange world of space in which float suspended specimens from the natural history of an unknown planet. Sometimes they appear to be of bone, or gelatinous globules and attenuated strings (F).

Magritte paints the bare walls of what Samuel Beckett has described as man's medium-sized cage, and then thrusts in intruders. A landscape comes out of its frame; a locomotive emerges from the fireplace (G).

Surrealism is entirely concerned with story telling in paint and this literary preoccupation is perhaps its weakness. It can be so firmly tied to its symbols that we cannot be certain of its future, since symbols change so quickly. Now that advertising is so dependent upon deep Freudian analysis the invasion of surrealism into this field has destroyed some of its punch. Our senses are blunted by familiarization.

The next most obvious step has already been made: to bring the dream picture itself to life. A few exploratory surrealist films have been made, but it is mainly the non-experimental cinema of the thriller and science fiction that has produced its own form of dream language.

(E) JOAN MIRÓ Woman, Bird by Moonlight, 1949 *London, Tate*

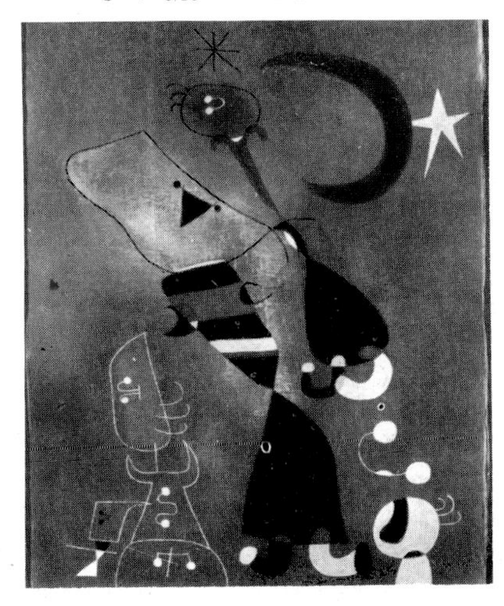

(F) YVES TANGUY Les Transparents, 1932 *London, Tate*

(G) RENÉ MAGRITTE Time Transfixed, 1932 *London, Tate (loan)*

CHAPTER 6

The Artist as Recorder of His Time

A

WE can obtain certain information by looking at works of art that, to the artist who made them, were incidental or even unconscious, and taken for granted. This to a later generation becomes very important. For example, the Egyptian and Assyrian painters and sculptors were recording the official history of kings, men, and gods. In so doing they tell us much about their everyday life, and even if we could not read Egyptian hieroglyphs or Assyrian cuneiform, even if we had no other records of these civilizations than a figure or two from each, we could still reasonably deduce certain things about them. The Egyptian apparently dresses in a tightly pleated garment of fine material, often translucent or gauzey (A). It is therefore likely to be cotton or linen, a vegetable fiber—not wool—and therefore we can assume that the people who wear it are part of a society of landowners and cultivators. Moreover, the regalia symbolizing authority are the reaping hook and threshing flail.

On the other hand, the Assyrian wears heavy-looking robes, thickly fringed and tasseled (B). He wears wool then, and his social system is based on owning flocks of sheep and goats, or herds of camels.

The former society was founded on land tenure and inheritance, and was conservative and stable, with a strongly marked hierarchy. The cities of the latter society depended upon semi-nomadic graziers, who followed seasonal pastures. It was more liable to economic fluctuation and exposed to successive conquests, and society was less stable. We can thus start to build up quite an accurate picture of the two great contemporary early civilizations from very little evidence (C, D). We acquire this information in an indirect way, for when an Egyptian sculptor carved the figure of a god, he certainly was not intending to leave a record of Egyptian dress for posterity. Even when he carved chariots or ships so accurately that we could use the reliefs as working drawings to rebuild these things today, he was still not telling us the

(A) Detail of gilded shrine from Tutankhamen Treasure, about 1350 B.C. *Cairo, Mus.*

(B) Assyrian figure dressed in the head and wings of an eagle, 9th century B.C. *London, B. M.*

(C) Huy's river boat: from "The Tomb of Huy" by N. de G. Davies and A. H. Gardner

B

C

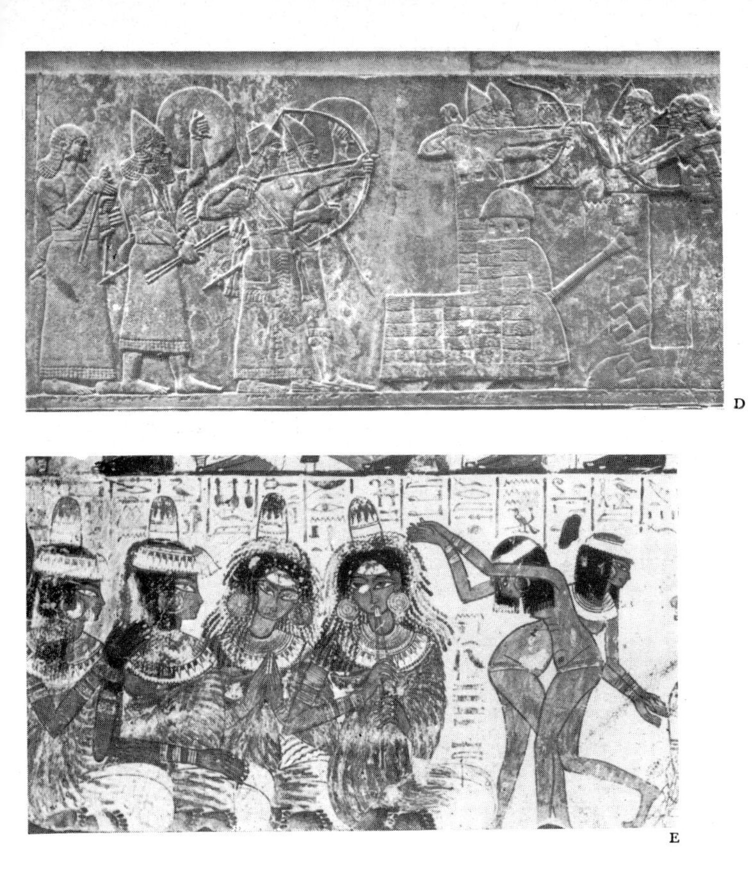

D

E

F

(D) Assyrian bas-relief: King Assur-nazir-pal and his army before a besieged city, 9th century B.C. *London, B. M.*

(E) Egyptian mural painting: Guests, dancing girls, and musicians. From a tomb at Thebes, about 1500 B.C. *London, B. M.*

(F) JAMES TISSOT The Visit, 1876 *London, Tate*

story of Egyptian vehicle or ship building, but of wars and conquests by land and sea. Peasants living their daily lives, hunting, ploughing, and building, musicians and entertainers, acrobats and jugglers, are all there on the walls of Egyptian tombs, painted and carved to the glory of their masters and as a record of their estates and possessions. This realistic description of their trades is their means of identification (E). We can use this information, but we cannot attribute an intention of recording this picture of society for future use to the artist, any more than we can assume that James Tissot in the 19th century intended to record changing fashions in ladies dresses, though he did so so accurately that we can date his work by the fashions portrayed (F, and p. 59). Tissot was concerned with storytelling in paint. The tales are often of the sentimental nature very popular among art patrons at that time, and his pictures were bought as painted anecdotes. Then came a reaction against this storytelling picture that was as emotional as the previous vogue for it. Now that this reaction is also passing, we can disregard Tissot's sentiment and turn to that side of his painting which is much stronger: his feeling for his own time and the loving way in which he recorded certain aspects of it.

Tissot's patrons were the rich merchants of his day, what we call self-made men. Princes like to buy or commission pictures that glorify themselves and their families and houses. The princes of the church commissioned pictures to the greater glory of God. The philosopher and scholar likes his pictures to be of a contemplative nature, telling of truths that lie behind the visible world.

As an example we may take a typical painting by Nicolas Poussin of Arcadian shepherds (*Et in Arcadia Ego*, p. 60). Any of us capable of looking at a picture can see that it shows some draped figures standing among trees and rocks in open country. We can see the colors of the sky and the robes, and it is all very pleasant. However, the picture was painted for patrons whose main education lay in the study of Greek and Roman literature. In Poussin's work every detail, every gesture is dictated by some sort of classical literary reference and, although we may like his pictures, we cannot really understand them in the way that Poussin intended unless we have had a classical education.

Indeed, without understanding his references, Poussin's figures often seem stiff and artificial, for they have to be forced to fit strong preconceived ideas.

It was the citizen merchant, banker or "expert," the doctor or the goldsmith, who was the patron for pictures of everyday life. They were people who wanted cabinet-sized pictures to hang in their rooms, and although their houses may have been large, they were not palaces requiring mural decoration. They preferred everyday scenes to subjects drawn from classical mythology, sometimes because they felt that the latter were not "respectable," more often because they had not been brought up to accept the conventions of Greek and Roman poetry and myths. They liked their portraits to be serious looking, prosperous, showing furs, silks, and jewelry as they really are, not too large, and most definitely something to leave behind for their successors to look up to. They liked still-life pictures of game and food, pictures of horses or of the interiors of bourgeois houses like their own, with a simple domestic incident, scenes of picturesque low life among villagers, and finally views of towns, the countryside, and the sea.

We find this kind of painting firmly rooted in northern Europe. Here the Roman influence had been less strong, and there were fewer classical monuments and models left behind. While the early Renaissance princes were setting themselves up on a large scale in Italy, and encouraging the Grand Manner in art, the northern painters followed a provincial way of their own. The later illuminated books of Flanders and Burgundy contain extremely realistic pictures, but when the Limbourg Brothers or Jean Colombe illustrated a classical or biblical scene, they dressed the Caesars or biblical characters in the dress of their own small northern European towns. Troy became a Gothic town, and we see all the medieval building trades engaged in its construction (A). Jerusalem itself becomes a brick and timber town with cobbled streets and market stalls.

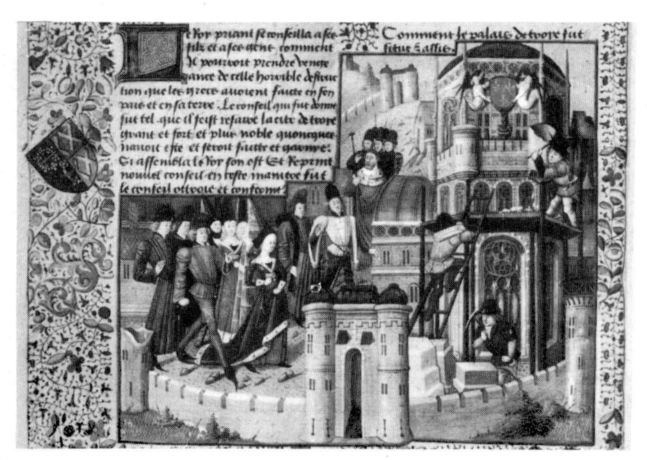

(A) JEAN COLOMBE The Building of Troy: from "The History of Troy," about 1500 *Paris, Bibl. Nat.*

One of the earliest paintings intended purely as a record is the so-called *Arnolfini* portrait by Jan van Eyck (p. 61), now thought by some to be a self-portrait of the Flemish painter and his wife. It is a betrothal portrait, a document. The painter wrote on his picture, "I was here and saw this." There is a direct relationship between the picture and the spectator. We are in the room with the couple and the little dog, the red bolstered bed and brass chandelier. We can even see the back of the couple reflected in the round bull's-eye mirror on the wall behind them. The Flemish interior, and all its furnishings, the clothes and jewelry are faithfully recorded for their own sake.

In the 16th and 17th centuries the Low Countries, Holland and Belgium, found themselves in an extremely advantageous position with regard to the rest of Europe. New voyages of trade and discovery to the Far East and to the West led to a boom in the import-export business and merchant banking. The door into Europe through which the bulk of the imports passed was the mouth of the Rhine. Social barriers and customs prevented the older aristocracy from becoming middle men and city merchants, and a new middle class sprang up which almost had a monopoly of trade. The Low Countries became very rich and independent.

One result of this sudden prosperity in a comparatively small area was an extraordinary outburst of productivity in picture making. This lively period of Dutch painting begins and ends with the 17th century and was founded on the analytical vision of van Eyck. The Dutch had to build their land before they could build on it, and orderly planning and economy became second nature to them. They painted their manmade landscape with that over-all clear light peculiar to a country never far from the sea. They painted their neat red brick towns, the houses and courtyards, rooms which are like views into an aquarium, still-life groups, and portraits of burgesses and their wives, not dressed as Greeks or Romans, or in ceremonial armor or draped like goddesses, but as they were, sometimes very plain, in their sensible well-made everyday clothes (B,C, and p. 62).

It is as if the painters gradually moved in from the open landscape through an increasing series of close-ups

B

C

D

(B) JAN VERMEER View of Delft, 1658 *The Hague, Mauritshuis*

(C) PIETER DE HOOCH Courtyard of a House in Delft, 1658 *London, N. G.*

(D) BARTHOLOMEUS VAN DER HELST Portrait of a Man, 1658 *Amsterdam, Rijksmus.*

(E) REMBRANDT VAN RYN Portrait of a Man, 1658 *Paris, Louvre*

E

to the intimacy of still-life. For these painters not only painted to satisfy their clients, they satisfied themselves. And what they sought after was a way of painting light. The landscapes and seascapes are full of light and air, and they were painted at all seasons. Their skies were not generalized as in classic Italian or French painting, with great rolling clouds providing upholstered comfort for the Olympian gods, but were born of a moment, of a particular season, place, and time of day.

The still-lifes, too, are not merely about good things to eat, as if the bourgeois patron was merely concerned with filling his eye as he would his stomach. The glasses of wine, the shining oysters, the silvers, the delicate spirals of lemon peel are vehicles for transmitting, reflecting, and holding light. The artist was absorbed in translating all the various textures of hard and soft surfaces, the bloom on plums, the fuzz of a peach, the crispness of silk, or the pile of velvet (p. 63).

In Dutch portrait painting the head, seen against a dark ground, set off by dark clothes, heightened by a geometric ellipse of white linen, appears to be its own source of light (D).

Rembrandt treated this light as if it would illuminate the character within (E). Eventually, to the disappointment of his friends and patrons, the search led him away from the painting that they could understand, to an inward vision, as if he were painting not what he saw before him but what existed in the remote corners of his own mind. He turned his back upon well-meaning friends and lived and painted alone.

His death coincided with the collapse of Dutch painting. It was as sudden as its beginning. The market suffered from overproduction and prices fell to practically nothing overnight. Quite a lot of gambling had gone on in the picture market, and this was replaced by a new and extravagant craze, gambling in tulips.

But the achievement remained, the idea that landscape could be painted without having to serve as the setting for a classical pastoral scene, that scenes taken from everyday life would be hung on walls, and that

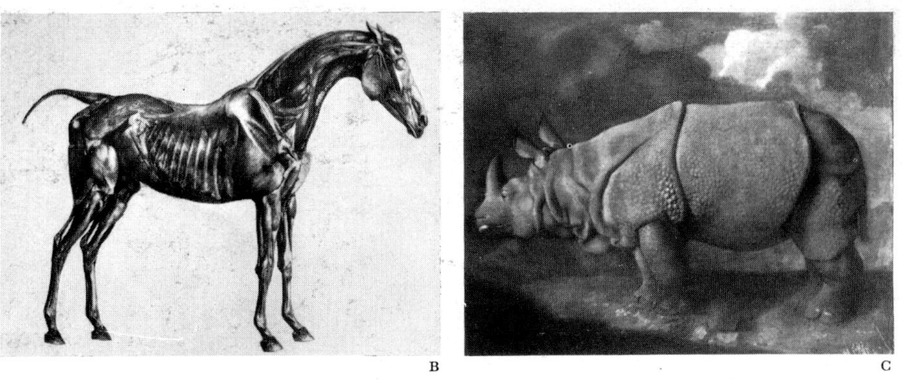

(A) ANTOINE LE NAIN A Woman and Five Children (detail) 1642 *London, N. G.*

(B) GEORGE STUBBS Engraving from "Anatomy of the Horse" *London, B.M.*

(C) GEORGE STUBBS Rhinoceros, 1772 *London, Royal College of Surgeons*

(D) JOSEPH MALLORD WILLIAM TURNER Rain, Steam, and Speed, 1844 *London, N. G.*

portraits could show people as studies of character and not as ideals of beauty, nobility, or spirituality.

In France, the Le Nain brothers took their subjects from the life of the common people, and combined this with an interest in the portrayal of artificial light (A). Jean Baptiste Chardin was trained in the Dutch school, and gave simple still-life subjects an architectural monumentality (p. 64). His conversation-pieces of mistress and maid, or a girl scouring pots, teaching a child his lessons, are painted with an air of detached but sympathetic calm. His paint is richly applied with a slightly granular texture. The tones and planes are sorted out with a scientific precision, and have a slight appearance of separation as in a careful mosaic. His composition is always firm and readily analyzed by geometry.

This scientific observation became the mainspring of some of the best English painting of the 18th and 19th centuries. English landscape painting has the botanic fidelity we should expect in a country where to be an amateur naturalist—and amateur only in the non-professional sense—was almost commonplace among the great painting patrons. Gainsborough's landscapes, inspired by the Dutch, are romantic but not artificial, and Richard Wilson painted his cool, clear views of Wales, seen through the warm glow of a late afternoon light.

George Stubbs was the most scientific of observers of the natural world. An anatomist very early in life, in him were fused scientist and artist into an inseparable, complete entity. No one observed and recorded what he saw more carefully, yet he is in control of nature in his work, not at its mercy. A strong geometrical foundation underlies all his paintings, and he considered geometry

as essential a part of the world as his sitters for portraits, his horses, their rural settings, harvesters, and the uncommon animals which made up his subjects (B, C, and p. 65). Stubbs was commissioned by the great 18th-century surgeon John Hunter to paint many of the pictures for his anatomical collection.

His work achieves Erasmus Darwin's great aim, "To enlist the imagination under the banner of science." The quotation equally fits the work of Joseph Wright of Derby, who painted some of the scientific experiments of his day, and was passionately involved in the portrayal of artificial and dramatic light from candles, forges, and volcanic eruptions (p. 66). The work of John Constable and Joseph Mallord William Turner ends this movement. Constable recorded his cloud observations as accurately and almost as quickly as a camera; Turner was much concerned with theory of light and color in order to paint light (D).

E F G

H

I

It was not a scientific but a moral attitude which revived realistic painting in mid-19th-century France. Jean Baptiste Camille Corot turned to nature and landscape as a reaction against what he considered to be false and inflated Romanticism, and Realism became a political slogan for Jean François Millet, Gustave Courbet, (E, H) and Honoré Daumier. The realistic movement split into two streams, composed of those who were concerned with the tonal rendering in grays of snapshot scenes of everyday life—Edgar Degas, Édouard Manet, Henri de Toulouse-Lautrec—and those who sought realism by painting what they saw in pure color without any preconceived academic ideas—Camille Pissarro, Claude Monet (G) and Pierre Auguste Renoir. The latter were loosely grouped under the title of Impressionist. The political label *revolutionary* was used in spite of denials by individual artists. Realism became synonymous with a concern for the underdog and reform. In England too, the realist illustrators of the "Illustrated London News" and "The Graphic," who unfortunately rarely produced any painting to match their powerful drawings, were working for a politically conscious public which had not long been given the power to vote.

J

(E) JEAN FRANÇOIS MILLET
The Woodcutters *London, V. and A.*

(F) EDGAR DEGAS
The Absinthe Drinker, 1876
Paris, Mus. de l'Impressionnisme

(G) CLAUDE MONET
La Gare Saint-Lazare, 1877
Paris, Mus. de l'Impressionnisme

(H) GUSTAVE COURBET
The Burial at Ornans, 1849
Paris, Louvre

(I) HENRI DE TOULOUSE-LAUTREC
The Dancer Chocolat in the Bar d'Achille *Albi, France, Mus.*

(J) SIR HUBERT VON HERKOMER
On Strike, 1906 *London, R. A.*

This equating of Realism with truth, and seeing it as a reaction against hypocrisy and complacency, gave us Lautrec's scenes of low life (I), Degas' *The Absinthe Drinker* (F) and Sir Hubert von Herkomer's *On Strike* (J). The moralizing pictures of William Holman Hunt and Ford Madox Brown depend equally upon realism. The

(A) GEORGE WESLEY BELLOWS Stag at Sharkey's, 1907
Cleveland, Ohio, Mus. of Art, Hinman Hurlburt Coll.

(B) ROBERT POLHILL BEVAN A Street Scene in Belsize Park, 1917
London, London Mus.

Ashcan school of American painting was an anti-romantic gesture. George Bellows' scenes of prize fighters are stripped of glamor in the same way that Degas treated his ballet dancers or his laundresses (A).

Today, realistic painting is still thought of as the product of certain social and moral convictions. In Marxist countries and among Marxist painters outside them, social realism is still founded strongly upon 19th-century principles. Renato Guttuso in Italy is probably the most powerful figure in social realism (C).

The non-Marxist New Realists are generally reacting against academic abstraction as well as being inspired by reformist ideas. Their aims color their realism with a highly personal point of view, that may lead to a kind of caricature through overstatement. This, far from being an artistic weakness, gives their painting a dynamic punch. However, the true record depends upon a certain amount of detachment in the artist, a certain cool aloofness, and the social document of today may be as unconscious in intention as that contained in William Powell Frith's *The Railway Station* (D), or *A Street Scene in Belsize Park* painted by Robert Polhill Bevan (B). Perhaps this form of documentary record is now the true province of the press photographer and the cinema, and the only form of realism left to the painter or sculptor is the portrait and still-life (p. 67).

(C) RENATO GUTTUSO The Discussion, 1959-60
London, Tate

(D) WILLIAM POWELL FRITH The Railway Station, completed 1862
Egham, England, Royal Holloway College

Bison: from the Lascaux Caves, about 12000 B. C.
Dordogne, France
Photo courtesy of Life Magazine, Time-Life Inc.

SEE PAGE 11

Two Kudu bulls, cave painting in Mtoko area of Southern Rhodesia, date unknown
Photo courtesy of Historical Monuments Commission of Southern Rhodesia

SEE PAGE 11

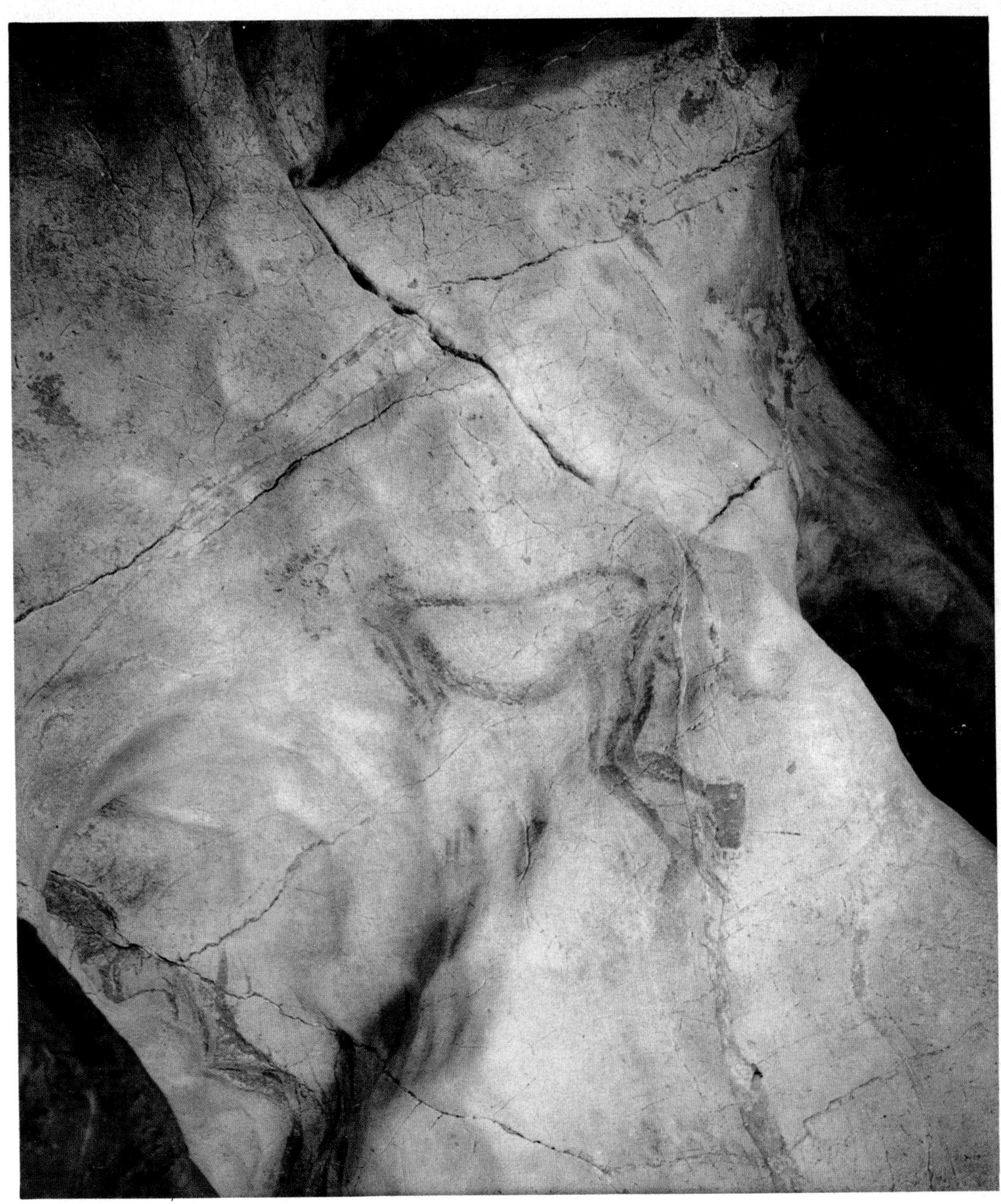

Antler Man, Cave of Les Trois Frères
Ariège, France
Photo courtesy of Abbott Laboratories

SEE PAGE 13

Fowling in the Marshes. Copy of fresco from the tomb of Nakht, about 1500 B. C.
London, British Museum

SEE PAGES 16 AND 96

PIERO DELLA FRANCESCA The Flagellation, about 1471 *tempera on panel* $22\frac{7}{8} \times 31\frac{7}{8}$ *in.*
Urbino, Ducal Palace, Gallery of the Marches

SEE PAGE 19

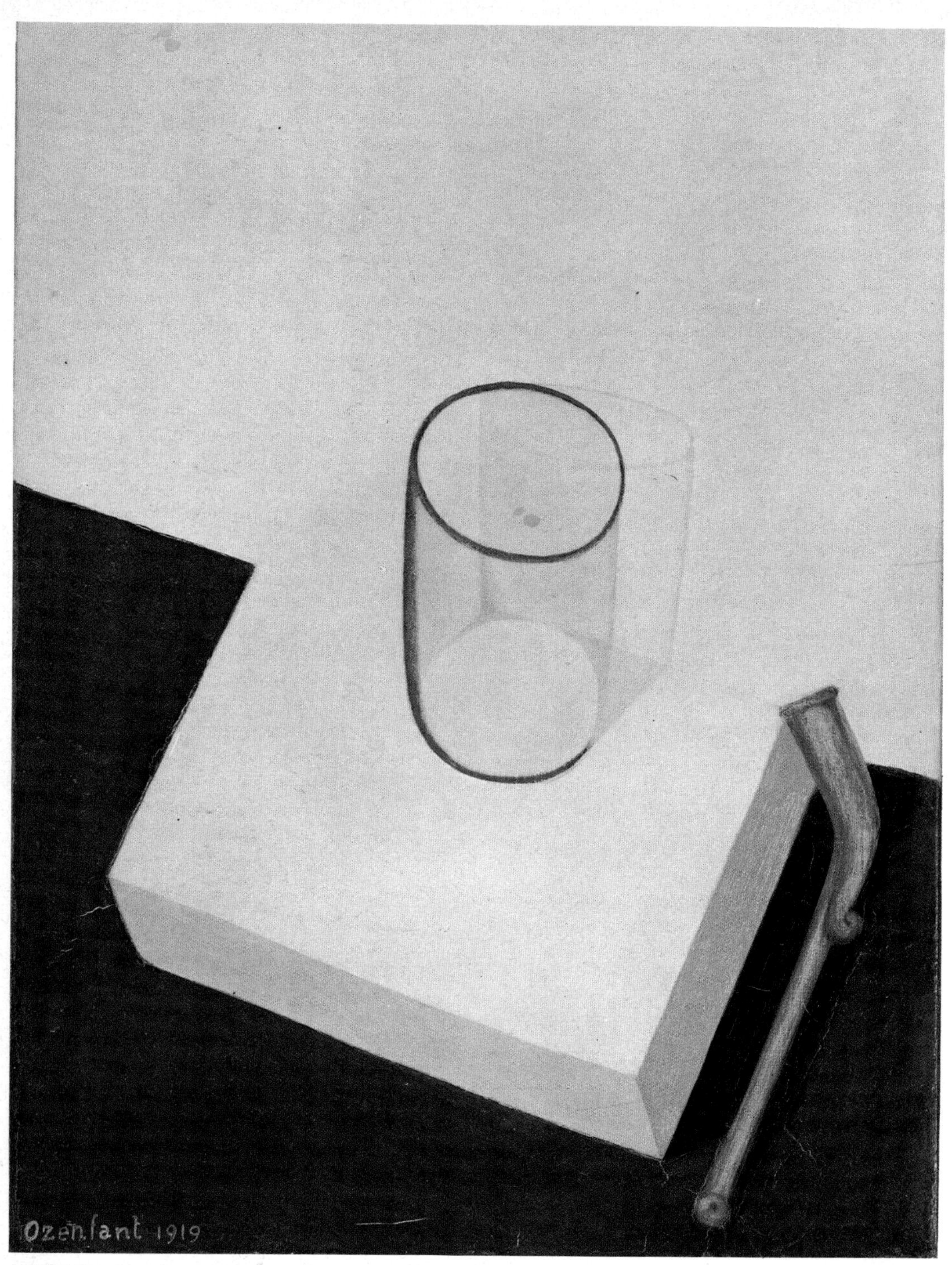

AMÉDÉE OZENFANT Glass and Pipe, 1919 *oil on canvas* $13\frac{3}{4} \times 10\frac{3}{4}$ *in.*
Philadelphia, Pa., Museum of Art, A. E. Gallatin Collection

SEE PAGE 21

PIETER BRUEGEL the ELDER The Adoration of the Kings, 1564 *oil on oak* $43\frac{3}{4} \times 32\frac{3}{4}$ *in.*
London, National Gallery

SEE PAGE 23

JAN STEEN Merrymaking in a Tavern *oil on canvas* $28\frac{7}{8} \times 25\frac{3}{4}$ *in.*
London, Wallace Collection

SEE PAGE 23

WILLIAM HOGARTH The Rake's Progress: Madhouse Scene, 1735 *oil on canvas* $24\frac{3}{4} \times 29\frac{3}{4}$ *in.* SEE PAGES 23 AND 156
London, Sir John Soane's Museum

FRANCISCO GOYA Peasants Fighting with Cudgels, about 1820 *oil on canvas* $48\frac{1}{2} \times 104\frac{3}{4}$ *in.* SEE PAGE 26
Madrid, Prado

JAMES GILLRAY The Plumb-pudding in Danger, 1805
London, British Museum

SEE PAGE 26

GEORGE GROSZ Man of Opinion, 1928 *watercolor* *18½ × 13 in.* SEE PAGE 27
New York, Joseph H. Hirshhorn Collection

LUCAS CRANACH the ELDER Lot and his Daughters (detail) 1529 *oil on canvas* $22\frac{1}{2} \times 14\frac{1}{2}$ *in.* SEE PAGE 29
Munich, Alte Pinakothek

Jm 1525 jor nach dem pfingstag zwischen dem ~~pfin~~ mitwoch und pfintzdag in der nacht im schlaff hab ich dis gesicht gesehen wy fill grosser wassern vom himell fillen. Und das erst traff das ertreich ungefer 4 meill fon mir mit einer solchen grausamkeit mit einem uber grossen rauschen und zersprutzen und ertrenckett das gantz lant. In solchem erschrack ich so gar schwerlich das ich doran erwachtt, ee dan dy andern wasser fillen. Und dy wasser dy do fillen dy woren fast gros und der fill ettliche weit ettliche neher und sy komen so hoch herab das sy im gedunken gleich langsam fillen. aber do das erst wasser das das ertreich traff schir herbey kam do fill es mit einer solchen geschwindikeit wint und brausen das ich also erschrack do ich erwacht das mir all mein leichnam zitert und lang nit recht zu mir selbs kam. Aber do ich am morgen auff stund molet ich hy oben wy ichs gesehen hett. Got wende alle ding zu besten

Albrecht Dürer

ALBRECHT DÜRER The Dream, 1525 *watercolor*
Vienna, Kunsthistorisches Museum

SEE PAGE 29

HIERONYMUS BOSCH The Garden of Delights (central panel) *oil on panel* $86\frac{5}{8} \times 76\frac{3}{4}$ *in.*
Madrid, Prado

SEE PAGE 30

RICHARD DADD The Fairy Feller's Master-stroke, 1855-64 *oil on canvas* $21\frac{1}{4} \times 15\frac{1}{2}$ *in.*
London, Tate Gallery

SEE PAGE 31

PAUL KLEE Senecio, 1922 *oil on canvas 16×15 in.*
Basel, Kunstmuseum

SEE PAGES 32 AND 120

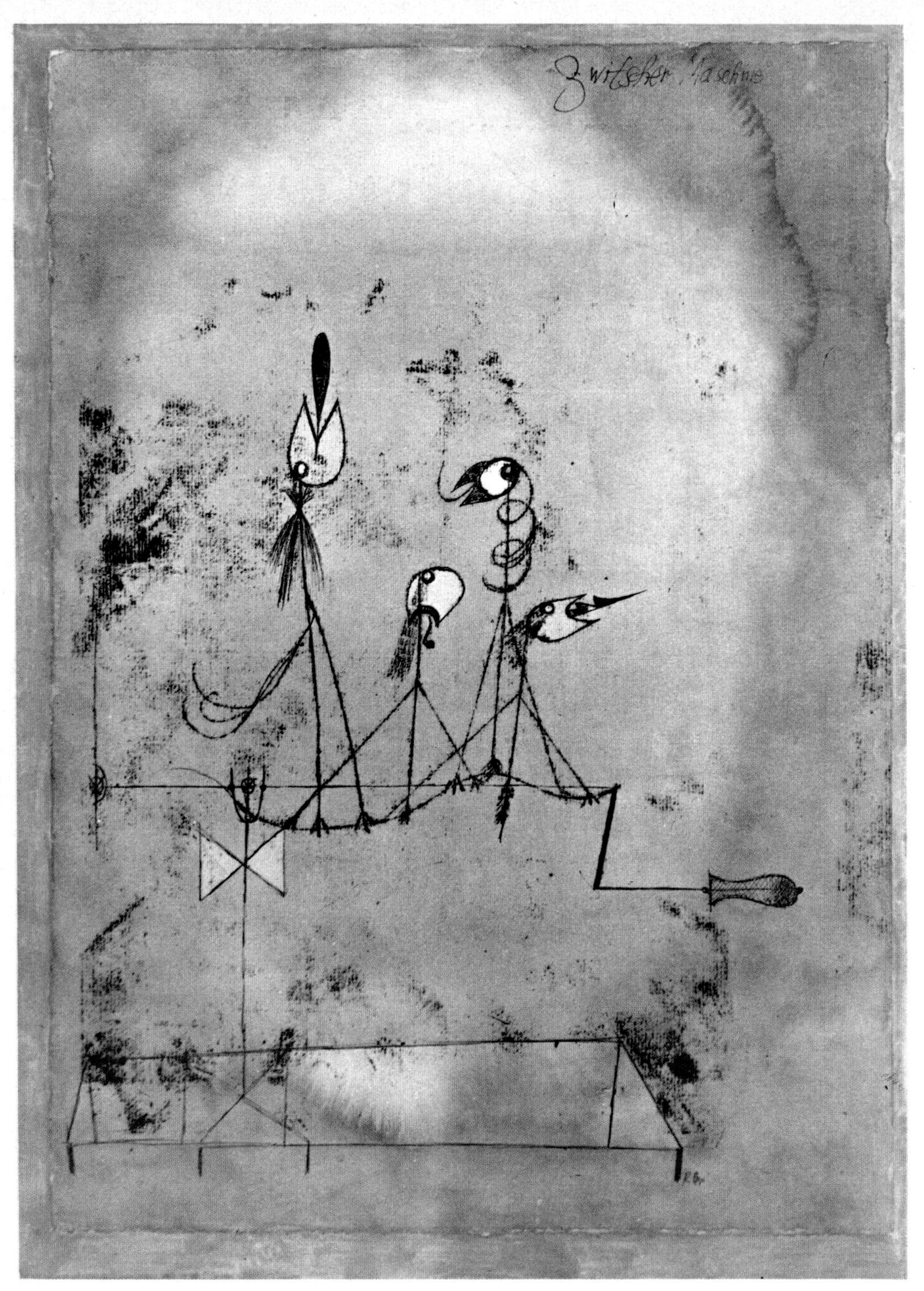

PAUL KLEE Twittering Machine (Zwitscher-Maschine) 1922 *watercolor, pen and ink* *$16\frac{1}{4} \times 12$ in.*
New York, Museum of Modern Art, Purchase SEE PAGES 32 AND 88

JAMES TISSOT The Ball on Shipboard, about 1874 *oil on canvas* $33\frac{1}{8} \times 51$ *in.*
London, Tate Gallery

SEE PAGE 35

NICOLAS POUSSIN Et in Arcadia Ego, about 1650 *oil on canvas 34 × 48 in.*
Paris, Louvre

SEE PAGES 35 AND 76

JAN VAN EYCK Portrait of Giovanni Arnolfini and his Wife, 1434 *oil on panel* $32\frac{1}{4} \times 23\frac{1}{2}$ *in.*
London, National Gallery

SEE PAGES 36 AND 103

JAN VERMEER The Artist's Studio, 1665 *oil on canvas* *47 × 39½ in.*
Vienna, Kunsthistorisches Museum

SEE PAGE 36

PIETER CLAESZ Still-life with Drinking Vessels, 1649 *oil on oak* $25 \times 20\frac{5}{8}$ *in.* SEE PAGE 37
London, National Gallery

JEAN BAPTISTE SIMÉON CHARDIN Still-life with Bottle, about 1756 *oil on canvas* $7\frac{1}{2} \times 13\frac{1}{2}$ *in.* SEE PAGE 38
Angers, France, Musée des Beaux-Arts

GEORGE STUBBS Hunter and Arab *oil on canvas 42×50 in.*
London, Private Collection

SEE PAGE 38

JOSEPH WRIGHT Experiment with the Air-pump, about 1768 *oil on canvas 72×96 in.* SEE PAGE 38
London, Tate Gallery

GIORGIO MORANDI Still-life, 1953 *oil on canvas*
Washington, D. C., Phillips Collection

SEE PAGE 40

Girl Athletes, 3rd-4th century A. D. *Roman mosaic*
Piazza Armerina, Sicily

SEE PAGE 74

TINTORETTO The Origin of the Milky Way, about 1578 *oil on canvas* *58¼ × 65 in.* SEE PAGE 75
London, National Gallery

FRANÇOIS BOUCHER Shepherd Piping to a Shepherdess *oil on canvas* $36\frac{3}{4} \times 55\frac{3}{4}$ *in.* SEE PAGE 76
London, Wallace Collection

ÉDOUARD MANET Le Déjeuner sur l'Herbe, 1863 *oil on canvas* $84\frac{1}{4} \times 106\frac{1}{4}$ *in.* SEE PAGES 79 AND 112
Paris, Musée de l'Impressionnisme

PAUL GAUGUIN Women of Tahiti, 1891 *oil on canvas* $27 \times 35\frac{1}{2}$ *in.*
Paris, Musée de l'Impressionnisme

SEE PAGES 79 AND 114

CHAPTER 7

The Artist as Entertainer

(A) Roman mosaic: Scraps on Floor (detail) *Rome, Lateran Mus.*

EVERYBODY at some time dreams of escape—of getting away from it all—of retiring from an accumulation of minor irritations and responsibilities. Men have escaped from the monotony and boredom of daily life by many means into an imaginary world of their own, sometimes by mental concentration on higher things. But this takes energy and thought, and men grow tired, and seek escape by an easier way, through pleasure real and imaginary.

Somewhere, men like to imagine, there must be an ideal life, where one can live for the moment, undertake heroic adventures without personal danger, eat and drink delicious foods, often in the open air, for the climate would never be too hot or too cold, where it never rains, and where every couple can make love without responsibility—a legendary Arcadia.

The original Arcady was not at all a soft place. The Greeks used the name to denote a place where all lived in harmony because, they said, it was such a wilderness and life was so hard that no one dared quarrel with his neighbor. The shepherds had no alternative but to be as kind as they could to one another. In the Greek view even the gods had their share of trouble and responsibility, and the Greek philosophers tended to frown on entertainment without some uplifting purpose—catharsis, a sort of refreshing purge. Plato thus has hard things to say about the sculptors and painters of his day. They had become, in his eyes, cheap entertainers who gave the common people realistic sensationalism and took their minds off true, ideal reality.

Plato denounced the arts in vain, for in a generation or so even the gods were converted. When the Romans inherited them, they saw them as supermen and superwomen, blessed with immortality and provided with splendid opportunities for every kind of scandalous behavior. The Greeks had taught by means of myths of the unavoidable consequences of men's actions. There is little comfort in these myths; simply harsh reality. The Romans turned the legends into entertainments, emphasizing their erotic quality.

The Romans tended to be materialists, interested in the good things of life, and they maintained this attitude even in the face of the breaking up of their empire. In fact, in the face of disaster, their philosophy developed into a stoic one of "eat, drink, and be merry, for tomorrow we die." It was during the decline and fall of the Roman Empire that much of its best architecture, painting, sculpture, and poetry was produced.

It is this period that has given us our sources of Roman classical mythology, and ever since the European view of the myths has tended to be colored by that particular escapist attitude, giving humanism its rather worldly air and providing a pictorial vocabulary for those visual artists who painted and carved for patrons demanding luxurious relaxation.

To judge the late Roman Empire on the evidence of remains found at Pompeii or Herculaneum is rather as if future historians could judge 20th-century civilization only by fragments of Monte Carlo, Brighton, or Atlantic City. Nevertheless, there does seem to be a great deal to support the popular view of the "decadence" of the last of Rome.

The Emperor Hadrian was an intelligent, reasonably moderate, and well-educated man, who was particularly proud of his "Grecian" view of life. This did not stop him from improving upon Greek sculpture by having expensive copies of the best Greek works made in marbles and precious stones that imitated real flesh, drapery, eyes, teeth, and hair, by their natural coloring. This banal element seems to have been inescapable.

It was considered amusing to pave a dining room floor with a mosaic picture simulating scraps of food, bones, ribbons, and even rubbish and ordure, complete with realistic, cast shadows, as if left there after a dinner party by guests—and dogs (A).

(A) Roman mosaic: Athletes, 1st century A.D.
Rome, Lateran Mus.

(B) Frieze of the Dionysiac Mysteries (detail):
from the Villa of the Mysteries, Pompeii, 1st century B.C. *Naples, Mus. Naz.*

Mosaic *paintings* range from incredibly realistic still-lifes made of minute tesserae to great carpeted floors of rich color and complex patterns. People had their houses decorated with mosaic pictures of race horses and jockeys, famous boxers, and bikini-clad dancing girls (A, and p. 68).

Roman wall paintings are of wax emulsion on plaster. The wax gives a beautiful semi-transparent, slightly polished patina like a soft enamel, quite different from the later dry, rather powdery quality of fresco painting. The subjects vary from the lovely windowless vaulted room of the Villa of Livia or the Palatini, Rome, where one is apparently surrounded by the most beautiful wooded thickets, rich with flowers and thick with song-birds, to the solemnly erotic "mysteries" of love on wall after wall at Pompeii (B).

Many of these sources of Roman entertainment art were unknown, of course, until almost the present day, and the great mythological and classically inspired painting of the past was based mainly on the poets' descriptions and fragments of sculpture. The Middle Ages knew the Roman myths, of course, but the strict moral teaching of the Church frowned on them. This new morality produced its own escapist formula, the legends of chivalry. In these the violence of the wandering, free-booting man at arms was converted into the noble image of the knight errant, who traveled, homeless, seeking to do good, asking for no reward. The love story is changed into romance of unrequited love. The knight declares his love for the lady who is far out of his reach, by rank, virtue, and perhaps marriage. In her name he would set out on adventures that symbolically led him to attain a blissful freedom of negative purity.

This is the theme of the "Story of Coeur," written by the landless King René of Anjou, and illustrated by an anonymous painter who was the contemporary of the Limbourg Brothers and Jean Fouquet during the 15th century (C). Both text and pictures epitomize the medieval romance, but the 1400's also saw the revival of Roman literature and poetry, of sculpture and architecture, and the Italian painters were already freeing themselves from the restrictions of medieval religious thought.

(C) MASTER OF KING RENÉ OF ANJOU Illustration from "Coeur d'Amour Épris," about 1460
Vienna, Nationalbibl.

D E F G H

(D) SANDRO BOTTICELLI
The Allegory of Spring, about 1478
Florence, Uffizi

(E) SANDRO BOTTICELLI
The Birth of Venus (detail) 1486
Florence, Uffizi

(F) The Greek Venus: Venus de Milo, 2nd century B.C.
Paris, Louvre

(G) The Roman Venus: Venus de Medici 3rd century B.C.
Florence, Uffizi

(H) GIOVANNI PISANO
The Cardinal Virtues: from the pulpit 1311
Pisa, Cathedral

(I) TITIAN
Bacchus and Ariadne, about 1523
London, N. G.

I

Sandro Botticelli's *The Allegory of Spring* epitomizes the new spring-time of the Renaissance—the rebirth. In his *Birth of Venus*, Venus rises from the sea with the traditional *pudenta* pose of the old classical sculptures (D, E).

Venus herself tells the story by her own transformation of successive schools of philosophy. In Greece, she was rather stern, aloof, and matronly rather than youthful (F). The Romans turned her into a coyly suggestive and very erotic young bathing beauty (G). She appears in the Middle Ages rather unexpectedly as a supporting figure for a pulpit: at Pisa in the 14th century, Giovanni Pisano carved her in her traditional pose as one of the Cardinal Virtues (H). With Botticelli she is reborn as a fresh open-faced young girl.

In spite of his pleasure paintings, *Spring* and *Venus*, Botticelli was a highly emotional religious painter. The nervous, elegant, and nostalgic world of these paintings was shattered by the revivalist preaching of Savonarola. Botticelli's conscience was deeply affected, and he returned to his religious painting.

The world of Venus was given a new dimension in Venice by Giorgione, who took her from her thin artificial Florentine dream world and put her down on the grass in the open air. The *fête champêtre*, the picnic, has all the ingredients of the Arcadian legend, the natural life free from manmade responsibilities and care, the soft open air, some music, and a beautiful woman. It is the pastoral poem of late Rome come to life. Our Lady is challenged by Venus, Christ by Apollo. The cherubs become cupids. The creation myth is replaced by the pagan *Origin of the Milky Way* (p. 69). Tintoretto's form and color are sumptuous and sensual, providing rich decoration for the princely houses where the Venetian nobility held court. A picnic is an intimate affair. Not so the *Bacchanale*, a large, rowdy drinking party, the allegory of the wilder passions dressed up in antique costume. Titian's Bacchus springs into the air from his leopard-drawn chariot before a startled Ariadne (I). As he leaps, the cymbals clash, and the riotous procession piles up behind the player. The picture is full of movement

(A) FRANCESCO PARMIGIANINO
The Madonna of the Long Neck, 1534-40
Florence, Uffizi

(B) BENVENUTO CELLINI
Salt Cellar, about 1540
Vienna, Kunsthist. Mus.

(C) JEAN ANTOINE WATTEAU
The Embarkation for Cythera, 1717
Paris, Louvre

frozen by geometry. The sounds of the scene have their exact equivalent in color.

The sensuously elongated Renaissance beauty even appears in religious painting. Francesco Parmigianino's *Madonna of the Long Neck* (A) at Florence is first cousin to the statue of Diana at Fontainebleau. Here the French King Francis I had Italian painters and sculptors employed to create a pleasure palace for him.

Francis had his mistress, Diane de Poitiers, pose for the goddess and as the Virgin too. Primaticcio enriched the galleries with plaster decoration depicting all the worldly pleasures. Even Francis's salt cellar was designed by the famous goldsmith and sculptor Benvenuto Cellini (B). This enormous center-piece, in the form of Amphitrite and Neptune, crowns the series of bronze, gold, and silver miniature sculptures of all kinds—door handles, knockers, inkstands, and candlesticks—that were made by the sculptors and jewelers of the day for all the great houses of Europe.

The 17th century saw the final assertion of the domination of the world by man, mirrored in the Baroque state which made a kingdom a stage set for the king, in the image of the lord of creation. This assumption of total responsibility brought with it its own form of melancholy and disillusion. An absolute ruler reduced his courtiers to political impotence; with all responsibility removed they were left with nothing to do but engage in personal intrigue. On duty the court was the essence of all that is formal, dominated by etiquette and protocol. Off duty life was equally informal. The rulers of Europe turned to Arcadia and an imagined ideal, simple life. They took the peasant and romanticized him into an idyllic shepherd, they saw the Indian and African as a child of nature who knew no evil in a tropical paradise. In France, the supreme Baroque state, Poussin stuck to the letter of his Virgilian texts in creating a rather formal Arcady, pointing out in his stoic manner that even in Arcady death finally ends all—*Et in Arcadia Ego* (p. 60). Sweeter, but no less melancholic, is the work of Jean Antoine Watteau. Cut off from much of life by long illness, he painted his imaginary world where couples laugh, caress, and listen to music in beautiful gardens. It is nearly always late afternoon or early evening. There are always couples on the point of departing for a more secluded place. In his great *Embarkation for Cythera*, the Isle of Venus, everyone is leaving, except, one feels, the painter himself who is left alone in front of his canvas (C). Watteau's mood, closely analagous to the world of the theater and music, fits perfectly with the idealized love sought after in endless intrigues and affairs by his patrons, but never realized. François Boucher was more direct and earthy (p. 70). His job was to provide Louis XV with a fit setting for his informal, off duty life, which, ever seeking satisfaction in love affairs, eventually collapsed in boredom. Boucher's figures are less original. They are directly derived from mythological tradition, but in them it is difficult to distinguish between a shepherdess

D

E

F

(D) FRANÇOIS BOUCHER Miss O'Murphy on a Couch (Nude on a Sofa) 1752
Munich, Alte Pin.

(E) JEAN HONORÉ FRAGONARD
Fête at Saint-Cloud (detail) about 1770
Paris, Banque de France

(F) FRANCISCO GOYA The Parasol, 1777
Madrid, Prado

and Madame de Pompadour, Diana at the Fountain, or Miss O'Murphy on a couch. This erotic quality of the *fête galante* dominates the portraiture of the time, and great ladies had themselves painted as Venus, Diana, and Hebe, the goddess of youth, in suitable undress derived from classical sculpture (D).

The demand for this type of painting was tremendous, and Jean Baptiste Joseph Pater, Nicolas Lancret and, above all, Jean Honoré Fragonard, produced minor masterpieces of *galanterie* (E). Engraving reached a high standard under pressure of increased production, and the medium carried the idea of the painting as a form of escape, like the novel, to a wide market. The French court was copied as an ideal throughout Europe. Every princeling had his miniature Versailles, and needed his complement of pictures, statuary, tapestries, and engravings to furnish his private apartments. In Spain, the young Goya was commissioned to design such tapestries for the rooms of the Crown Prince. He was specifically to copy the manner of Boucher. However, there was no pagan tradition of mythological painting, it being forbidden by the Church and Inquisition. There was only one previous example of such painting in the country: *The Toilet of Venus*—popularly known as *The Rokeby Venus*—by Velázquez.

Having no ready-made references to work from, Goya turned to the life of peasants in the country that he knew well. Although his peasants are unnaturally clean and well fed, polished up into a suitable setting against which a nobleman could take his ease, they are drawn from experience and have an air of solid reality that makes them quite different from their French counterpart (F).

Absolutism was followed by revolution, first in France and then through the rest of Europe. *Galanterie* was branded as an untouchable product of the *Ancien Régime*. Painting had to be noble, inspiring, and uplifting. An idealized Rome was still set as an example, but it was the heroic Republican Rome, Rome the creator of great works, not the consumer of luxuries. The *Odalisques* of Jean Auguste Dominique Ingres are cold, stern ladies. He turned to the harem and the Turkish baths instead of

A

B

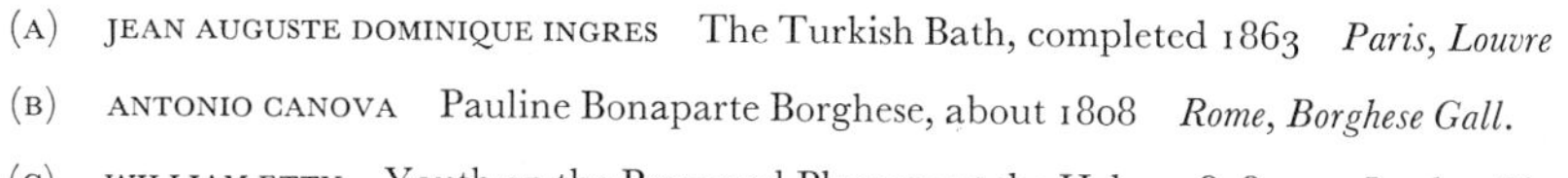

(A) JEAN AUGUSTE DOMINIQUE INGRES The Turkish Bath, completed 1863 *Paris, Louvre*

(B) ANTONIO CANOVA Pauline Bonaparte Borghese, about 1808 *Rome, Borghese Gall.*

(C) WILLIAM ETTY Youth on the Prow and Pleasure at the Helm, 1818-32 *London, Tate*

(D) SIR EDWARD POYNTER A Visit to Æsculapius, 1880 *London, Tate*

C

D

Arcadia (A). The East combined the exciting and exotic with the new scientific archeology that was replacing mythology. Ingres abandoned classical sculpture as his model too, developing a sinuous arabesque line that gives his pictures a tense balance between coldness and sensuality. This, too, exactly fitted the tastes of the new patrons. They were middle class and rich, and concerned with their own respectability. They refuted frivolity both personally and because of its political association with the *Ancien Régime*. They needed their sensual works of art, but these had to be given a respectable excuse. They heavily draped their drawing room interiors and covered the legs of their chairs for decency's sake, while they filled their glass conservatories with white marble nude statuary. Classical antiquity was respectable and learned; the 18th-century version was not. They invented their own imaginary version of a Golden Age of Greece (B).

Similarly in England, typical of this new Arcadia is William Etty's *Youth on the Prow and Pleasure at the Helm* (C). Etty at least handled his paint and chose his color with some boldness, but the tradition degenerates in the overworked cold and gray paintings of Lord Leighton, Sir Lawrence Alma-Tadema, and Sir Edward Poynter, with their fashionable bathing beauties dressed in chitons and togas at marble tanks, surrounded by pergolas and rose-strewn terraces (D).

The 19th-century painters borrowed freely from any period. Roman classicism was opposed by Gothic revival. The Pre-Raphaelites revived the legends of medieval chivalry. To them the Middle Ages, not Arcadia, was the Golden Age, and they looked upon the Renaissance as something like a second Fall of Man.

The public formed long queues outside the Royal Academy, London, or the French Salon exhibitions, to look at storytelling pictures, whose explanatory captions were nearly as long as the queues. Successful pictures had to be roped off, and guarded by policemen to hold back the crowds.

The same queues form today outside the cinemas. They seek the same entertainment. The cinema can handle a chariot race or gladiators in the arena, or Cleopatra at her bath, on a larger scale than any Victorian painter, with the addition of sound and movement. Here cavalry charges come to life and dash across the screen, giving the audience all the thrills with none of the dangers of war.

Serious painters tried to keep to the real tradition of

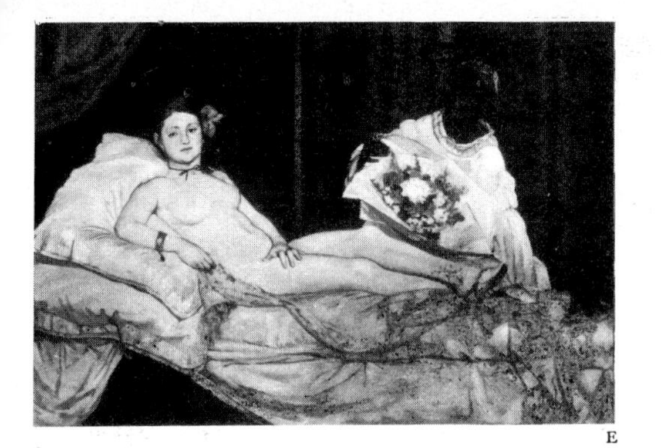

E

F

G

(E) ÉDOUARD MANET Olympia, 1863 *Paris, Mus. de l'Impressionnisme*

(F) PAUL CÉZANNE The Bathers, 1898-1905 *Philadelphia, Pa., Mus. of Art*

(G) LEON BAKST Costume design for "Scheherazade," 1910

(H) AUGUSTE RENOIR Bather with Crossed Legs, about 1904-06 *Switzerland, Private Coll.*

pleasure painting. Manet took the theme of the picnic, the *fête galante*, and turned it into everyday realism, giving the theme a seriousness which turned it from its original purpose (p. 71). However, he was accused of obscenity and immorality, while the official salon was full of the most thinly disguised purely erotic painting. Manet's *Olympia* has much of the great Venuses of Titian in her attitude (E). Cézanne turned to the theme of bathers and produced a masterpiece which abandons sensual pleasure for philosophy (F). The dancers and prostitutes of Degas and Toulouse-Lautrec promise nothing but disappointment and disillusion—they are too real and their message is the true one. Gauguin kept to the theme of the noble savage, and actually went to Tahiti to find her (p. 72). He imposed on his Tahitian pictures brilliant colors, yellow earth, red sky, and purple figures already preconceived in his own imagination.

It was Renoir (p. 151) who really discovered the essence of pleasure painting. His nymphs and goddesses are his ideal snub-nosed, wide-mouthed, red-haired beauties. They vibrate with color and real flesh and blood (H). His still-life painting is as sensual as his bathing girls. From him Matisse took up the theme of the *Odalisque*, the pleasures of love and music, and sumptuous still-lifes.

The modern masters made their own direct contribution to entertainment in the most literal sense too. Under the direction of Serge Diaghilev, practically all the significant painters of the time made settings and costumes for the Russian ballet, the modern equivalent of the Rococo theater (G).

H

The unattainable Venus has now become the moving shadow, and desires are projected onto the cinema screen. She is no longer invented by the artist, but by a team of producers, agents, and cameramen. Her image quickly fades and is constantly being replaced by a newer up-to-date version. It is to this new image rather than ancient myth that the artist-entertainer turns. The *pop* painter takes the ephemeral popular idol or goddess, and by paying a homage compounded partly of love, cynicism, and brutality, tries to turn her into a more lasting image in paint.

(A) Relief from Tel-el-Amarna, about 1350 B.C. *London, B. M.*

CHAPTER 8

Art and Emotion

SOME artists heroically ignore the anxieties and fears inherent in man's condition, in order to create a contemplative clearcut world of idealistic philosophy. Others are psychologically compelled to enter fully into the dark world of doubt, fear, and insecurity, and can only purge themselves by giving their feelings some sort of physical expression, as if the setting down of such fears can relieve their minds of their burdens.

This can be done directly as in the straightforward portrayal of such agonies of mind—the Grünewald *Crucifixion*, for example, or Goya's *Disasters of War*. Painting and sculpture can also be highly charged with emotion in a much more indirect way than in the choice of subject. Anxiety and distress can be conveyed by the choice of form and color.

Some forms are simple and stable—those that are simply described by means of geometry, for example. Others can be distorted and complex, and in this way convey instability. Among the symptoms of human sickness are loss of weight, thinness. The body droops, becomes weaker and more languid, as if the bones themselves were melting. The sick man, the drooping plant, become too weak to stand. Sometimes physical sickness brings mental suffering, sometimes the morbid mind weakens the body.

Certainly attenuated, elongated sinuous forms have long been strongly associated with morbidity, and their occurrence at regular intervals in the history of artistic creation has been labeled decadent. This elongation appears at moments of crisis and change, from brief periods of disturbance, such as those in Ancient Egypt under the revolutionary pharaoh Akhenaten, and the work at Tel-el-Amarna under Amenophis IV (A), to the period of *Art Nouveau* when the apparent stability of 19th-century Europe was beginning to crumble.

This direct association of form itself with emotional disturbance is sometimes labeled Expressionist. Perhaps a better word would be anthropomorphic, meaning the attribution of human emotions to the non-human and inanimate world. Thus, in much of van Gogh's painting the landscape is highly disturbed (p. 121). Hills, trees, and clouds are all distorted and contorted like a human face undergoing and reflecting great emotional stress. Cypress trees writhe in sympathy with the artist's own agitated condition. Or so it seems at first glance, and this would appear to be borne out by the artist's own mental illness leading to suicide.

Now we know a great deal about van Gogh, especially from his own letters; he was a prolific correspondent, and wrote clearly and well about his painting. In his letters to his brother Theo, van Gogh talks about his painting in quite a cold-blooded calculating way. He says a great deal about color theory; how, for example, he intends to paint a series of pictures exploiting a particular pair of complementary colors to their limit—violet and yellow, or blue and orange. If we look closely at the pictures, we can see clearly that the paint-fresh strokes, although strong and clearly defined, were not applied in a fit of passion. Instead, solid blocks of carefully mixed and chosen colors are built up in little slabs, as if they were the pieces of stone or glass that a mosaicist uses—tesserae.

These slabs of paint follow around the form of what he is painting. They follow the contours and are concentric, spreading like the ripples on a pond. Eventually, they collide with another concentric series of strokes generated by another picture detail. They make shapes that are convex, which when they meet leave little concave "holes" to be filled up, small curved triangles and other polygons.

We can see exactly the same sort of thing happening in a detail of mosaic. Again, the tesserae must follow the form and echo it; a mosaic artist cannot paint straight across the form, only around it. So that around an eye the mosaic waves spread out until they meet those spreading from the nose and cheek. This echoing produces an exaggeration of form. The intense gaze of the dark-eyed Byzantine figures that stare one out of countenance are in part at least due to the rigid, inflexible medium.

Van Gogh paintings and Byzantine mosaics echo each other in spiritual and emotional intensity. We can only guess that van Gogh painted with a great deal of control. Our suppositions are backed up by the fact that although he was mentally disturbed, the bad attacks came only when he was unable to paint.

We know for a fact that the Byzantine mosaics, with which van Gogh's pictures have such an affinity, could only have been carried out under conditions of utmost discipline.

However unearthly, however intensely spiritual and emotional the figures of Christ, Our Lady, saints, emperors, and empresses seem at Ravenna, staring with enormous dark sad eyes, floating upon a luminous golden ground, they were painstakingly built up by teams of craftsmen over a long period of time. A mosaic, made up out of thousands of carefully matched tesserae, cannot simply be run up in a fit of religious enthusiasm. The emotional content, conveyed by the enlargement of the eyes, the emaciated features, the elongated form, are carefully worked out according to a tradition. These symbols of spirituality are as well understood as the mechanics of the highly disciplined technique. Their use does not preclude the carrying out of recognizable portraits such as those of Justinian and Theodora (B), or the Archbishop Maximian. In the same way, van Gogh's self-portraits (p. 122) and those of his other sitters are recognizable persons, and the landscapes recognizable places.

The Byzantine formula was capable of mechanical repetition in the work of the anonymous Russian and eastern European icon painters, who learned their craft by copying one another, each generation in turn being the prototype for the next (C). El Greco, the Greek, who was taught in Venice and who settled in Spain, took this formula and, combining it with free brushwork and high coloring, produced a highly sensational form of painting that served admirably as an emotional counterblast to the puritan Reformation (D, and p. 123).

He seems to have painted his crimsons and purples as transparent glazes, and then, while they were wet, painted pure white into them. Each form is modeled up to a highlight independent of its neighbor. The colors range from a light chalky hue to the deepest intensity over each single area. This gives the whole picture an energetic restless surface that powerfully reinforces the tormented agony of writhing limbs and elongated emaciated form. The pictures appear to be bathed in a

(B) Portrait of Theodora (detail) mid-6th century *Ravenna, S. Vitale* (C) TVER SCHOOL Russian icon, 15th century *London, V. and A.*

(D) EL GRECO Christ Driving the Traders from the Temple (detail) about 1595 *London, N. G.*

B C D

ghastly glare. The figures are like contorted columns of rising smoke from separate fires.

To compare El Greco with the traditional icon painter is to define at once the difference between the independent fine artist and the folk artist. The tradition is no longer a tight framework in which to work. It becomes a tool to be made use of at will, a technique ready to be turned into something else.

Although van Gogh was far from being a naive painter, the formula or system that he evolved in his search for purity of color and the need to find a direct relationship between drawing and painting, was taken up in the same way by his successors and put to a different use.

The 19th century outwardly conformed to a most rigid moral and social code of behavior, based not on a spiritual ideal, but on the material necessity of carrying society safely through a succession of violent social changes. Behind this façade men wrestled with the problems and doubts that are born afresh with each generation. Freud brought men's secret fears into the open and severely damaged the structure that society had built to hide them. At once poets and painters gave expression to the self which Freud had revealed.

Edvard Munch, the Norwegian painter, copied the restless forms of van Gogh's painting and used them to produce deliberate anthropomorphic art. In his painting *The Cry* (also know as *The Scream*), the girl on the bridge screams with all her body. The bridge, the sky, and the rushing water scream in sympathy with her. They are of the same tortured form as the terrified girl. Munch's subjects are sick rooms, the death bed, and neurotic invalids. Strange assemblies of figures dance in what might be an asylum, quiet, restrained, afraid to speak to each other, with hidden violence just beneath the surface (A, B).

His color is used in the same emotional way. There is a somewhat crude symbolism: blood red, green sickness, black death, plus complementary colors derived from Impressionism and van Gogh. Combinations of complementary colors clash, grate physically on the nerves to effect a feeling of vertigo, in a deliberate attempt to produce sympathetic sickness and emotional disturbance in the onlooker.

Munch exhibited in Berlin in 1892. German painters were already using Impressionism as a conscious act of revolution against the Neoclassic academy. What was almost a technical revolution in France became a political issue to the Germans; immediately, their use of Impressionism became a much more dramatic and personal affair. It was not merely sympathy with Munch's morbid personality that influenced German painters, but his direct linking of the medium of paint to the expression of personal feelings. A group of north German painters very much under his influence formed a society. They called themselves The Bridge group —*Die Brücke*—using the symbol at several levels—to

(A) EDVARD MUNCH The Cry, 1893
Oslo, Munch-Museet

(B) EDVARD MUNCH The Dance of Life, about 1900
Oslo, Nasjonalgall.

(C) ERNST LUDWIG KIRCHNER
Berlin Street Scene, 1913
Stuttgart, Staatsgal.

AUGUST MACKE Street Scene
nany, Private Coll.

(E) OSKAR KOKOSCHKA
Die Windsbraut (The Tempest) 1914
Basel, Öffentliche Kunstsamm.

(F) FRANZ MARC Tyrol
Munich, Staatsgemäldesamm.

symbolize the bridge between the individual and expression, the individual and society, the old century and the new. Above all The Bridge was the idea of a crossing-over point, of going somewhere.

The Germans made Expressionism something peculiar to themselves. It is true that there are certain resemblances to the parallel movement in France, also derived from the work of van Gogh and Gauguin—Fauvism—and the Fauves were given their nickname (Wild Beasts) because of the violent impact of their pictures upon the senses. But Fauvism is really a new development of sensual painting; its content is largely serene, luxurious, it is not charged with the neurotic tension of Expressionism. Fauvism was born of intellectual freedom and Expressionism was still part of a struggle for this freedom.

Ernst Ludwig Kirchner (C), the leader of The Bridge group, and Emil Nolde are perhaps the most totally Expressionist. They coupled the use of violent colors with rapid handling of paint. They summarily dismissed irrelevant detail in their concern to catch the emotion of the moment in its passing. Their work is harsh and strident. Their paintings assault the spectator. They are the painters' act of retaliation against public indifference.

The Bridge was dissolved in 1913, and was replaced by a south German movement, *Der Blaue Reiter*—The Blue Rider—that was more lyrical and dreamlike than the northern painters. The *Blaue Reiter* group was also more open to other influences, particularly Cubism. August Macke (D) and Franz Marc (F), Paul Klee and Wassily Kandinsky were the most representative painters of the group. Both Macke and Marc were killed in World War I. Kandinsky developed violent Expressionism into pure abstraction, and Klee, whose picture *A Young Lady's Adventure* is a dreamy counterpart to Munch's *The Cry*, became concerned with poetic contemplation rather than violent action.

The movement attracted a number of painters from outside Germany, particularly from the persecuted minorities in eastern Europe. Man as a victim of impending doom was a strong concern of the movement, and its attraction for those whose experiences had already included a foretaste of inhumanity is easily understood. Indeed the Expressionist movement as a whole was a readymade object for attack by National Socialism, itself a counter-revolutionary movement. This form of government that turned Germans into refugees, and set older refugees on the road once more, both spread Expressionism and gave it an added significance. The prophecies of hidden violence, the warnings in paint, had come true.

Expressionism lost its provinciality and became international, recognized as a voice of protest of its time. Painters went to Paris, London, and New York. Oskar Kokoschka is perhaps the true lone wolf of Expressionism. His early picture *The Tempest* has strong elements of El Greco's influence in composition, color, and the treatment of form (E). Kokoschka has always combined his highly personal view with an equally strong appreciation of place in landscape, and the person in portraiture. He creates an inseparable mixture of emotion and observation, telling us equally his own feelings and yet of his subjects' independence of them (p. 124).

This later phase of Expressionism is darker, more somber. The brilliant complementary colors, the sweet lyricism of the *Blaue Reiter* painters are replaced by a more Rembrandtesque *chiaroscuro*. The emphasis is on light and shade. The painters' subjects are taken from the butcher's shop and the slaughter house, the dumb slaughtered beasts being identified with the massacre of innocents, foretelling of genocide. The paintings of Chaim Soutine in Paris are of sides of meat and still-lifes with calves' heads. Scumbling—the dragging of light paint over a darker ground in irregular streaks and spots—and thick *impasto* build up the subjects in high relief on the canvas.

As political tension grew during the 1930's, Picasso overlaid his Cubist structure with strong emotional content. His *Woman Weeping* (p. 125), painted during the Spanish Civil War, shows the despair of the bereaved in pictorial terms. Her eyes are like shattered panes of glass. She tears a handkerchief between clenched teeth. The linen folds are painted hard and sharp like the blade of a knife. Her tears well from rigid, tubelike mechanical tear-ducts. The colors are muted, but harsh, discordant, and irritating.

Francis Gruber's models stand in gray-brown studios like emaciated concentration camp victims, pathetic living skeletons. They are like Munch's neurotic casualties of life, yet the flat *Art Nouveau* patterns of the Norwegian painter are now replaced by three-dimensional realism. The figures are surrounded by light and air. Very similar are Alberto Giacometti's paintings, in which thin figures are almost entirely eaten away by the surrounding atmosphere (A, B).

Francis Bacon has used over and over again the image of screaming men and women with shattered glasses taken from Eisenstein's film of the Potemkin mutiny and Odessa riots (C, D). His slashed, screaming figures are imprisoned in cage-like constructions similar to those of Giacometti, added to which are strong influences of El Greco and Velázquez. Bacon also painted a homage series after van Gogh and all these are dedications rather than imitations. His figures are mutilated, caged in sound-proof glass. They bear wounds that are themselves teeth in mouths. Although slow in execution, the paintings bear the final strokes of rapid handling, giving the impression that the incidents have been painted from life with not a minute to spare. They are like press photographs or film stills. Bacon has exploited to the full the expressionist content. That other quality of Expressionism, its thick, juicy surface of paint, was exploited in England by David Bomberg (E) and others. In particular Frank Auerbach has turned *impasto* into relief sculpture. The canvases are worked and overworked until the paint is six inches or more in thickness. The paint in form and color resembles volcanic lava slowly flowing down the canvas.

A B C D

Karel Appel in Holland literally attacks the canvas on which he is working as if it was a physical enemy. Here the calligraphy of the Expressionists is forced to the extreme, setting down the agony and fury of the moment in a frenzy, and recording the gesture by the trace of paint it leaves behind (F).

But perhaps above all it is in the field of sculpture that Expressionism is to be found at its most potent and still developing in original ways. The monument to the destruction of the city of Rotterdam by Ossip Zadkine, the tormented figures by Jacques Lipchitz, are powerful images of man's protest against inhumanity (G, H).

After two world wars in which no man was spared, and with the living reality of atom war fears ever present, the early 20th-century Freudian revolt seems almost a private and academic affair. Present-day Expressionism is

E

F

(A) FRANCIS GRUBER Job, 1944 *London, Tate*

(B) ALBERTO GIACOMETTI Woman Standing in Studio 1949 *Photo: Hanover Gall., London*

(C) Still from "The Battleship Potemkin," 1925 Director, Sergei Eisenstein

(D) FRANCIS BACON Portrait of Foster Dulles, 1952 *London, Marlborough Fine Art Ltd.*

(E) DAVID BOMBERG Tendrine in Sun, Cornwall, 1947 *London, Marlborough Fine Art Ltd.*

(F) KAREL APPEL Amorous Dance, 1955 *London, Tate*

(G) OSSIP ZADKINE Monument to the Destruction of Rotterdam, 1951 *Rotterdam*

(H) JACQUES LIPCHITZ Study for a Monument, 1953 *London, Tate*

G

H

very much concerned with public fears and threats. Nevertheless, if these large-scale menaces were removed, man would once again be left with his private fears. Indeed, these are ever present, and the mass menace is born of them in turn. As long as there are artists with enough conscience and feeling to spare for their fellow men, there will be painting and sculpture to record it.

Of course, expression is a quality that all visual art has. The artist expresses something of his own state of mind when he is at his coldest and most detached. However much a painter may try to turn himself into an inanimate and anonymous camera, some sort of expression must come into his work. The most disciplined of painters, the Dutch still-life artists, a Chardin or a Stubbs, still "sign their work all over." It is like the individuality of handwriting. The artists who favor austerity will always say, "Leave expression alone—it can take care of itself." If a man has something to express it will come out automatically.

Expressionist anthropomorphic painting is not self-expression alone, and a great deal of harm has been done by confusing Expressionism as an idea with mere self-expression. The term self-expression is used here not to belittle it, but to emphasize that it is something that *all* painting and sculpture have in common.

To take the powerful emotions that all men have, and give them recognizable symbolic forms is quite another matter.

CHAPTER 9

Art and Style

When we have an idea that we think is a good one, we usually want to tell other people about it. We generally do this by telling them in spoken words, or, if we cannot see or telephone them, we write the words by means of commonly understood symbols and send it to them.

This is the use of language. Language is the means by which we convey ideas. Words are one language, mathematics another; drawing, painting, and carving are yet other languages. In writing, the subtle combination of the traditional use of words plus an indefinable personal choice of them, the invention of new meanings, the giving of an old phrase a new twist, is what we call style.

In the visual arts we use the word style in the same way, to describe a compound blending of the tradition or school in which an artist works with his own original contribution, such as the way he might handle his medium. It describes the artist's use of his language.

Language, written and spoken, is always changing. Slang, the poetry of everyday life, depends on change for its telling effect. It is the new phrase or word that brings a point home. Nothing is more out-of-date than yesterday's popular catch phrase. But the ideas conveyed by slang change much less quickly. The fact that language does change constantly reminds us that ideas do not necessarily get stale with age. They are brought back to our attention by being expressed in a new way.

It is important to understand that ideas and language are not the same. One is the thought, the other the medium for giving the thought physical reality. The two often do become confused. A time when such confusion was at its greatest was in the 19th century, and we still suffer from its results. If we take, for example, the popular historical novels of Sir Walter Scott we find that, as far as was possible at the time, they may be said to be archeologically correct. His dialogue is sprinkled with plenty of *thees*, *thous*, and archaic phrases and mannerisms, and clothes, weapons, and buildings are fairly correctly described.

However, in *idea* his novels are completely Victorian. The psychology and personality of his medieval characters are completely of his own time, mid-19th century. What they do, think, and say, and how they react are

(A) Gothic architecture:
Canterbury Cathedral, 12th century

(B) Victorian Gothic architecture:
The Houses of Parliament, London, 1840-60

(C) Greek archaic figure (detail)
6th century B.C. *Athens, Acropolis Mus.*

(D) Roman portrait bust:
Julius Caesar (detail)

(E) MICHELANGELO David (detail)
1501-04 *Florence, Accad.*

governed by Victorian standards of morality. The language is medieval, but the ideas conveyed by it are those of several hundred years later. At the same time, to turn to the language of form, the Victorian architect mistook pinnacles, pointed arches, and gargoyles, the language of the medieval architect, for the idea of Gothic architecture, and could not see that the use of such language did not recreate the Gothic world the Victorians so much admired (A, B).

In the making of a work of art the idea must come first, and then the suitable means of expression is evolved from it. An artist with no ideas can learn the language of drawing in a mechanical way, but his work will be dead.

Places and times have produced their own universal languages of style. The term classical sculpture conjures up something in our minds that Greek, Roman, and Renaissance work have in common. This is in great measure due to the language of sculptural form. Whether the work was severe and aloof, as in the Greece of the Parthenon, or emotional, as in Hellenistic times, or intensely realistic, as in Roman portraiture, the elements of which it is composed are all very similar. It was quite early when a standard symbol for an eye was evolved of unchanging cross section, with a curious device to portray a translucent pupil. This is achieved by cutting out quite a deep groove in the shape of a horseshoe, with the ends upward, round the lower part of the pupil. The groove extends round the pupil to leave a solid, reflecting circle of stone joined to a peninsula of solid material at the top. This blob is never quite dead center, and the groove is swelled and diminished. The solid stone reflects light just where the highlight would appear on the pupil; the rest is translucent shadow (D, E).

This became part of the sculptor's standard alphabet or vocabulary meaning "eye," and it persisted through Greece, Rome, the Middle Ages, and Renaissance unchanged. The other features such as ears, nose, mouth, and hair all have their standard forms. These were the foundation upon which various periods or individual sculptors built their own personal style. It is completely analogous to the universal language of Latin, or the worldwide use of the Roman alphabet.

The language of Cubism is another. Its well-defined planes, the tendency to reduce complex forms to simple solid geometry, the hard edges and highlights, are very much the language of a machine age. Its structural solidity reflects an optimistic outlook based on scientific discovery, and the application of scientific reasoning to all man's problems. The dissolution of form in Cubism and its highly relative treatment of space are the equivalent in paint of the new cosmology based on theories of relativity developed at the turn of the 19th century. Again, inside this framework that we call Cubism, individual masters have put this language or style to uses that are poles apart. The strict Cubists were content to explore form purely and simply. The *De Stijl* painters used Cubism to remodel the world to their own puritanical fashion. Chagall and Klee used Cubism to tell us of fairy tales and dreams (A, and pp. 58 and 126), Léger to paint heroic canvases which he saw as banners of socialism (B).

The contrasting 17th and 18th century styles of Baroque and Rococo reflect the two sides of European society. The use of classical form, treating it as if it were soft and malleable, twisting columns, breaking pediments with sculpture, making stone appear to be flying off into space, and making hard marble look as if it were weeping tears, marches parallel with man's faith in his domination of nature, a philosophy culminating in political absolutism. The Baroque plan, whether of a garden, a city, or a palace, is like a great seal stamped across the face of Nature (C, D).

Off duty, the Baroque man sheds his responsibility and daydreams of a simple carefree back-to-nature existence. The heavy carved Baroque garlands become undone in the Rococo boudoir, like a woman letting down her hair, unlacing and unribboning her tight artificial stays and pannier skirts of the time. The ribbons fall across the walls, the fruit and flowers tumble down in carefully contrived accidents, and the pictures that go with them are of lovemaking after a picnic-concert in a natural garden.

The Gothic style is one of attenuated form. Heads, hands, and feet are elongated, drapery folds are given a strongly vertical emphasis that echoes the great churches, and figures have a heightened spirituality that lifts them out of this world, until they really do seem to float free of the earth (E).

The advantages of a universal language in the visual

(A) MARC CHAGALL The Green Donkey, 1911
London, Tate

B C

(B) FERNAND LÉGER The Builders, 1951
Biot, France, Mus. Fernand Léger

(C) Seated Saint with Bishop's Staff: from the Mercy Altar, about 1763 *Vierzehnheiligen, Germany, Pilgrim's Church*

arts at any one period are fairly obvious. It means that from one generation to another successive artists can stand on the shoulders of their predecessors. It means that young artists can be taught the language early, so that by the time they have matured, and have ideas of their own to express, they have the full technical means of doing so at their disposal.

The young sculptor in classic times was not taught how to carve an eye by observing nature directly, but was taught to carve the accepted symbol for an eye. Then, when he became a sculptor in his own right, he would use this symbol in his own way, or, if he was carving a portrait, he could concentrate absolutely on making a likeness, that is to say, he would concentrate on *what* he was doing without ever wondering *how* he was going to do it. An 18th-century painter did not learn how to paint trees by looking at them. Instead he learned the formula for drawing trees. On top of a clump of leaves their flattened planes blend together to produce a uniform smooth curve. Below this clump, the leaves hang down as ragged points giving a looping broken line. This can be seen clearly in the sketches of a painter like Gainsborough (F). The individual trees would have their character superimposed upon this formula as a result of observation and the artist's own inclination. Students learned the technique by copying masters' drawings. Goethe learned how to draw in Weimar from a minor German painter, Johann Heinrich Wilhelm Tischbein, who worked in Rome. He was sent drawings,

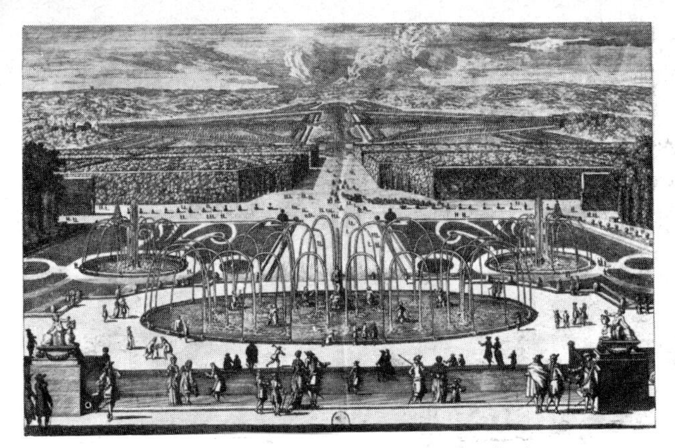

(D) Fountains and Gardens at Versailles (engraving)
Paris, Bibl. Nat.

(F) THOMAS GAINSBOROUGH
Sketch (detail of trees)

and returned them with his copies for criticism to and fro across the Alps, a form of correspondence course.

The disadvantages are inherent in the advantages themselves. A lazy student learned the formula and got by with passable imitations. The style or formula at times became more important than the work itself. Language predominated over idea, and style was held to be sacred for its own sake. Artists—not only visual artists, but writers, musicians, and architects—could pick and choose styles from the past to avoid the sometimes overpowering responsibility of being part of one's own time and making one's own contribution.

(E) Pilasters of the Royal Portal
Chartres, France, Notre Dame Cathedral

William Blake thought that he was working in and reviving the style of Michelangelo and the High Renaissance in figure drawing. If his strong and eccentric strain of originality had been suppressed the result would have been ludicrous. Indeed, it was held to be so by many people who saw no further than Blake's own expressed intention. He was saved by accident. A lesser man who could have been a fine artist also emulated the Renaissance masters. Alfred Stevens was a highly talented draftsman of the 19th century, but he mistook the language of Raphael and Michelangelo for their intentions. Whereas they drew on a foundation compounded both of an understanding of classical form plus original observation and research, Stevens copied outward resemblances. Michelangelo's drawings are built up from the inside out. He too drew directly from models, but subordinated them to his knowledge both of the sculptural tradition and the direct study of anatomy. His shading or tone, that which makes his drawings look solid by means of light and shade, is gained from a continual process of correction that can be clearly seen even in reproduction. The figure or head is sketched in lightly. As successive corrections are made, the lines are made blacker and stronger to obliterate those that went before. He never erased, but corrected over and beside the "wrong" lines, using them all the time to make certain that errors were not unconsciously repeated. The drawings are virtually built up layer by layer from the inside. The aim of Stevens and other would-be neo-Renaissance masters of the 19th century

A

B

(A) MICHELANGELO Studies for the Libyan Sibyl
New York, Met. Mus. of Art
Purchase 1924, Joseph Pulitzer Bequest

(B) ALFRED STEVENS Studies
London, V. and A.

was to produce an immaculate drawing. Stevens worked directly from the model, and his idealization consisted of smoothing out and depersonalizing the form into generalities about the figure, rather than the research into form that drove Michelangelo on. Stevens, by copying the style without understanding the idea, drew from the outside in, instead of from the inside out. He tried to give his drawing solidity by copying the shadows he saw on the form, and depended on the light at the time that he saw the pose. The light in Michelangelo's drawing is not only of his observation, but of his making. Michelangelo could make sculptured drawing look alive, whereas Stevens turned the living figure into dead stone (A-D).

It was this kind of misunderstanding of language and idea that finally killed the idea of universal language in the arts, and gave the word Academic a derogatory meaning.

Today young students still copy sculpture without knowing why. Instead of learning the details because one day they will use them, they copy them because they are told to, and there is a vague tradition that one should do so. As if this burden was not enough, the young artist soon finds that in order to find his own style or language, he will really have to live through the whole history of painting in himself before he can do so, for the modern masters have become more and more personal and inimitable. They do not found obvious schools. Since there are so many personal tongues speaking at once, the person for whom all this painting and sculpture is made, the interested layman, has to spend much more time learning about how to look at modern art than did the layman in any of the periods of the past. This requires time, patience, experience, and the opportunity to see a great deal of work.

C

D

(C) MICHELANGELO
The Tomb of Giuliano de' Medici, 1526-31
Florence, S. Lorenzo, Medici Chapel

(D) ALFRED STEVENS
Wellington Monument, 1856-70
London, St. Paul's

CHAPTER 10

Art and Beauty

(A) SANDRO BOTTICELLI The Birth of Venus (detail) 1486 *Florence, Uffizi*

SHOULD a work of art be beautiful? The question, and the argument that arises from it, are not new. Rembrandt was thought both in his own time and later to have a perverted mind and to be in love with deformity and ugliness.

Critics have fought bitter battles over Realism and Idealism in art. The realists have been accused of deliberately being provocative in a sensational way, by cultivating ugliness, whether it be Cromwell's "warts and all" type of portraiture, or the inclusion of factory chimneys in Impressionist landscapes; or even a genre painting such as Sir Luke Fildes's *The Widower*, a laborer feeding a child in a cottage, of which "The London Times" critic said that a drawing room is no place for muddy boots, even if they are only paint on canvas.

Can an ugly subject make a beautiful work of art, or must a true work of art only express ideal beauty? Can a Venus by Botticelli, an old woman by Velázquez, a flayed carcass of raw meat by Rembrandt, a firing squad by Goya, old boots by van Gogh, a minotaur by Picasso, and a sunset by Turner all be beautiful paintings in the same terms? (A-D, and p. 92 A).

To begin with a distinction must be made between the

(B) DIEGO VELÁZQUEZ An Old Woman Frying Eggs, about 1622 *Edinburgh, N. G. of Scotland*

C

(C) REMBRANDT VAN RYN
Slaughtered Ox, 1655
Paris, Louvre

(D) VINCENT VAN GOGH
The Boots, 1887
Baltimore, Md., Mus. of Art, Cone Coll.

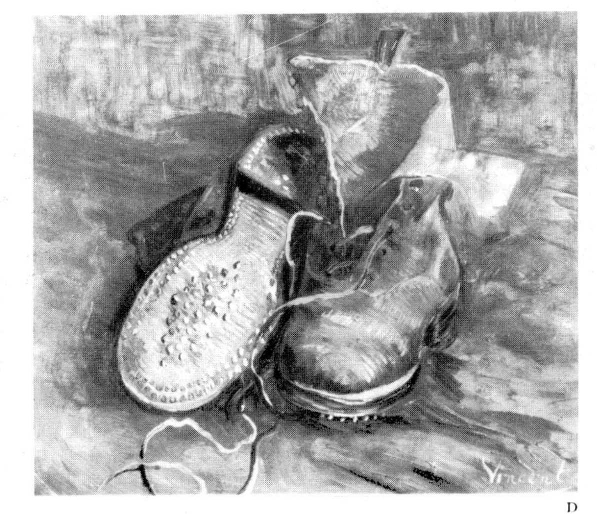

D

(A) PABLO PICASSO Minotauromachy, 1935 (etching)

(B) EDWARD HOPPER Nighthawks, 1942
Chicago, Art. Inst., The Friends of American Art Coll.

subject and a work of art. A sunset might be beautiful, but it is not a work of art. It is the result of certain natural causes. We call a nightingale's song beautiful, the croak of a raven ugly. The nightingale, however, is not a better musician than the raven; as far as the birds themselves are concerned, they are both doing the same thing. The fact that we prefer one to the other is accidental. Each makes his own appropriate noise.

Although in everyday speech, when we admire a tree or a view we might call it a natural work of art, strictly speaking we cannot use the word in this way. The phrase is self-contradictory, for a work of art by definition must be artificial and not natural, that is to say, all works of art are things that are made by man.

The work of art can have its origin in nature. A composer may be inspired by a bird's song, a painter by a sunset or by a beautiful woman. Or he may be inspired by what at first sight seems to be outside nature. A painter who is disillusioned by the everyday world may turn from it to an ideal world in his mind. But his mind, and the ideas that are formed there, are still as much a part of nature as he is himself. Piet Mondrian's horizontal and vertical black lines on a plain canvas (p. 128) are as "natural" as his early paintings of trees, although we cannot readily identify them with our experience from everyday life as we can a recognizable drawing which says "tree" to us (p. 170 A, B, C, D).

This element of automatic recognition is a very important factor. Let us take the pictorial representation of an automobile. We might say that a photograph in a catalogue (p. 129) is realistic. Because of the way a camera sees, we can only see one end and one side of the car at once. We rely on our experience of automobiles to tell us that the object is the same on the other side, and is symmetrical either side of a line along the body. Sometimes in a catalogue one may see an artist's drawing of an automobile in which parts of its body are cut away by the draftsman, to show us what goes on inside (p. 130). Now we never see cars running about like this, but if we want to know about the construction in order to choose wisely when we buy one, then we might say that this drawing is more realistic than a photograph of an actual car. If we are concerned with making automobiles, then we need blueprints, a set of engineer's drawings which show every single detail in flat views. These have to be read with some considerable mental effort in order to know what the finished automobile will look like.

These drawings may be said to be the most realistic of all. They show every tiny detail as it is, and leave nothing to chance. There is no guesswork, everything is measured. They take nothing for granted except our ability to read the drawings. But the drawings are not easy to read; an engineer has to have a long training to understand them, and needs considerable experience in their interpretation on top of that.

So we seem to call realistic that with which we are most familiar, and that which we have learned to read. This is an act of recognition, and recognition is based on experience. Sometimes this is taken for granted. We learn to read both actual trees in nature and newspaper photographs automatically. We learn how to read an engineer's or architect's drawings by making a conscious effort, and we have to be helped by someone who has already learned the code.

Anything outside our range of experience is automatically regarded with a certain amount of suspicion and mistrust, as when one is brought face to face with a stranger. In this case we overcome our natural defensive attitude by asking questions, but we do not often wait to ask questions of an unfamiliar work of art.

This automatic experience, what we call feeling in everyday life, is part of our non-thinking reaction to realism and beauty. Sunsets and pretty faces are considered to be beautiful in everyday life, because of pleasant associations as well as abstract qualities like *shape* and *color*. Other things are not so pleasant, old boots, flayed carcasses, a grim suburban scene (B), or a junkyard. To most people, quite rightly, scenes of cruelty and violence are not only repellent but cause nausea and sickness.

The artist is a man who is trained to see and go on seeing. His feelings may be the same as any other person's. He can admire a splendid view or a pretty girl, and abhor cruelty, death, poverty, and corruption, like anyone else. But he trains himself to look more closely, and to analyze his own feelings. A pair of old boots are not useless and ugly objects to be thrown away. Their shape and color, when seen in a certain way, become an interesting problem in drawing and painting. He sees them as accidental sculpture. This is no sentimental feeling for old boots as old "friends" with all sorts of romantic associations of long tramps in the country. His attitude is strictly formal and objective. He looks at the boots as if for the first time.

Rembrandt saw a flayed ox not only as flesh and blood, a reminder of corruption and the way life must feed on life, but as glistening rich, iridescent color, the crimson streaks against the pearly quality of raw fat, a challenge to his brush and a stimulant to his mind.

In order to condemn atrocities Goya put himself heart and mind into his work, holding nothing back. In using every ounce of his ability, he was committing himself as a fine painter and draftsman as well as a man, and whatever his subject, beauty of line and form always predominates in his work.

The word "form" can have varied meanings, all of which complement one another, none of them contradictory.

First, there is a pure kind of form, the idea as it exists in the mind. This idea becomes a piece of furniture, a picture, or statue, by using tools to work on materials. The work of art then has its own form, words on paper, a musical composition, paint on canvas, carved wood, stone, or cast metal. This is a second but more tangible kind of form.

Then there is also the form of the subject of a picture itself. This can be the form of a tree, of a person, of a pair of old boots, or of another work of art, an antique statue or picture from another age.

The first form is pure essence of idea, only existing in the mind of the thinker. The second is the form of the idea given physical existence by tools and materials. The third is that form that all things that exist have, and that is peculiar to each object.

Recognizing this is one of the artist's most difficult tasks, and one which anyone interested in art must try to follow. The artist must be able to see old boots, or anything else, as form apart from its associations. He must see that beauty and perfection can be striven after, so that a subject that is not beautiful may be turned into a work of art. This requires thinking as well as feeling, and thinking means spending time and concentrating on unfamiliar objects. Form is closely related to ideas. Style, we have seen, changes quickly, and ideas do not. There is an everyday language of beauty which works through our feelings and by-passes our minds. Fashion drawings, magazine illustrations, and photographs, still and moving, have to make an immediate impact. No one wants to stop and think about a picture illustrating a love story or advertising clothes. We want to get the message right away. Every age creates sets of symbols that mean beauty when the people of their time see them.

If we take a fashion drawing and analyze it as form, we see that no living person could really look like that. It is absurd. Various qualities that are considered to be beautiful are exaggerated. One period may consider thin legs to be attractive, and legs in the drawings become impossibly attenuated. One period likes a thin flat figure, another an exaggerated bust and bustle. In everyday life it is absurd for us to analyze these drawings as form, but by doing so we can see why fashion drawings, and fashions themselves, date so quickly. Yesterday's fashions are absurd, those of the day before nostalgic, those of the past romantic. Even faces themselves date. In making historical films each decade thinks it is accurately reconstructing the past, yet in looking at a series of stills of, say, films about the 18th century, from the beginning of the cinema onwards we can pretty accurately date each by its own idea of beauty, superimposed over towering hair styles and pannier skirts (A, B, C, D).

Fashion, like slang, must always be up-to-date, and nothing dates more quickly. Form lasts. Works of art by a master always last, because their form is stronger than their fashionable and temporary symbols of beauty. Botticelli's Venus is out-of-date. The Venus de Milo is unfashionable. Rubens' enormous women would probably be found unattractive as pin-ups by most people today. Amedeo Modigliani's beauties (E) are as out-of-date as the shop-window dummies they inspired during the early 1920's, that is to say as ideas of beauty. Yet good painting and sculpture is never out-of-date, and these are all such.

E F

(E) AMEDEO MODIGLIANI Portrait of Madame van Muyden *São Paulo, Mus. of Art*

(F) DANTE GABRIEL ROSSETTI Monna Vanna, 1866 *London, Tate*

A B C D

(A) Fashion plate from "La Mode Artistique," 1885

(B) Design for woman's costume. The House of Worth, 1948

(C) Film costumes from "Madame de Pompadour," 1928
Director: Herbert Wilcox

(D) Film costumes from "Du Barry was a Lady," 1943
Director: Roy del Ruth *(Metro-Goldwyn Mayer Inc.)*

On the other hand, the beauties of John Singer Sargent, Sir Philip de Laszlo, Dante Gabriel Rossetti, Sir Edward Burne-Jones and many others, date as quickly and as completely as fashion drawings. Good fashion drawing always remains good drawing, and the study of yesterday's symbolic beauty is interesting. The trouble with the fashionable but formless portrait of the beauty of their day is that it suffers from being elaborate and pompous as well.

Our unconscious conditioning by everyday life is always changing. We wake up one morning and find that the key no longer fits the lock in our minds that releases the word "beauty" automatically. Sargent's sitters, whom he intended should look like the cool, clever hostesses off the Edwardian stage of Pinero, Wilde, and Shaw, are left forever on canvas with retroussé noses, raised eyebrows, giraffe necks, and not much else. All we see in Rossetti are bulging eyes, and an overpowering anxious expression that once symbolized passion but now appear to be symptoms of goitre (F). Even William Etty's luscious nudes suffer from their Victorian fashion-plate look. With their sleek brown hair pulled back into a tight bun, they remind us of Queen Victoria herself.

A great deal is written about the magic of the old masters, but probably the one thing that ensures that a modern master will one day be an old master is the lasting quality of his form.

CHAPTER 11

Art and Realism

(A) Assyrian winged human-headed lion, 883-859 B.C. *London, B. M.*

WE call a work of art realistic when we recognize something in it that is related to our own experience. Although an Assyrian winged lion is outside our range of worldly experience, we can recognize the elements that it is made of, a bearded head, bird's wings, and a lion's body. In fact, what disturbs most people is not that the creature itself does not exist in nature, but that when the Assyrians carved it in the round they gave it five legs. We can accept the symbolism, but we say that any five-legged creature is impossible (A).

We must take certain things for granted here. In an earlier chapter we saw that the Assyrians did not think that lions have five legs any more than we do. Then the way in which the work is carried out shows such a degree of precision and control that we cannot assume that this was an unnoticed accident, a mistake that was overlooked. The precision is comparable to that of machine manufacture in a modern factory, and, as we saw earlier, we may think of the Assyrians as drawing their winged lion as an engineer draws, that is to say, as a series of absolutely side, or head on, or overhead series of views. These views were then added together on the surface of a block. As they were left as solids the Assyrians were unable to undercut the block to incline one of the forelegs backwards in the front view, to coincide with the same leg in the side view.

This discrepancy does not seem to have worried either the sculptors or their public, for no attempt was made to reconcile these views.

The Assyrians could see three-dimensional form as well as we can today, but their mental attitude towards the portrayal of volumes in space, and their idea of space, was evidently quite different from ours.

A three-quarter photographic view of an automobile not only has a definite spatial meaning, but it is also a picture of the car at a certain instant in time. We see just how the light was at that particular moment. If the photograph is of several cars moving along a road, then it is even more tied to a particular relationship of space and time. We see where the vehicles were at that instant with regard to each other, probably recognize the particular place, and the time of day, and perhaps the season of the year. We know how far away the cars are, for those that are nearest look larger than those in the distance.

An engineer's drawing of a car tells us everything that there is to know about the idea of the car, but stands outside the world of space and time with regard to any particular automobile. The engineer is concerned with certain ideals of accuracy and efficiency that are necessarily modified in the everyday world when the car is made.

Egyptian and Assyrian artists were, like the engineer, unconcerned with everyday space and time. Figures vary in size, but according to importance and rank, not position in space (p. 44). Figures that we know should be behind one another seem to be above one another. The result to us is incongruous until we learn to set aside our habit of expecting size to be related to distance. When we realize this, then we can read the artist's work as he intended it to be read.

We find Greek vase painting to be much the same. The front view of a chariot drawn by four horses is an engineer's or architect's elevation, with horses, chariot, and driver, all apparently on the same plane (A). When they are shown side by side we find that sometimes a very simple kind of oblique projection is used to show objects, men, and horses overlapping (p. 131). Again, there is no change in scale throughout.

teristic of medieval art. The plates appear to be flat disks seen from above. The cup is seen from a side view. These two pictorial statements apparently completely contradict one another. How can we see the plates from above and the cup from the side at the same time, when all are supposed to be side by side on the same table? If we believe that there is a certain kind of technical progress in the history of art, we might be tempted to say that the artist did not know any better, or simply could not draw, and label the picture as primitive.

It is more reasonable to suppose that the artist was considering each object singly, in its own right, with its own particular quality. He first of all wanted to make it clear that the table or altar had sides and a flat top, and combines elevational drawing with a simple oblique projection. The plates are flat and round, and the best way of showing flatness and roundness is to draw from

A

(A) Greek vase: Chariot, about 500 B.C.
London, B. M.

(B) Abel and Melchisedeck,
6th century
Ravenna, S. Vitale

(C) Abel and Melchisedeck (detail)
6th century
Ravenna, S. Vitale

(D) A besieged city:
from a 15th-century manuscript
London, B. M.

The Egyptians were concerned with rank and protocol, the Greeks with an unreal accuracy, the medieval artists with the particular qualities of objects themselves. There is a mosaic in the Church of San Vitale at Ravenna representing the sacrifices of Abel and Melchisedeck, two incidents combined in one picture (B, C). A table is set with plates and a cup whose symbolism deliberately links the Old Testament story to the Christian Mass. The table is tilted unrealistically, in the manner that we have learned to accept as being charac-

above. From the side they might appear as only thin slabs. The cup, however, seen from above, would be indistinguishable from a plate. The artist chooses the side view to show the essential feature of any cup, its round bowl plus some sort of base to stand on. In avoiding what to him would be confusion and ambiguity, and the possibility of mistaking two objects for each other, he produces a kind of relationship between the two, which may be spatially ambiguous but which to him was obviously of no concern at all.

B

C

Medieval miniaturists are equally forthright. When they painted the picture of a town under siege, attackers and defenders might be mistaken for giants among dolls' houses, standing up above waist-high walls (D). But the most important thing to both illustrator and reader was that the leaders and heroes of each army be given due credit. They had to be recognized clearly, and the means of identification was the armorial blazons on clothes, armor, flags, and shields. These had to be capable of being read clearly, and thus were enlarged. The painters knew that houses and towns are much bigger than men as well as we do. In fact, they thought that this common-sense kind of "information" could be taken for granted, and that scale and distance in art were unimportant. The medieval idea of realism was obviously one of recognition, just as ours is, but of a different kind. Again, these artists cannot be accused of not being able to draw, or of being primitive and naive, or of always copying and recopying and never working from nature. If we turn from these pictures to their marginal decorations, we find then that the artists were capable of minute examination and exact portrayal of every kind of flower

D

(A) Detail of illustrated page from "The Hours of Charles of Orleans" 15th century

(B) Roof boss, 13th century
Southwell, England, Minster

A

B

and insect, of tiny pastoral scenes and incidents of everyday life. If we look at the carved foliated decoration in Gothic cathedrals, we see all manner of plants carved with botanical accuracy, often enlarged many times in size in order to be seen from a distance. The artists' control of observation and medium is such that we cannot accuse them of incompetence, or inability to draw (A, B).

Classical form, inherited from Greece and Rome, never entirely died in the Middle Ages. Like Latin, a universal language persisted, although it became provincial, ungrammatical, and rustic at times, and adapted to meet new philosophies and changing points of view. This persistence was not entirely an automatic affair. At times scholastics would make an attempt to improve the language of philosophy by studying classical texts, and artists would also make determined efforts to acquire classical form. Roman remains were always there for everyone to see in Italy, and in 13th-century Pisa fragments of statuary and Roman tombs were even formed into a collection of sorts.

A Pisan family of sculptors copied these and incorporated a fairly competent knowledge of classical form into work which was purely medieval in idea. Straightforward transformations of a Roman Hercules, complete with his club and lionskin cloak, into a Christian symbol of fortitude and faith, and of Venus into one of the Cardinal Virtues, both adorn the base of Italianized Gothic pulpits and testify to the extent of the sculptors' acquaintance with the classical past (p. 75 H).

Perhaps their work is epitomized in a relief panel executed in 1260 by Nicola Pisano, the senior member of the family, for the pulpit in the Baptistery at Pisa (C). The subject is the Nativity. The same panel contains the Annunciation, the birth of the Virgin herself, and the shepherds watching their flocks in the fields. The main figure of the Virgin is a dignified Roman matron straight from the top of a tomb. The form of the head and the drapery are purely classical, a copy but not a blind one, made with skill and understanding. The Virgin is reclining on a couch, Roman fashion. Immediately to the spectator's left, and actually half-hidden by her is the second Virgin of the Annunciation. In the foreground is the scene of her birth. Here the "nearer" figures are much smaller than the main one. Tucked in at her feet are the flocks of sheep. The incidents mount up one above the other.

To the modern mind, trained to think in terms of one space and one time, the panel seems crowded and confused. The form is not confused, but carefully controlled. We must therefore conclude that this superimposition of separate events is also intentional, and that neither the sculptor nor his public had any difficulty in recognizing them.

The incidents shown are idealized, as became the portrayal of the life of the Virgin. However standard systems of measurement of space and time may have been applied in medieval everyday life, we can be certain that the ideas of abstract space and time were not the same as ours. In some ways they were freer. When the philosopher and theologian St. Thomas Aquinas, roughly contemporary with the Pisani, wrote critical commentaries on Aristotelian texts, he addressed the philosopher as if he were alive in the room with him. Time does not enter into criticism. St. Thomas does not say this or that idea is out-of-date. Instead he asks if it is true or false, and actually argues in person with the old philosophers who were denied only one thing by time, the Divine Revelation of Christianity. There was no sense of history. Classical and biblical figures are often shown in ordinary everyday dress. Ideal time was eternity, and the medieval thinker did not try to measure out eternity by the everyday hourglass or clock. Space and time are impersonal, outside everyday life. There is no here and now in the life of the Virgin. It is a moment in eternity which persists as long as eternity. There are not two Virgins in the relief but one. Paradoxically there is not one space but many. Above all, the story, the content gets across to the spectator.

It is useful to describe the end of the Middle Ages and the beginning of modern times by the word Renaissance, the "rebirth." The name was given to the change by scholars who saw the 15th century as a kind of boundary, on this side of which all things were revived and finally reconciled with Christianity: the classical texts, architecture, painting, sculpture, and the physical sciences.

Particularly in the arts, man is supposed to turn his eyes away from a naive medieval Heaven to become more concerned with things on earth. He drew from nature and not according to formulas, and studied the antique sculptors once more.

This, however, is not quite true. The Pisani and many other medieval artists studied and knew the antique world. The monkish illuminators knew how to work from nature when they chose to. Nobody could have observed birds, insects, and plants more carefully than they, and no one could have studied natural form more closely than the sculptors who turned the oak leaf, the vine, the blackberry, and even tiny saxifrages into great stone roof bosses and frieze decoration.

The change is really one of definition. It began linguistically. Latin was the language of learning. The workshop of learning was the set piece argument or debate. As today, philosophers and teachers had to decide what words meant before they could agree to differ. So they turned to the old Latin texts to improve their grammar and their arguments. In doing so, a great deal of the thought of the old Roman philosophers and poets stuck in scholars' minds along with the vocabulary, and on this was based the new philosophy of humanism. This is not to be confused with humanitarianism. A humanist could be either saint or villain. The philosophical school is so called because it is supposed to be more man-centered than the idealism of the Middle Ages, which is charged with looking to the next world rather than this.

The philosophy of the Renaissance is more concerned with here and now, the redefinition of space and time, of man's relationship to the universe and to his God; this has its counterpart in the arts. Here indeed is one of the main sources of evidence, for the change is beautifully illustrated, not by philosophers whose texts need special training on our part in order to understand them, but by men who were very much concerned with everyday life. These men were the sculptors and painters.

(c) NICOLA PISANO
The Nativity: from the pulpit, 1260
Pisa, Baptistery

CHAPTER 12

Renaissance Time and Perspective

PERSPECTIVE literally means clear-seeing. We are so used to thinking of perspective as having to do with railway tracks that apparently meet on the horizon and with other schoolroom maxims, that it is something of a shock to realize that its discovery and use is visual evidence of a philosophical revolution. The painter controls the portrayal of three-dimensional form in space on a two-dimensional canvas, in such a way that the scene is directly related in the most personal way to the spectator. It gives him the impression that he is there, witnessing events taking place in a world like that of his own experience in everyday life (A, and p. 135).

One of the earliest of the new pictures was the fresco of *The Holy Trinity* painted on the wall of Santa Maria Novella in Florence (p. 132). It was painted by the young Masaccio in about 1427. It shows God the Father sending the Dove of the Holy Spirit to the crucified Christ. Either side of the cross are the Virgin Mary and St. John. Kneeling below them again are the portraits of the donors who commissioned the picture. All figures are very nearly life size. They are not related hieratically, by order of importance, but realistically, as they would appear in space. The donors are recognizable portraits. They are of the same size and included in the same space as the holy figures. The whole scene takes place in a barrel-vaulted chamber which seems to penetrate the wall, an illusion of a side chapel. All the linear boundaries of the architecture converge on a central vanishing point. The eye-level is that of the spectator himself. The architecture is severe in form, but elaborate in fine detail. In fact, this classical Renaissance vault was painted before any such work was actually carried out architecturally. It may have been designed by Filippo Brunelleschi, who was said to have been Masaccio's master in perspective studies. Brunelleschi was originally a master goldsmith whose studies in geometry led him both to clarify the working rules of perspective, and also to practice architecture and engineering. When he undertook the formidable task of covering the great octagonal crossing of the cathedral in Florence with a dome, he

(A) MEINDERT HOBBEMA The Avenue at Middelharnis, 1689 showing perspective lines
London, N. G.

conceived a double-shelled structure after making studies of Roman domes. He is one of the first Renaissance universal men, who tried to understand all things and relate them in an all-embracing philosophy.

The technique of pictorial perspective was taken up with great enthusiasm and spread quickly, passing from workshop to workshop. At first new techniques and old ideas existed side by side. *The Rape of Helen* (p. 133) is based on realistic space, but still has an impossible simultaneity of events. As with other technical innovations in the fine arts, both before and since, the love of perspective for its own sake became the generative source of much of early Renaissance painting.

Architectural form, which is itself strictly controlled by geometry, is ready-made for perspective treatment; to do the same thing with living form is more difficult. In order to make bodies, heads, and limbs fit straight lines, ellipses, and vanishing points, they had to be turned into the simple forms of solid geometry, or at least contained within cylinders and blocks that could be used as a linear perspective frame.

In *The Rout of San Romano*, by Paolo Uccello (B, and p. 134), the accidental debris of the battlefield, broken lances, dropped shields, discarded helmets, and fallen bodies are carefully arranged along vanishing parallels. The fighting knights and their horses are frozen into Euclidean solids as if turned to stone. The horses' bellies are barrel-like. Even nostrils and hooves become exercises in relating curves to vanishing points. The battling armies have themselves been overcome and imprisoned

B

(B) PAOLO UCCELLO The Rout of San Romano, about 1452-57 *London, N. G.*

(C) PIERO DELLA FRANCESCA
The Finding and Verification of the True Cross, 1452-64 *Arezzo, S. Francesco*

for ever by that geometrical law and order that is the complete antithesis of the confusion, blood, and dust of the battlefield. "How sweet is perspective!" exclaimed Uccello, and this might have been echoed by Piero della Francesca. Piero's treatise on perspective shows how to construct the most complex forms in space, reducing them to their component spheres, cylinders, and cubes. To Piero perspective studies were inseparable from those of proportion. The world of his paintings, as of those of Uccello and Botticelli, is light and clear, no matter how dark and violent the scene portrayed (C). It is a simple world where all form is related harmoniously, a world contained by a thin hairline boundary. Shadows are reduced to a minimum to show the modeling on form, as if it were relief sculpture. Here there is one space, one time, and no ambiguity. It reflects the philosophy of the early Renaissance world. In a new wave of optimism men believed that reason would solve all problems. They pictured a man-centered world where the sun and planets moved round the earth in simple concentric circular orbits. At the center of the universe was the earth, and here at the focal point of all stood man, able to hold this world in the hollow of his hand.

The study of perspective brought social changes too. It was now necessary for the artist to understand mathematics, proportion, and geometry, and these were already part of the education of a gentleman. The artist changed from an almost anonymous member of a craftsman's guild to a self-conscious individual who considered himself equal to his patrons, socially and mentally. The change can be most clearly seen in the case of Leonardo da Vinci. The illegitimate son of a provincial notary, he adopted a completely aristocratic form of life,

C

and forced his patrons to accept him as one of themselves.

With Leonardo, the simple linear pictorial world begins to change. Leonardo regarded art and science as one, but it was as an artist that he began, and it was knowing that the artist portrays not just what he sees but what he knows to be true, that led him to ask so many questions about the nature of the physical world. Among these researches were his anatomy studies, which introduced him to the darker world of corruption and decay. Not only that, but Leonardo, like his fellow philosophers, soon found that the more they discovered the less they knew. The world was not such a simple place after all. "The sun does not move," wrote Leonardo. Not only did the sun not move, but the earth did not even go round the sun in simple circles. Man found himself on the edge of the universe, not at its center. Research into the nature of light and the observation of form led to darker, more obscure painting. The hairline

A B C D

(A) LEONARDO DA VINCI
Studies of the Head and Shoulders of a Man, 1510
Windsor, Royal Library

(B) MICHELANGELO
The Last Judgment: detail of Christ, 1536-41
Rome, Vatican, Sistine Chapel

(C) TINTORETTO The Ascension, about 1592
Venice, Church of the Redeemer

(D) EL GRECO The Resurrection, 1608-10
Madrid, Prado

(E) CARAVAGGIO The Supper at Emmaus, about 1600
London, N. G.

E

boundaries disappeared, and form became blurred at the edges. As the simple picture of the world dissolves into doubt, so painting seems to dissolve too. Figures no longer appear to have their origin in sculpture. Instead they appear to be of translucent living flesh with blood beneath the skin (A).

The subject matter changes too. The works of Leonardo and Michelangelo express deep disillusion and noble despair. What had been regarded as absolute knowledge becomes a matter of faith and hope once more. In the Sistine Chapel, instead of man demanding what he thinks he is owed by right, he begs for mercy (B).

The Baroque painters, named for their apparent eccentricity by a later age, followed. They still used perspective, but in order to portray dissolving rather than defined space. They used geometrical analysis of the human body in order to portray figures in space that seem to move in a violent manner, or are seen dramatically foreshortened. Where previously perspective was used to make pictures seem more like the everyday world, it was now used to make the impossible seem real and acceptable. The paintings of Titian and Tintoretto are beyond human experience, but are completely acceptable. Ellipses and spirals replace simple arcs and circles, matching the new cosmology of astronomers of the post-Galileo period (C).

Caravaggio uses perspective in an exaggerated way, to involve the spectator in the scene itself. In *The Supper at Emmaus* (E) the detailed observation is accurate, but the actual span of the apostle's arms is outrageous by conventional standards. The utmost limit of distortion is reached in the world of El Greco, where religious enthusiasm borders on hysteria, but here again it must be understood that this exaggeration only has its emotional effect upon the spectator who has been brought up to look at the painter's world with the language of perspective (D).

Nowhere is the contrast between the old world of the infinite, where simultaneous events caused no problem of interpretation, and the new world of here and now, one place and one time, more clearly shown than in Flemish and Dutch painting. The Arnolfini portrait by van Eyck (p. 61) is intended to be a social document, and the witnessed betrothal contract of the couple who stand hand in hand. Van Eyck inscribed the painting, "I was here and saw this." We are just as intimately involved in the scene today. In actual fact, under analysis, the perspective grid of the interior is not accurate. The walls, floor, and bed vanish to different eye-levels, and vanishing lines do not meet. It seems therefore that van Eyck painted the scene by copying as accurately as he could the relative positions of the room and its contents, perhaps by using mirrors and marking the co-ordinate points very carefully on them. As he looked about the room the eye-level and vanishing points would be constantly changing as he moved his head. But the technique of the perspective imposes a fixed viewpoint on the artist. He is like a man sighting a rifle on a target, with one eye shut and his head perfectly still, just as Dürer shows us in his treatise. Thus however realistic a perspective scene appears to be, it is still a highly schematic and abstract view of nature. The painter must draw his eye-level on the canvas, fix his vanishing points, and then, however much he looks about him to observe and record details of the scene when he puts them onto his canvas, he must fit them carefully into his preconceived structure of space.

This is how Hobbema must have painted his avenue of feathery-topped trees (p. 135). The eye-level of the man walking along the road is that of our own, and this immediately brings us into the scene and establishes our relationship with the landscape, as if we were advancing to meet him. In this painting we can almost tell the time of day and the season of the year by the light.

The highly organized interiors of Jan Vermeer, Pieter de Hooch, and Pieter Saenredam, are all strictly controlled to contain the view within a limited area (F, G). This roughly corresponds to our natural arc of vision. When the artist sets up a perspective he is at liberty to continue his vanishing planes from the horizon right down to his feet. But here another element of distortion enters, for in everyday life we cannot see objects straight ahead and at our own feet simultaneously. We have to look up or down. Parallel floor boards at the far end of a room appear to get closer together. If we look down on them from above they appear to be parallel without converging. If they were painted like this on a canvas, they would appear to stand upright like the planks in a palisade. This is a problem that always troubles the portrait painter who undertakes a full-length standing figure, for at one moment he looks straight at the head, then down on to the feet. If he simply copies what he sees, then his figures apparently stand on tiptoe. This is, in fact, what the Byzantine,

F

G

(F) JAN VERMEER Young Woman Standing by a Virginal, after 1670
London, N. G.

(G) PIETER DE HOOCH
Maternal Bliss, about 1675
Amsterdam, Rijksmus.

(A) The Archangel Michael:
part of ivory diptych, 6th century
London, B. M.

(B) DIEGO VELÁZQUEZ
Portrait of Pablo de Valladolid, about 1635
Madrid, Prado

(C) ALFRED SISLEY
Snow Scene, Marly-le-Roi, 1859
Paris, Mus. de l'Impressionnisme

Early Christian, and Romanesque artist did, and thought nothing of it (A, and p. 136). Since people have become aware of perspective, and have been taught how to see by it, this particular kind of portrayal looks "wrong" to them.

Portrait painters like Velázquez avoided the problem altogether by "faking" their portraits, and not having the figures standing on any plane at all (B). There is no distinguishable change of plane between floor and background. Other portrait painters put their sitters up on a raised platform in order to avoid this duality of contradicting views.

It is this simple principle that underlines the so-called break-up of space in modern painting. Although the Impressionists claimed to work from nature, they still imposed the rules of perspective on what they saw (C). It was Cézanne who tried to paint exactly what he could see without first building a structural framework. In his later still-life paintings we can see how he painted along and around the objects, fruit, pottery, drapery, that he placed on a table top (p. 137). He carefully marked the points where fruit or linen "cut" the edge and where they impinged on one another, finding all their relative positions by eye and by measuring against a brush handle held at arm's length working up one side, then across, and so on down the other side. When Cézanne had worked his way across his still-life he, of course, ended up by looking in another direction to that in which he began. As he drew and painted, he constantly changed all his vanishing points and eye-level, rather as van Eyck did in his interior. However, in his pictures Cézanne is closer to his subjects and the differences are far more marked, and also are left "uncorrected" visually.

The two parallel sides of a table may thus diverge rather than apparently converge, owing to this changing view point. The form may be displaced, for Cézanne did not draw through his solid objects but round them, and the horizontal planes do not always coincide. These displaced horizontals are reminiscent of geological faults and slips seen in a rocky landscape or a diagrammatic cross-section from a geography book.

Again, when he painted a landscape he worked from one form to another. When we look into the distance we may clearly distinguish hills, fields, houses, and trees, although they appear smaller and more crowded together. If we try to draw all that we can see, we find that

D E

(D) ALBERTO GIACOMETTI Seated Man, 1949 *London, Tate*

(E) FRANCIS BACON Seated Man with Turkey Rug, 1960-61 *London, Tate*

unless we strictly observe a perspective framework this distant area grows vertically on the canvas as we try to fit in all this detail.

This is what happened in Cézanne's work. The vertical distortion is completed by his continuing to draw what he saw almost to his own feet. Thus what we see in a late Cézanne is in one way outside the range of visual experience, and this is why we tend to say that his paintings look unreal and use words like distortion to describe them. In fact they are not so at all, but describe what we see in the one-eyed or camera's eye view.

If we stand half way along a wall, and look straight across, at right angles to the main axis, at one of the side walls, we can see that the ceiling line must slope down on either hand to right and left. Looking harder, we see that since this line is continuous it must actually be curved. However, we *know* that this line is straight, and what we know contradicts what we see.

This sort of experience is of the order of those ambiguities and paradoxes of spatial representation that form such a major part of modern painting from Cubism onwards. Cézanne showed the way, not by inventing theories about painting but from simple practical experience. His followers turned practice into theory, and this coincided with the change from the fixed ideas of Newtonian physics, and the solid universe pictured by it, to the new concepts of relativity. Just as early Renaissance painting mirrors the concentric man-centered world, and as the Baroque echoes the ellipses of Kepler and Copernicus, so the new, split space of the Cubist painter came into being just at the same time that Einstein's Relativist view of the universe was beginning to gain general acceptance.

Yet at the same time the Renaissance perspectivist's portrayal of space is as alive as ever. The camera, through whose lens we have become used to seeing so much of the world in magazines or on cinema and television screens, sees exactly in this way and conditions our own view of life.

The technique itself is still important to the film and television picture maker, and particularly important for the architect. By its means the architect can see for himself and show others what his buildings should look like before they are built.

Above all, true ideas never completely die, and must always have some relevance. Perspective is more than an academic training in straight lines, converging parallels, and eye-levels. More broadly it means the controlling of apparent space on a canvas. The painter must feel that he can hold space in the hollow of his hand. Once perspective technique has given him this experience, it is with him for ever whether he consciously obeys the rules or not. It is as clear in the work of Giacometti or of Francis Bacon as it ever was (D, E).

CHAPTER 13

Renaissance Painting and Light

ALTHOUGH it must have been seen for centuries that the distant scene in landscape appears to become more and more blue the farther it is away, Leonardo da Vinci seems to have been the first to try to analyze the phenomenon. In his notebooks he suggests that it must be due to moisture in the atmosphere. He also notes how the smoke of a bonfire appears blue under certain conditions of light, and supposes that these atmospheric blues are related to the blue of the sky.

It was John Tyndall, the physicist, who first accurately explained the phenomenon in the mid-19th century, and it is now named after him—Tyndall's effect. The blue sky is filled with dust motes and tiny globules of moisture. These are comparable in dimension to the shorter wave-lengths of the visible spectrum, the blue-violet end. The longer waves of red and yellow pass through this filter of particles; the blue-violet waves are scattered and reflected. The intensity of the blue depends upon the size and density of the packing of the particles.

The intense blue of the wings of Brazilian butterflies such as *Morpho Rhetenor* (p. 138) is a similar blue. Here it is the tiny scales and configurations on the upper surface of the wing that reflect the blue light. The blueness is increased by the actual pigmentation of the wing, which is a dark warm brown. This deeper layer absorbs all the yellow-red light so that none is reflected to interfere with the blue. This brown is the only pigment on the wing, as can be clearly seen if the wing is held *against* the light. Then all the blue color seems to evaporate from it and it becomes a gauzy brown membrane. This *structural* blue color, so called because it depends on light alone and not on pigment, is found everywhere in nature, in the jay's wing and the pigeon's breast, in the green of a mallard's head or the iridescent peacock's tail, and in many fish and reptiles too.

Any emulsion of fine particles suspended in a fluid medium will produce a similar result. If we spill milk upon a mahogany table, the milky smear looks blue (p. 139). Milk is an emulsion, a mixture of tiny particles of fat suspended in water. Paint is another such mixture of tiny particles of pigment in some sort of fluid medium, such as linseed oil. If the pigment is opaque, then its grains will scatter blue light and the paint will turn blue optically. This blueness will be quite independent of pigmentary color or color mixtures, but obviously will be more apparent in lighter colors, that is to say colors with a fair amount of white in their composition. This includes, of course, the whole range of flesh colors, and this is where the effect is most valuable.

A milky solution is said to be turbid, and the painter's technical phrase to describe this milky blue effect is that of turbid media.

There is no record of the discovery of the effect of turbid media. It is the secret of Leonardo's atmospheric painting—*sfumato*—and indeed is the only secret of the techniques of the old masters, and then secret only because romantic criticism has demanded that the great masters must have had a magic or secret formula. Like so many other secrets, the system itself is extremely simple.

The painter starts with his prepared ground on panel or canvas. This is basically dense and light reflecting, usually white. On this ground he draws his subject in very thin red-brown paint, using it rather like a wash or ink. At this stage he is free to make alterations or changes as he wishes, but he must also finally decide on all major points of composition. Let us suppose that he is painting a head. It may be a portrait, or an invented head such as those in Leonardo's *The Virgin of the Rocks* (p. 140). The head is painted in this red-brown wash. The tones follow the final modeling, but are much exaggerated. The shadows are very dark, and are carried well over into the lighter parts of the composition. The drawing is not a rough sketch, but a careful study.

When this first layer of paint is dry, the next is laid on. This is a ready-mixed pale yellowy-pink flesh tint with plenty of white body to it, and just enough oil and turpentine to make it workable. The pink, warm flesh tone is applied quite densely in the lighter parts of the head, on the brow or cheek, for example. This layer is smeared out over the brown underpainting into the shaded half-tone areas, perhaps with a brush, but quite often with the ball of the thumb or the side of the hand (p. 141).

Where this attenuated layer becomes a thin film over the underpainted shadow, it takes on a cold, bluish hue like the spilt milk on the table. The brown underpainting absorbs the yellow-red light wavelengths and stops them from reflecting back, while the pigment particles in the top layer scatter and reflect the blue.

The darkest shadows are left alone, as first painted. Thus with only two layers of paint, we have the following scheme. First, on top, a warm light area. Next, an imperceptible shading off into a cool half-lit layer, which in turn gradually trails off into deep warm shadow.

Finally, detail such as cold white highlights are painted in, and fine lines added to represent hair, eyelashes, eye pupils, lips, braids, and so on. These were sometimes painted in tempera, a mixture of oil and egg yolk which, like mayonnaise, permits the addition of water in order to thin it down.

This scheme of painting is very close to what we see in nature. The paint varies in thickness all over the picture according to whether it reflects or absorbs light, again very much as we actually see, for lit surfaces reflect light while shadows seem to soak it up and absorb it.

The system is technically sound for it ensures that the painter paints from thin to thick or lean to fat, his oiliest layers being those on top. It is also a very quick method of painting, consisting of only two main coats of paint, although it calls for great skill in drawing and does not permit the painter to change his mind once he has embarked on a picture. Obviously, any overpainting or alteration weakens and destroys this subtle optical effect.

The paint is kept very clean and lustrous, for the painter does not need to blacken or otherwise darken his shadows by adding and constantly mixing pigment on the canvas itself.

Having made his observations on the behavior of light and atmosphere in landscape, Leonardo never applied his knowledge to the painting of landscape itself. Instead he either invented or at least brought to perfection a means of modeling figures which is parallel in its working to that of the atmosphere. It is certainly one of the main reasons why his religious and mythological figures, based not on life but on his knowledge of anatomy allied to an understanding of the classical tradition in sculpture, seem to be so convincingly realistic, although they remain above and outside any human experience.

The technique became the accepted foundation of all oil painting. In the hands of lesser followers of Leonardo it could become black and wooly. It was in Venice, that half-eastern city where color was at least as important as form, that the two, modeling and brilliant color, were allied. Titian made full use of it, exaggerating the redness of the ground. A by-word for mastery and brilliance of pure color, his later work is limited to five or six colors only. His robust flesh painting is achieved entirely by these indirect means. Tintoretto went even further in making the paint work for him. By roughening the canvas texture, and working on a very dark light-dissolving ground, he dragged his loaded brush in such a way across the canvas that the strokes are like the trails of rockets or comets.

In Antwerp, using the same system of painting, Rubens was able to reduce this already simple system to an assembly line technique. His assistants were so well versed in his method that they could paint giant canvases, which, as painters say, are "signed all over" Rubens, but on which the master never worked at all. In the autographed work, *The Straw Hat*, the blueness around the eyes, the faint shadow of the hat brim, the bloom on the skin, and the liquid depth of the pupils, are all achieved by this technical method.

Rubens was a great public figure and used the method to create large-scale public works of art (p. 142). Rembrandt, who became a near hermit, used the same method to create intensely personal works of art single-handed. In *Woman Bathing in a Stream*, (p. 143), we can see how the whole of her right arm is painted in this way as clearly as if we were looking over the painter's shoulder. The brush loaded with flesh tint was dragged down the length of the drawn-in arm. The paint starts to run out towards the wrist, and the arm starts to dissolve in shadow. Then, when the painter came to the hand holding the bunched-up shift, he pressed hard against the picture, squeezing out a blob of dense paint into the back of the hand, finally dragging the merest smear over the knuckles, turning away from the light once more (p. 108 A).

It is impossible to copy a painting of this sort by even the most careful means. Indeed, the more careful the copyist the further away he will be from the real thing. The optical effects are indescribably subtle and cannot be matched by mixing paint. The only way to copy such an effect is actually to reproduce the original brush stroke, and even the master himself can never do this in exactly the same way twice. When the painter is making his medium work for him in this way, there must always

(A) REMBRANDT VAN RYN
Woman Bathing in a Stream (detail) 1655
London, N. G.

(B) REMBRANDT VAN RYN
The Return of the Prodigal Son (detail) about 1668
Leningrad, Hermitage

be an area where pure chance will come into play.

Not all Rembrandt's work is as easily analyzed as this. He often repeated the two-layer process over and over again on one picture, allowing each proceeding layer to dry out. His later works seem to be built up of geological strata. He modeled and remodeled in optical half-tones, and then freely laid on thin colored glazes in the very last stage. His brush strokes do not follow around the form as in Titian or Rubens, but run across it and sometimes counter to it. Yet however much he worked and reworked his pictures, they grew more rather than less luminous (B).

The word luminous is perhaps the one adjective that sums up this method of painting, for by using it painters were painting with light itself. In Rembrandt's work the illusion is so complete that the pictures themselves seem to be translucent, like dark stained-glass windows. The source of light is an important ingredient of his religious paintings. Symbolically, in *The Holy Family with Angels*, the source of light is a visitation of angels, or the Christ figure itself (p. 144). As well as this magical quality which led so many 19th-century painters astray in a search for the secret varnishes, waxes, and other media, that the old masters were supposed to have used, there were also great practical advantages.

Almost certainly all portraits were made from drawings of the sitter. Therefore as long as the physical likeness was achieved, the abstract formula for light and shade on flesh was acceptable. An indirect technique was suitable for an indirect method of portraiture painted mainly in the sitter's absence.

It was a much quicker method than one might think. The painter either manufactured his own paint, or had an assistant do it for him. Linseed oil dries by taking in oxygen. This may be taken directly from the air but just as easily by contact with a chemical rich in oxygen. Most white and brown pigments are oxides. Thus a mixture of white pigment—lead oxide—and linseed oil will dry as quickly without contact with the atmosphere as with. In order to keep their stock of paint moist, present-day manufacturers have to add non-drying oils such as olive oil to their tubes of paint, and these considerably lengthen the drying time of artists' colors.

The master painters could control the drying time of their paints themselves. Drying could be speeded up by using exposed and pre-oxidized oils, by loading the oil with pigment until it was almost too stiff to work, and then by adding the minimum of turpentine to make it usable.

An underpainting could be applied which would be hard in a matter of a day or so. Rembrandt could build up an impasto of thick white and umber paint that would stand up like sculptural relief, and yet be iron hard in a comparatively short time.

The use of this system accounts for the tremendous single-handed output of painters who were free from time-consuming trial-and-error methods. The technique was teachable almost by rote. It was so fundamental that it could serve as a foundation in which an individual master was free to build his own personal style.

The life-like appearance of the great mass of 18th-century portrait painting is due to this technique. In the hands of a provincial master such as Allan Ramsay (p. 145) it could be the means of portraying great psychological insight as well as the likeness his patrons demanded.

In the hands of a minor painter, it could still help him to produce a credible and acceptable painting. In the 18th century, for example, a host of very average portrait painters flourished in England and America who, in spite of certain deficiencies in drawing and handling of paint, turned out portraits that are considered "realistic" and competently painted, all entirely due to their having learned a sound technique by heart.

The technique was still used well into the 19th century. The two English masters, Turner and Constable, are often cited as the forerunners of Impressionism. If we are to define Impressionism as a certain freedom of handling of paint, of bravura brushwork, and omission of irrelevant detail, then we can point to many other examples of this sort of painting. By this definition the painter of the Ebbo Gospels would have to be described as Impressionist (p. 146). Indeed, there have been very free painters at every period from the Roman wall painters onwards.

If by Impressionism we mean a break with previous tradition, as indeed it was, we have to look for other characteristics as well as broad handling, one of which is an entirely new attitude towards atmosphere and light, and a new observation of nature.

For however free painters in the classical tradition might seem to be, however close to nature a Constable landscape sketch (p. 147) appears, it is still painted according to this synthetic preconceived idea. Constable often worked on a dark brown ground. Sometimes it was a piece of plain board which was sized but not covered with white. This ground gave him his half-tone. The brush strokes of his free landscape sketches seem often to stand out on this ground in three-dimensional relief. His sky sketches were painted rapidly from direct observation on prepared boards, often quite a rich red in tone, and he made full use of optical or structural blues in contrasting the shadowed underside of a cloud against its warm, creamy white crown.

We can see quite clearly how Constable worked when painting a landscape on such a board. He painted his sky down towards the horizon, leaving the trees as unpainted silhouetted shapes against the light sky. Next, the foreground was put in, the paint being thinned out towards the horizon to give depth to the scene. Finally, the trees would be dashed in with dabbing brush strokes, leaving the dark ground to provide natural shadow.

Turner himself took a great interest in physical theories of light. In particular he read Goethe's treatise in translation and annotated his copy. Goethe's theory is substantially that of Leonardo developed on a more didactic basis. In his effort to provide an over-all philosophy that would embrace every phenomenon and reduce all knowledge to unity, he was obviously attracted by a view that light was homogeneous, all one.

Like Leonardo before him, Turner found that the homogeneous theory of light worked particularly well as part of a painter's experience. He rarely painted directly from nature, always from drawings made on the spot and taken to his studio. He also had a phenomenal visual memory, able to turn out authentic scenes of sea and ships in the seclusion of a house deep in the country.

His light effects are of light itself. He glazed and smeared thin films of paint over one another, sometimes as milky glazes, sometimes as pure transparent color washes, until we cannot see where one ends and the other begins (p. 148).

However, Turner's color, not his technique, and Constable's concern with nature, not his method of painting, certainly helped those searching for a new spirit in painting.

Because the classical technique of painting was a synthetic studio method, it became identified with those outworn studio subjects which had become "Academic" clichés.

The Impressionists turned to Newton for a prismatic theory of color, and for the time being the Renaissance technique in a debased form was left entirely to the Salon painters of popular nudes masquerading in classical disguises.

CHAPTER 14

Impressionism and Post-Impressionism

A

B

ALTHOUGH the indirect method of painting in oils predominated from the beginning of the 16th century until the mid-19th century, a few painters here and there had attempted a more direct technique. By direct is meant a way of painting what the painter sees before him by mixing paint and matching the picture with the subject tone for tone. Of particular importance is Frans Hals's late portraits. Hals tried to paint directly from his sitter instead of from drawings. He was interested in "character," and attempted what we should call psychological portraits. The sittings had to be kept short, and Hals seems to have often tried to paint a portrait at one sitting. In order to do so he could not wait for successive layers of paint to dry, and painted wet paint into wet. As a result the luminosity of the paint was destroyed, and he had to match his half-tones and shadows by graying his paint. The paint tends to be of an even thickness all over his canvas. The form is built up of innumerable small measured strokes of paint whose size and complexity vary with the variations of light and shade on the particular form he was copying. The paintings have an appearance of flickering dabs of light and shade all over (A). At the time his patrons complained that they could see nothing but brush strokes and dabs of paint, and that the form was unrecognizable. Hals became as unpopular and was considered as eccentric in his own way as Rembrandt, and died neglected in poverty.

A less mannered example is the work of Velázquez (p. 149). In his so-called gray paintings, he too worked directly from his sitters and mixed his matching half-tones, but he worked broadly and achieved a subtlety of blended tones parallel to those of the masters of indirect painting such as Rubens.

The studios of the 18th-century Venetian painters, Canaletto and Guardi, were committed to carrying out large mass-produced views of Venice and other towns in Europe, from London to Warsaw (B).

They also used a direct method, the limited series of tones being arranged almost by numbers. In the work of their assistants in particular, a flicked-in highlight becomes an affected mannerism.

Goya, too, was a master of direct painting as well as indirect. In his case it is derived partly from choice, in his study of Velázquez and ambition to emulate him, and partly from necessity, in that in his career he was commissioned to design tapestries for the Santa Barbara factory in Madrid (C). These designs had to be capable of interpretation by weavers less skilled than those of the Gobelins in France, and with a narrower range of colors available to them. The designs had to be simple in tone and color, and rather flat, and were painted in distemper. Later, in the cupola of San Antonio de la Florida, Goya was to use a direct technique in a mixture of pure fresco with a distemper-like tempera overlaid on top (D). Here the direct range of tones, slashing bravura, and

(A) FRANS HALS
Portrait of a Man (detail) about 1639
London, N. G.

(B) FRANCESCO GUARDI
Venice, Piazza San Marco (detail) about 1765
London, N. G.

(C) FRANCISCO GOYA
Boy on a Sheep (tapestry design) 1791
Chicago, coll. Cormick

(D) FRANCISCO GOYA
Fresco (detail) about 1798
Madrid, S. Antonio de la Florida

(E) FRANCISCO GOYA
Old People Eating Soup, 1819-23
Madrid, Prado

C

D

simplicity of form have caused the work to be described as the forerunner of modern painting. The same has been said of his so-called black paintings, carried out in his old age when living alone, isolated and deaf, in the Quinta del Sordo—the House of the Deaf. Here Goya peopled the walls of his dining room with terrifying figures, as if to purge his mind of nightmares. The life-size figures are slashed in as if the painter were fighting a duel with his witches. We can see how he jabbed and slashed or scrubbed on the paint. Each free gesture is recorded as if by an instantaneous photograph. The simplified and exaggerated planes of the form seem to anticipate Cubism (E).

E

But Goya was an isolated example, and his influence lay in his subject matter and political concern in the events of his time, rather than as either a technician or recorder of pure form. Modern painting has a quieter origin, and there is no sudden revolution. Dissatisfied with an academic tradition that had become a series of meaningless clichés, a group of French painters in the mid-19th century turned their backs on the studio and the Grand Manner, and turned to nature as if to start painting afresh, from scratch, and without any preconceived ideas. Their subjects were modest, country scenes and country people.

Corot, leader of the new school, attempted to work directly from nature (p. 150). In order to do so he was forced to adopt a direct method of painting. His method consisted of mixing completely opaque paint on his palette. White was added to every color in some degree, and while an increase or decrease in the pure color alone would alter the hue or intensity, the quality of lightness or darkness had to be achieved by adding black. Thus Corot was really painting with a series of tinted grays. These not only had to be matched to the landscape or figure but also to each other, as if he were constantly adding weights to one side or other of a pair of scales to balance the "values" of tone. Thus he was constantly mixing paint on his canvas as well as on his palette. The paint would build up on the canvas until the surface was covered with a thick opaque layer, which did not vary in density according to the light and dark areas. Enlarged and reproduced in monochrome, details of a Corot landscape are remarkably like a photograph of similar subjects. In fact he tried to subordinate himself entirely to recording what he saw, as if he were a scientific instrument for doing so. His handling of paint is extremely careful. He only varied his strokes to match the difference in scale of detail between foreground and

(A) CLAUDE MONET Impression: Sunrise, 1872
Paris, Mus. Marmottan

distance. In fact, most 18th-century painters were much freer than Corot and the early Impressionists in their handling of paint.

Corot's followers grouped themselves round Édouard Manet. Manet was very much a "gray" painter, influenced as much by Velázquez and Goya as by Corot. *Le Déjeuner sur l'Herbe* (p. 71) caused a scandal at the Salon des Refusés of 1863. Manet took the subject of a nude girl talking to men in an open-air setting—the theme in fact of Giorgione's masterpiece. The scandal arose from the uncompromisingly realistic and unromantic treatment of the theme.

The name Impressionist was given to the new school by a journalist in 1874, at a show that the group, barred from the official salon, had organized for themselves. The name was taken from the title of one of Claude Monet's canvases, *Impression: Sunrise* of 1872 (A). The group had become much concerned about the lack of color in Corot and early Manet, and tried to revive brilliance of coloring while still working from nature. This meant having to analyze what color is and how it is seen. The painters became concerned not only with the relative values of tones, but how colors on a canvas affect one another. Shadows were seen not to be brown or black any longer, but as colors that contrast with those in the light. Thus complementary colors became important, and painters turned to Newton's color theory, or, to be more specific, to Eugène Chevreul's book on color, which is a practical application of Newtonian theory.

Chevreul was a scientist, a chemist, who had been called into government service to research into the dye stuffs industry and tapestry manufacture. Since the time of Louis XV, the Gobelins tapestry factory had been dominated by painters who demanded that the weavers should copy the effect of painting as accurately as possible. In their efforts to follow every shade and nuance of a large oil painting, the weavers had had to dye an enormous range of tones and colors. There is a limit to the minimum quantity of any one color that can be dyed, no matter how little is needed, and the warehouses became full of superfluous and unusable dyewools. Moreover, the more subtle the mixture, the grayer and

(B) CLAUDE MONET
Rouen Cathedral, 1894
Paris, Mus. de l'Impressionnisme

(C) CLAUDE MONET Water Lilies, 1904
Le Havre, France, Mus.

(D) PIERRE AUGUSTE RENOIR
Road Climbing through Long Grass, 1875
Paris, Mus. de l'Impressionnisme

(E) PIERRE AUGUSTE RENOIR The Judgment of Paris, 1914
Philadelphia, Pa., coll. Henry P. McIlhenny

(F) GEORGES SEURAT
A Sunday Afternoon on the Island of La Grande Jatte, about 1886
Chicago, Art Inst., Helen Birch Bartlett Memorial Coll.

more fugitive it tends to become, so that the tapestries fast lost their colors. The result was the bankruptcy of the industry. Chevreul's revolutionary suggestion was that a wide range of colors could be made by mixing comparatively few of the threads themselves in different quantities, so that the colors blended to the eye. He also showed that colors side by side affect one another's color and tonal values simultaneously.

The book was written for a new industry based on synthetic chemical dyes. These new colors were also available ready-mixed in tubes for the painter. In fact, without the advent of these, there could have been no outdoor painting and no Impressionism.

As the Impressionists became more interested in light and color theory, they undertook the difficult task of painting pure light by direct methods. Indeed, the subject became completely subservient to the idea of painting light and color.

Here they ran into difficulties. The longer one looks at a view, the more one sees. The longer one looks at colors, the more color one sees, and the more one becomes aware of the effect they have on one another. The painter's eye was constantly adjusting itself, changing quite as much as the light itself.

Each stroke of pure color called for alteration elsewhere on the canvas to maintain the balance. The canvas became more thickly encrusted with wet paint, and painting wet paint into wet paint not only changed the color as the artist worked, but tended to even all color out to a range of grays again. Even the most brilliant colors will cancel each other out if used in this way. Also, the disturbance of the medium by constant overworking caused colors to lose their luster physically.

Monet, in his series of Rouen cathedral, found himself caught up in the very grayness he sought to avoid (B). He only solved the problem in his very late paintings of water lilies (C). Here pure color is applied in quite large, separate islands and patches, with a minimum of mixing on the canvas. Renoir, having mastered Impressionism quite early (D), sought for a more disciplined form, and even returned for a while to the study of Ingres and Neoclassicism. He eventually found complete freedom by returning to a modified highly personal version of the classic Venetian painters' technique, working on a red ground, making full use of optical effects, and yet combining these with Impressionist color theory (E, and p. 151).

Georges Seurat, in the course of a remarkable, fruitful but short working life, turned purely to Chevreul. He took Monet's use of pure color in broken patches a stage further, and painted in tiny dots of pure color, a technique soon named *pointillisme* (F, and p. 152). Instead of mixing his color on the palette or on the canvas, Seurat mixed his colors "in the air" between the canvas and the spectator. By the juxtaposition of spots of pure blue and yellow-green, he could optically produce any degree of green from blue-green to yellow-green, according to which predominated. Pure reds and yellows gave him his oranges, and pure blues and reds his violets. All three produced a whole range of apparent browns and ochers.

The adoption of such a scientific method meant that a high degree of control was imposed upon the whole

(A) ANDO HIROSHIGE Ohashi Bridge in Rain, 1857 *Philadelphia, Pa., Mus. of Art, et al.*

(B) VINCENT VAN GOGH Copy of Hiroshige's woodcut *Amsterdam, Stedelijk Mus. V. W. van Gogh Coll.*

(C) PAUL GAUGUIN The Vision after the Sermon — Jacob Wrestling with the Angel, 1888 *Edinburgh, N. G. of Scotland*

(D) PAUL GAUGUIN Riders on the Beach, 1902 *Essen, Folkwang Mus.*

A

B

C

D

picture. As might be expected this control did not end with the tone and color alone, but extended to the composition as well, and Seurat made full use of geometry in organizing his pictures. Eventually horizontal elements such as the horizon, a pier, or a bridge, and vertical ones such as masts, trees, people, or factory chimneys, become more important as harmonic divisions on the canvas than as objects in a landscape, and we have a return to the equivalent of the philosophical painting of Piero della Francesca.

The Dutch painter van Gogh began by trying to emulate Rembrandt without understanding the master's technique. The increasing blackness of his pictures was bringing him to despair when his brother Theo, who worked for a Parisian dealer, introduced him to the work of Camille Pissarro (p. 183) and Monet. Immediately van Gogh became an Impressionist. He continually wrote to his brother in great detail of his highly organized series of pictures exploiting, say, all the qualities of complementary colors such as yellow and violet, or of orange and blue. Complementary colors are those that react most violently upon one another, and are the diametric opposites of a Newtonian rainbow arranged as a disc, which, as Chevreul demonstrated, can be used to calculate and predict color effects. In an effort to sort out his colors van Gogh evolved his own personal technique. He first mixed the color he wanted on his palette, and then carefully laid this color on his canvas in thick short slabs. Each brush stroke is quite distinct from its neighbor. The effect is of a mosaic of paint-stroke tesserae. The short brush strokes follow the form, outlining and echoing each detail. The concentric brush patterns spread outwards from each center of form like the ripples on the surface of a pool until they encounter a similar series spreading from another part of the picture.

Paul Gauguin, stockbroker turned painter and companion of van Gogh for a few violent weeks in Provence, was no amateur. By the time Gauguin had reached his middle twenties he was an accomplished Impressionist.

The boldness of line and color in the Japanese print had already appealed to the Impressionists who collected and copied them (A, B). Their influence was most marked in Gauguin, who turned also to Persian and Indian handling of color. He painted landscapes and scenes in Brittany (C) and Provence in flat clear colors, arranged in well-defined shapes, and eventually became a completely neo-Oriental painter, abandoning Europe for the South Pacific (D, and p. 72).

CHAPTER 15

Cézanne and the Cubists

THE Impressionists were accused of being social revolutionaries and anarchists, rather incongruously since Manet and Degas were both extremely conservative, and Cézanne owned a bank. The label arose partly from their subject matter and partly from the way they painted. Degas was regarded as sordid because he did not idealize his laundry women and ballet dancers, or disguise his nudes with classical allusions (A). Toulouse-Lautrec was regarded as a renegade aristocrat whose interest in low life, prostitutes, cabaret dancers, and jockeys was perverted (B, C). Seurat was accused of taking an unnatural delight in ugliness because he chose to include factory chimneys in his landscapes (p. 152). Monet's crepuscular light-drenched out-of-focus pictures of railway stations, cathedrals, and the Thames, were held to be the work of a childish lunatic (D, and p. 184).

Nothing now seems less revolutionary than these paintings. Reproductions of them hang in schoolrooms, and they are taken for granted by children, who seem to be born with the ability to see them.

We all of us see in clichés, artists and laymen alike. The difference is this, that the creative artist is not content to use signs that have become conventional, but in his search for what is the truth for him he constantly modifies and changes these signs. We often say that such an artist is ahead of his time. What we really mean is that the public has not yet learned how to read his work correctly. He himself lives with his work, grows up with it, and sometimes cannot understand why other people cannot see as he can. On the other hand, people do not expect to have to learn to see, and therefore condemn that which is unfamiliar.

A

B

C

(A) EDGAR DEGAS Seated Dancer Tying her Slipper, 1886
Paris, Durand-Ruel et Cie.

(B) HENRI DE TOULOUSE-LAUTREC
The Two Friends, 1894
Albi, France. Mus.

(C) HENRI DE TOULOUSE-LAUTREC
At the Races, 1899
Albi, France, Mus.

(D) CLAUDE MONET
La Gare Saint-Lazare, 1877
Paris, Mus. de l'Impressionnisme

D

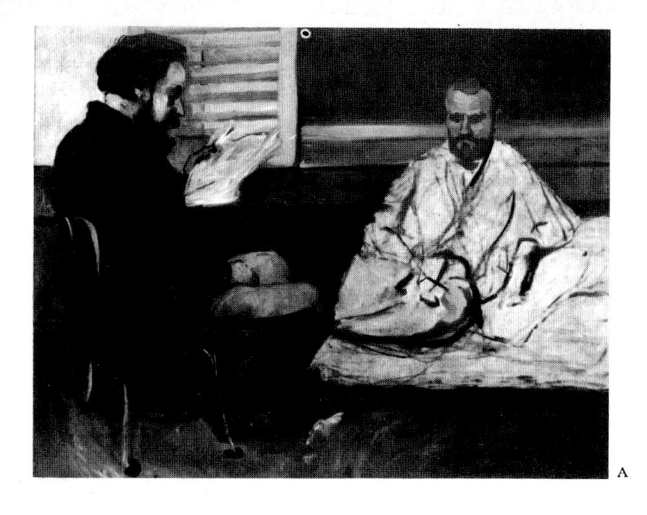

A

B

C

We should always be expecting the artist's vision to change and be prepared to learn his language, before we can understand and criticize his work. The 19th-century critics, who apparently did not understand Impressionism, were quite right. There was a revolution going on. And, as they justly complained, it was a technical one. It was a revolution that was almost over by the time they first realized that it was going on. It was a paradoxical revolution carried on by men whose last intention was to be thought revolutionary. What the Impressionists all craved for was recognition and respectability. And none more so than Paul Cézanne, the most abused of them all, and one of the most unsuccessful in his day.

Just as van Gogh's primary ambition had been to re-create the heroic phase of Dutch painting, so Cézanne saw himself as the successor to the great French Romantic painters of the 19th century, Delacroix and Géricault. Against his father's wishes he went to Paris as a painting student. Here, among students who were carefully painting brown tonal pictures, he became an object of derision and, soon discouraged, returned home. In spite of himself he could not give up painting and drawing, and, older and tougher, returned to Paris and the schools. It is comparatively easy for us to see the strength and tenacity of the old Cézanne in the work of his youth; we are able to make comparisons. At the time they appeared to be so grotesque, clumsy, badly drawn and painted, that even his close childhood friend Émile Zola tried to persuade him to give up, and, when unsuccessful in this, called him a madman. And this in spite of the fact that Zola considered himself one of the most advanced and anti-traditional thinkers in France (A).

Cézanne became bitter and withdrawn, but persisted in painting. He returned home to Provence. In the meantime the Impressionists had discovered the brilliant light of Aix-en-Provence and Arles, and Cézanne was received sympathetically by Pissarro, who taught him to see with an Impressionist's eyes. By the 1870's, when he was in his early thirties, Cézanne had mastered Impressionism, and was embarking on his unique development of color and space in painting that was to occupy him to the end of his life, and particularly for the next thirty years in which he lived in virtual isolation. Van Gogh, living and working within calling distance of Cézanne at this time, speaks of him as if he were a painter of another place and time (B, C).

Cézanne's ambition was to unite painting directly from nature with the solidity and durability of Poussin. He therefore became interested in the theory of color

(A) PAUL CÉZANNE Paul Alexis Reading a Manuscript to Émile Zola, 1869-70
São Paulo, Mus. of Art

(B) PAUL CÉZANNE The House of the Hanged Man at Auvers-sur-Oise, 1873
Paris, Mus. de l'Impressionnisme

(C) PAUL CÉZANNE Mont Sainte-Victoire, about 1886
London, Courtauld Inst. Gall.

(D) PAUL CÉZANNE Still-life with Plaster Cupid, about 1895
London, Courtauld Inst. Gall.

(E) PAUL CÉZANNE The Black Marble Clock, about 1870
Paris, Stavros S. Niarchos Coll.

(F) PAUL CÉZANNE The Lake of Annecy, 1896
London, Courtauld Inst. Gall.

D

and form, always relating theory to practice. Of particular interest was Chevreul's analysis of the simultaneous contrast of tone and color. Chevreul, as we saw in the previous chapter, had noticed that a peculiar optical illusion arising from the tapestry weavers' use of solid color tended to destroy the form. If we imagine a series of tones evenly graded in steps like a musical scale from black to white, each occupying an equal area large enough to give each its own clear definition, and each touching its neighbor, the difference between every tone and its neighbor makes a clear, hard line. Now where any one tone borders its lighter neighbor, it will appear darker. Similarly when it touches its darker neighbor, it will appear lighter. Thus although we know that each solid gray area is really of a uniform tone, it will have the appearance of being light at one edge and dark at the other, when bordered by tones lighter and darker than itself. The result is that our strip of tones laid out like a keyboard appears to be made up of counterchanged segments, and the strip has a ribbed concave appearance like that of a fluted column. This was the effect that Cézanne saw and used.

E

We know that Cézanne was a very slow painter. He would sit staring at his subject for hours before making up his mind about a brushstroke. Sitters became impatient and refused to pose. Flowers faded and fruit decayed in his still-lifes. He took to using artificial fruit and flowers, and unchanging bits of china, clocks, and plaster casts (D, E).

The harder he stared at a particular passage of tone, the more he became aware of the contrasts which bordered it. A dark edge appears to have its own corresponding vibrant light line if we look at it long enough,

F

Chevreul said. In order to achieve three-dimensional solidity, Cézanne painted up each plane that he saw with its own related contrasts. This has the effect of giving each small section of form its own complete tonal scale from light to dark. The result is rather like a bas-relief. The major change in a Cézanne landscape, from immediate foreground to farthest distance, becomes dominated by a whole series of equivalent tonal changes which depended upon the number of local changes of plane that the painter cared to use—in other words, how much detail he cared to put in (p. 117 F).

The same is true of a still-life (p. 137). Thus the over-all space in a Cézanne became deliberately limited. Some painters paint a horizon at infinity, as Turner did. In a Cézanne we can in imagination run our fingers over these steps of form to the horizon, which is no farther from the nearest apparent plane than the background of a carving in relief.

At the same time that Cézanne painted from one tone to another, he also painted from one complete object to another. He plotted points where one edge crossed or cut another as a mapmaker might, or as a mathematician draws a graph. At the same time, fearful of losing his contact with the subject by imposing any preconceived idea upon it, he did not set up a perspective projection to guide and co-ordinate all the forms into a single view-point space. We have already seen how, by moving his gaze from one part of the subject to another, he also changed his view-point and drew apparent vanishing lines accordingly. Thus these range through an unlimited series both horizontally and vertically, and result in tabletops that apparently diverge and vertical elongation in landscapes.

To his contemporaries, taught how to see from a single view-point and to think that this was the only possible and, therefore, the correct way to see, the resulting discrepancies of form, the apparent splits and divisions of solid objects, were proof only of incompetence at best and of a deliberate insulting challenge at worst.

They were neither. They were an automatic result of a certain persistent outlook.

Cézanne deliberately limited his color while simplifying his form. He obtained the most brilliant effects with a series that ranges from blue to orange. Thus his greens tend to be blue-greens; his yellows are related to either blue and are lemonish, or to orange and are ocher. This imposes an over-all unity of color. Each plane has its own range from cool-blue to warm-orange relating to its own

A

range. By means of this contrast Cézanne makes his color multiply its range and increase its effects by optical illusion. It is as if his colors can breed. To keep his purity of tone and color, he, too, eventually separated each brush stroke, even sought to separate the brush stroke from the form itself. All form was seen as simple planes—treating nature as the cylinder, the sphere, and the cone, to quote Cézanne himself. Cézanne tried to make his painting as impersonal as possible. To match his platonic idea of form he developed a single diagonal brush stroke, which he used regardless of the actual form he was depicting.

The diagonal brush stroke runs through his later paintings like the vertical strips of woven wool in a tapestry. The result is highly paradoxical. In searching for complete anonymity, Cézanne reveals in a most intimate way his strong personality.

Cézanne is a one-man compendium of the language of modern painting. In his work we find the synthesis of form into planes; the breaking up of space and freeing it from a single viewpoint; the structural use of color; the assertion of the brush stroke which stands in its own right; the careful placing of co-ordinate points on the canvas; the domination of the subject, which becomes the starting point for speculation by the painter rather than an end in itself. And yet all these are blended together in an "attempt to seize a harmony between numerous relations."

Cézanne was, and still is, very much a painter's painter. It was only among his fellow artists, Monet, Pissarro, Renoir, that he found any friendship and encouragement. His influence was posthumous. He had no pupils or followers. He did not found a "school" in

C

D

(A) GEORGES BRAQUE The Table, 1911
Paris, Mus. d'Art Moderne

(B) ALBERT GLEIZES Tableau, 1921
London, Tate

(C) JUAN GRIS Portrait of Picasso, 1912
Paris, Bignou Coll.

(D) LOUIS MARCOUSSIS The Table in Front of the Balcony, 1936
Paris, Mus. d'Art Moderne

his own time, but in the succeeding generation his influence was so sudden as to be almost a revelation.

The period of *La Belle Époque*, 1900-14, was the time in which classical Cubism was founded and reached its peak. The movement was begun by the young Georges Braque. Pablo Picasso, who had been following Degas and Lautrec, almost simultaneously started painting in pure planes.

These two took the pictorial language of Cézanne and pushed it to its extreme. Having seen his work, they could no longer see the world save through his eyes. Cézanne's relative view of space coincided with the shock of physical relativity, that was as shattering and as stimulating as the hypotheses of Galileo or Newton had been in their time. It was the dawn of the new machine age, and the Cubist's sharpening of the world into hard planes had an affinity with the machine aesthetic. Above all, it was a period of optimism, of confidence based on science, and Cézanne had shown how to build pictures that took the ephemeral accidents of nature, and turned them into structures interlocked, balanced, and buttressed to last for ever.

At first, the Cubist subjects were those that lent themselves to this treatment in a fairly obvious way: landscapes of which buildings were the focal point, such as Braque's early painting of l'Estaque. Then, of course, still-life, where jugs are cylinders, books are rectangular prisms, and so on (p. 185). Picasso soon applied the technique to figure painting (p. 186). The obvious comparison was made between a Cubist-treated head and African masks (p. 187). Indeed, ethnographic objects of this kind became to the Cubists what the Japanese print had been to the Impressionists. After a short period of individual, largely intuitional searching, the two painters embarked upon a series of classical Cubist pictures which so closely approach anonymity that it is very difficult to tell their work apart.

In these the form is completely fractured, broken up into shattered splinters of planes. They turned Cézanne's limited color scheme into a simple range from blue-gray to brown, with perhaps a touch of ocher here and there. Some of these pictures can be seen to be identifiable portraits upon close inspection (p. 188), but mainly they are still-life paintings. The subjects are bottles, glasses, tobacco pipes, and musical instruments, chiefly the violin or guitar (A). Sheet music is used, and sometimes half-obscured stencil letters may begin to spell Bach. Often these paintings are opalescent ovals of light in the middle of a rectangular canvas.

After this academic language had been formulated, Cubism crystalized into big solid forms once more. The movement was joined by Albert Gleizes, Louis Marcoussis, and, most notably, another Spaniard, Juan Gris (B, C, D). The more recognizable Cubist studies that followed take what was incidental to Cézanne, the "split" form, and turn it into a deliberate duality. As in archaic and medieval art, once more one can see two views simultaneously. The top of a jug is shown superimposed upon its side elevation. Objects stand upon checkered tables, painted as upright as a wall. A certain hard, timeless quality is achieved which is very like both the art of the ancient world and the Middle Ages. For the second time in history an eye in full view is placed on a face seen in profile. Profiles are superimposed upon frontally drawn heads. As if in punning mockery, real or *trompe l'oeil* materials are stuck or collaged into still-life paintings. Wood-grained paper simulates the real thing, wallpapers and newspapers are used as themselves, sheet music, bills, and tickets are stuck onto painted tables (A).

Classical Cubism had coincided with political, social, and scientific ideas that it matched. The coming of World War I in 1914 was as much a shock to the *avant garde* as to the prosperous bourgeois. The old world of both was destroyed by it, and a period of reaction set in.

Nevertheless, Cubism has been the persistent thread running through all modern painting. The hardening of form and seeing it as planes are found in painters as individual and as idiosyncratic as Paul Klee (p. 57) and Marc Chagall (p. 126). Some like Jacques Villon have held to it in a more or less pure form. Social realists like Fernand Léger (p. 127), Diego Rivera (p. 180 A), and Renato Guttuso (p. 40 C) have used it as the foundation on which to build their figure compositions on an enormous scale.

The sculptor, working in solid material in the round, has not the same problem of giving substance to the medium as the painter has. Nevertheless, it was painting that influenced sculpture in the modern movement, not vice versa. Apart from the sculpture produced by painters themselves—Matisse, Picasso, and Braque all worked in the round at one time or another—sculptors such as Ossip Zadkine and Jacques Lipchitz also emphasize the geometrical plane aspect of form. The main characteristic is that a twist is generally given to the plane, warping it in three dimensions, the one act absolutely denied to the painter (B, C).

Used loosely, Cubism has become the popular generic term to describe all modern art willy nilly, often as a term of abuse. Although the actual period of Cubism was short-lived, its influence is still such that it may be said that it is comparable to any great academic movement of the past. The innumerable individual variations bear out rather than deny this, for the capacity to contain every kind of personal interpretation has been the hallmark of all true academic systems.

What was not foreseeable was that once painters set themselves down in front of nature and painted according to their own perception, free as far as possible from preconceived ideas, then however sincere each painter might consider himself to be, the result was bound to be extremely personal and subjective. All men see differently, and without a common sign language with which to say what they see, they must each invent their own. Thus by a very simple act the forces were released which were to result in the tremendous and bewildering variety of individual facets of modern art.

(A) PABLO PICASSO Collage *Paris, coll. Georges Salles*

(B) OSSIP ZADKINE Woman with Fan, 1920 *Saint-Étienne, France, Mus. d'Art et d'Industrie*

(C) JACQUES LIPCHITZ The Acrobat on Horseback *Paris, Private Coll.*

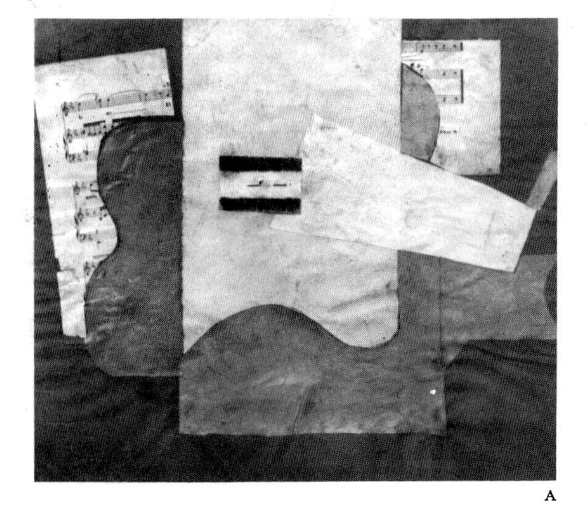

A

B

C

VINCENT VAN GOGH Road with Cypresses and Star, 1890 *oil on canvas* $36\frac{1}{4} \times 28\frac{3}{4}$ *in.* SEE PAGE 80
Otterlo, Holland, Rijksmuseum Kröller-Müller

VINCENT VAN GOGH Self-portrait, Saint-Rémy, 1890 *oil on canvas* $25\frac{5}{8} \times 21\frac{1}{4}$ *in.* SEE PAGE 81
Paris, Musée de l'Impressionnisme, Gift of Paul and Marguerite Gachet

EL GRECO The Agony in the Garden of Gethsemane, about 1580 *oil on canvas* $40 \times 51\frac{1}{2}$ *in.* SEE PAGE 81
London, National Gallery

OSKAR KOKOSCHKA Summer I, 1922 *oil on canvas* $43\frac{3}{4} \times 55\frac{1}{8}$ *in.*
Krefeld, Germany, Private Collection
By permission of Roman Norbert Ketterer, Campione d'Italia

SEE PAGE 83

PABLO PICASSO Woman Weeping, 1937 *oil on canvas* *$23\frac{1}{2} \times 19\frac{1}{4}$ in.*
London, Private Collection

SEE PAGE 84

MARC CHAGALL I and the Village, 1911 *oil on canvas* $75\frac{5}{8} \times 59\frac{5}{8}$ *in.* SEE PAGES 88 AND 120
New York, Museum of Modern Art, Mrs. Simon Guggenheim Fund

FERNAND LÉGER Two Women Throwing Flowers, 1954 *oil on canvas 38×51 in.* SEE PAGE 88
London, Tate Gallery

PIET MONDRIAN Painting No. 1, 1921 *oil on canvas* $38 \times 23\frac{3}{4}$ *in.* SEE PAGE 92
Basel, Private Collection

S3 Bentley Continental "Flying Spur" with coachwork by H. J. Mulliner. 1963
By courtesy of Rolls-Royce Limited

SEE PAGE 92

Catalogue drawing of a Rolls-Royce, 1963
By courtesy of Rolls-Royce Limited

SEE PAGE 92

Greek vase: Harnessing a Chariot, about 510 B.C. *height 18 in.*
London, British Museum

SEE PAGE 96

MASACCIO The Holy Trinity, about 1427 *fresco*
Florence, S. Maria Novella

SEE PAGE 100

BENOZZO GOZZOLI The Rape of Helen, early work *oil on wood 20 × 24 in.*
London, National Gallery

SEE PAGE 100

PAOLO UCCELLO The Rout of San Romano (detail) about 1452-57 *tempera on panel* *72 × 125¾ in.*
London, National Gallery

SEE PAGE 101

MEINDERT HOBBEMA The Avenue at Middelharnis, 1689 *oil on canvas* $40\frac{3}{4} \times 55\frac{1}{2}$ *in.*
London, National Gallery

SEE PAGE 103

Christ in Majesty, 12th century *wall painting*
Berzé-la-Ville, France, Cluniac Priory

SEE PAGE 104

PAUL CÉZANNE Still-life with a Basket, about 1890 *oil on canvas* *$25\frac{5}{8} \times 31\frac{7}{8}$ in.* SEE PAGES 104 AND 118
Paris, Musée de l'Impressionnisme

Tropical butterfly: *Morpho Rhetenor*
By courtesy of D. B. Janson, London
Photo by Gerald Howson

SEE PAGE 106

Spilt milk on mahogany
Photo by Gerald Howson

SEE PAGE 106

LEONARDO DA VINCI The Virgin of the Rocks (detail) begun 1483 *oil on panel* $78\frac{3}{4} \times 48$ *in.*
Paris, Louvre

SEE PAGES 106 AND 156

Flesh tint being smeared over warm red ground
Photo by Gerald Howson

SEE PAGE 107

SIR PETER PAUL RUBENS The Landing of Maria de' Medici at Marseilles, about 1625
oil on canvas $155 \times 92\frac{1}{2}$ *in.*
Paris, Louvre

SEE PAGES 107 AND 156

REMBRANDT VAN RYN Woman Bathing in a Stream, 1655 *oil on canvas* $24\frac{1}{4} \times 18\frac{1}{2}$ *in.*
London, National Gallery

SEE PAGE 107

REMBRANDT VAN RYN The Holy Family with Angels, 1645 *oil on canvas* $46 \times 35\frac{3}{4}$ *in.* SEE PAGE 108
Leningrad, Hermitage

ALLAN RAMSAY Portrait of David Hume, 1766 *oil on canvas 30 × 25 in.*
Edinburgh, Scottish National Portrait Gallery

SEE PAGE 109

Portrait of St. Luke: from the Ebbo Gospels, 816-833 *vellum* *10¼ × 8 in.*
Epernay, France, Bibliothèque Municipale

SEE PAGE 109

JOHN CONSTABLE A River Scene, with Farmhouse near Water's Edge, 1830-36 *oil on canvas* *10 × 13¾ in.* SEE PAGE 109
London, Victoria and Albert Museum

JOSEPH MALLORD WILLIAM TURNER Windsor Castle from the Meadows, about 1807 *oil on thin veneer* *$10\frac{3}{4} \times 21\frac{1}{2}$ in.*
London, Tate Gallery

SEE PAGE 109

DIEGO VELÁZQUEZ Philip IV of Spain, 1655-60 *oil on canvas 27 × 22 in.* SEE PAGE 110
Madrid, Prado

JEAN BAPTISTE CAMILLE COROT The City and the Rocks, 1827 *oil on canvas*
Paris, collection Georges Vian

SEE PAGE 111

PIERRE AUGUSTE RENOIR Mossy Roses, about 1890 *oil on canvas* $13\frac{3}{4} \times 10\frac{1}{2}$ *in.* SEE PAGE 113
Paris, Musée de l'Impressionnisme

GEORGES SEURAT The Bridge at Courbevoie, 1886 *oil on canvas* *18 × 21½ in.* SEE PAGES 113 AND 115
London, Courtauld Institute Galleries

CHAPTER 16

The Mass Production of Works of Art

MASS production is generally thought of as something comparatively new, and specifically as a result of the use of machines. Its essence is not in the machine itself, which is an extension of the hand tool into a tool of greater accuracy and with its own sources of power, but in the division of labor and the organization of production teams. The team is organized as a production line, where each man or machine does one repetitive operation out of all those necessary to the finished product.

This organized method of production has been known for a long time in the world of art. The sculptors of ancient Egypt, and later those of Greece, operated in this way. A block of stone was quarried to the necessary size, from much smaller than life-size to a colossus, depending upon the requirements. Whatever the size, a drawing of the figure was squared up on the sides of the block from a laid-down series of proportions. The block was trimmed to fit the drawing exactly. The least skilled of the workmen or apprentices would then carefully cut away superfluous stone to the outline on all faces. The figure was now roughed out, and looked rather like a square-faced 19th-century wooden toy (A). The next operation was the cutting out of the figure in the round, checking surfaces against a series of templates or profile patterns which were also enlarged from a set standard (B). This was semi-skilled work. At this stage a bladed chisel was not used, but a pointed hardened punch. These punches ranged from slim single-pointed tools to broad-ended multiple-point tools. The punch was held at right angles to the surface of the form being cut, and the stone was almost powdered away in grains, not chipped away.

(A) Unfinished statuette of horse found at Sparta *London, B. M.*

(B) Unfinished torso from Naxos, 6th cent. B. C. *Athens, Nat. Mus.*

A B

The operation was similar to that of the modern pneumatically-powered bush hammer, used to finish off concrete.

The final finishing and polishing was left to the master sculptors. If the piece was to be a recognizable portrait the head was left until the very end, so that any mistake made along the line would not ruin an expensive operation. The head was carved by the master sculptor himself, from a plaster or clay cast made from the sitter's face.

Mass production calls for standardization. The materials must be constant. All parts must fit together. Details such as the screw thread of a nut and bolt must conform. So it was with sculpture. The drawings were standardized and filed like blueprints. They were not squared in dimensions but in ratios, so that they could be enlarged to fit any surface. The poses themselves were unified and standardized, as were symbols of rank. Methods of showing drapery or hair were constant, and however much the likeness would vary from one sitter to another, the actual method of carving the individual features themselves was standardized.

Thus in a portrait, the same symbol for an eye in stone was always carved, but its actual shape and proportion would be carefully measured from the cast of the sitter. The final outline ridges to the features would be cut with a hardened chisel, and the whole would be rubbed down and finished with polishing stones. The amount of labor involved was tremendous. As the tools were bronze, the punches needed constant attention, particularly when working the very hard basalts and granites of which the

Egyptians were fond. The ultimate precision of Egyptian work can only be compared to modern engineering machine-tool production. Not that this is a quality in itself, but it is a measure of the achievement of intention. Most of this work, all of a high uniform quality, is as anonymous a product as the automobile is to the average purchaser, who knows the maker's name but rarely the designer's. Like the automobile or airplane, the product was the result of a highly organized team. The carvers worked all over a large sculpture simultaneously, not finishing off one piece before another. Often it would have been impossible to obtain a view of the whole before completion. This meant that the team had to have unquestionable faith in each member doing his job thoroughly and accurately, sticking absolutely to the drawing, again very like the modern engineer does.

Carvers and painters were tradesmen. They served an apprenticeship and gradually worked their way up, the most skilled or most talented eventually becoming the final carvers and team leaders. They were taught by copying details, learning the system, and working from established rules, not directly from nature. These rules could be taught absolutely. The artist's intelligence was finally called into play in the application of these rules to a given subject, a scene from village life on the wall of a tomb of a minor official, the portrait of a scribe, in wood and life-size, or of a seated pharaoh 50 feet high.

The Greeks used Egyptian technology, but the scale of operation was smaller and the result more personal and open to change (A, B). The Greek sculptors still used the punch and not the chisel. They worked in crystalline marble, and the constant hammering concussed the stone and gave it soft opacity. Even the final polishing did not erase all trace of the punch, and the sculpture was left with a grainy texture. This pitted surface is highly sympathetic to the touch. Left as it is, it is translucent yet skin-like. It is slightly porous and a good surface on which to apply encaustic colors, that is to say pigment bound in a wax base that is finally finished off with a heated iron. Also it provided a keyed surface for skimming over with plaster. The latter was often used as a protective coat for sculpture and marble architecture, and also colored with encaustic paints. Although the Greeks had no religious restrictions limiting the sculpture to set poses, and figurative sculpture gradually changed from the figure with one leg advanced and arms at the side to one in dramatic counter-balanced attitudes, the standard details remained fixed. The symbols for features, hair, or the anatomy of the kneecap, were as set as our Roman-based alphabet, and were to remain so until the end of the 19th century. Like the alphabet, the smaller the standard parts the greater the flexibility of the system.

This alphabet is the basis on which a school or academic system is based. Any student or apprentice was expected to copy standard details until he had completely mastered his technique and their form. As soon as he was capable of doing so he assisted the master. Then, eventually, he became a master in his own right. On the foundation of the academic system he could make his own contribution as an original artist, or, if he was not capable enough, at least he could turn out an efficient job in the tradition in which he had been trained.

In other words, he learned to see an eye first of all as the sculptor carves it, then, secondly, as the eye of an old or young person, a man, a woman, a mythological or religious figure, or a portrait sitter.

Production techniques varied, but the language of form did not. To speed up their output, the Romans used drills more frequently than the Greeks. A line of holes was drilled, and the honeycomb of stone hacked away with a sideways stroke. The introduction of iron chisels instead of bronze meant that a harder, sharper, and broader edge could be used, and they began to be used rather more like wood-carving chisels. The sculptor started to score cross-hatched grooves along the form, taking off much more stone at a time, and emphasizing broad planes, rather than "peeling" off the layers of stone slowly and painstakingly.

(A) Egyptian statue: Khan-em-Uast, son of Rameses II *Cairo, Mus.*

(B) Greek archaic Kouros *Athens, Nat. Mus.*

A B

In the Middle Ages the distinction between mason and sculptor diminished. At first the Church was the main organizing body of all the arts, and the schools were monastic communities. Many monasteries were almost completely art factories, specializing in carving, glass, or book production. As the cities grew and lay communities prospered, masons and other monastery-trained artists left to become free masons, working on the great secular cathedrals rather than the abbey churches. From the free masons and other town-dwelling artists arose the guilds, trade unions that fixed prices and controlled the training of young artists.

Thus in classical times the artist was a civil-servant, an employee of a Ministry of Works. Subsequently he was a member of the Church, which undertook private and courtly commissions. Finally, he was a private member of a corporation, which executed works for Church, or state, or a private citi[illegible]. T[illegible]e artist's history tells the story of society.

All this time sculpture predo[illegible]n that it was the yardstick, the primary and c[illegible]ompendium to be referred to on all questions [illegible] and drawing.

The system of producti[illegible]r works of art was organized on parallel lines[illegible]bvious that the construction of Roman and I[illegible]ine mosaics must have entailed the building up of [illegible]highly skil[illegible]team, from the provision of the origin[illegible] design to th[illegible]nufacture and sorting of tesserae, the erection of sca[illegible], the training and organizing of the plaster workers and the numerous assistants to lay the mosaic itself. There is a direct link between mosaicists and medieval stained-glass workers, colored-glass artists having migrated from Venice and Ravenna to Limoges, the center of the glass and enamel industry in western Europe, as early as the middle of the 10th century.

The large Renaissance frescoes were carried out with a system of divided labor too. The over-all conception was that of the master who was head of his *bottega*, or workshop. Advanced pupils enlarged the master's sketches (C) to full-size cartoons, often having to add original passages as they did so. Then, when all was ready, all members of the *bottega* would go on to the site of the fresco. The final layer of wall plaster was applied, the scaffolding erected, and then the drawing transferred to the wall (D). The final layer of plaster was made of lime which had stood in a pit for twenty years, mixed with fine-washed silver sand and marble dust, and applied area by area to the drawing. With lime water as a medium, water-bound color was painted onto the wet

C D

(C) MICHELANGELO Studies for the Libyan Sibyl
New York, Met. Mus. of Art, Purchase 1924, Joseph Pulitzer Bequest

(D) MICHELANGELO The Libyan Sibyl, 1508-12
Rome, Vatican, Sistine Chapel

plaster. A natural transparent crystalline surface formed as the plaster dried, locking the water color behind it. A true fresco could only be painted onto wet plaster. The drying time of plaster was about four hours, so that the painter had to work on single units, a head, or an arm, or an area of drapery. The plaster was cut back to the outline of the shape, and given a beveled edge to key it invisibly to the neighboring area of plaster. On large areas the painters had to work quickly, for if a joint had to be made in the middle of an area of form, there was no guarantee that the next patch would dry to an exact color to match, and the dividing line would remain visible. Thus it was necessary that all such divisions should coincide with an actual ouline in the design. Once an area was begun there could be no alteration without cutting the plaster away and starting all over again. There was no margin for error or room for displays of "artistic" temperament, as Michelangelo found out to his cost in the Sistine Chapel. Here, after several false starts due to either technical mistakes or clashes of temperament with his team of assistants, he found himself finally working alone with the aid of a plasterer.

Even by Michelangelo's time there was still no hard and fast division between the creative artist and the skilled craftsman. Leonardo would always have had himself taken to be a gentleman, but his clients were very conservative in their attitude towards him, even though they themselves were often "self-made" men in

A B

the modern sense of the word. In 1483 Leonardo, in partnership, undertook a commission for an elaborately carved and gilded altarpiece for the Chapel of the Brothers of the Immaculate Conception in Florence. Leonardo undertook to paint the centerpiece, *The Virgin of the Rocks* (p. 140). The frame was valued at 700 gold pieces, the picture at 100. When Leonardo saw what he had actually achieved in his picture he asked for more money. The litigation went on for years, and he finally took the picture back. It was his treatment as a scholar and gentleman at the French court which made him finally decide to leave Italy for good.

(A) PETER PAUL RUBENS Sketch for the Maria de' Medici series, about 1625 *Munich, Alte Pin.*

(B) Louis XIV visiting the Gobelins Factory (tapestry)

(C) JOHANN ZOFFANY Life Class in the Royal Academy, 1772 *London, Royal Coll.*

(D) ALFRED STEVENS Design for fireplace, 1851 *London V. and A.*

It was not only large-scale fresco painting that had to be carried out by team-work. Rubens' studio in Antwerp was a factory in every sense of the word. His assistants, some of whom were well-known artists in their own right, were not only graded to the stage of each picture upon which they were allowed to work, from grinding and mixing colors, preparing canvases, transferring squared-up drawings, and working on the final picture, but also were trained to specialize in the final stages as animal painters, portrait painters, painters of drapery, linen, silk, and satin, painters of still-life fruit and flowers, even to a final specialization in the ability to put the bloom on fruit or the sheen on shiny surfaces. The enormous canvases were hung on rollers, and the painters worked on wheeled stages at several different levels. Rubens so skilfully organized the technique that he could be certain that pictures done in his absence would be as much a Rubens as if painted by himself (A, and p. 142.) His clients knew that they were buying pictures that he had not touched and were quite satisfied. His attitude was not thought to be at all commercial; in fact, he was as well known as a diplomat and ambassador as a painter, a gentleman and courtier in his own right. And like so many other Flemish and Dutch painters, he was also a picture and antique dealer and speculator.

Still later and working on a more intimate scale, a painter with a large portrait business, such as Sir Joshua Reynolds, had to rely on mass production methods. Not only did he employ a large team of assistants to paint the clothes and backgrounds, but he also pre-prepared portrait canvases. A sitter could choose a completed half-figure or bust with the head and face left blank, clothed in one of a number of dresses, suits, or uniforms. Such canvases were part of a portraitist's stock in trade. Again, on a finished canvas most of the work might be done by assistants. The master would add the final touches, and, jointly approved by himself and his sitter, the picture would receive his signature.

Hogarth deliberately worked for the mass market. After his paintings were engraved *en suite* as set pieces, the *Marriage à la Mode* or *The Rake's Progress* (p. 49) for example, he simply raffled off the originals for whatever

C

D

he could get for them, relying on the sale of prints for his money. And he did very well, so much so that he had to have the copyright laws revised to protect himself.

A further change came with the foundation of the various European academies. Under the authoritarian rule of Louis XIV, the arts in France became virtually a nationalized industry (B). The Academy's function was to replace the old guilds as a body regulating standards of workmanship, and it also added censorship to its duties. It was only much later that teaching became a function of an academy. When the Royal Academy was founded in London in imitation of the French, a school in which members taught was an important part of the organization (C). Here painters could train pupils in a rather more anonymous way, not being responsible for the actual welfare and work as for apprentices under the old scheme. Industrialization brought a sudden and large increase in the number of schools teaching art, all more or less modeled on academy lines. The demand was twofold, for mass-produced decorative art and mass-produced pictorial art. The former demanded that artists should be trained as painters, but required to design for printed textiles, or as sculptors but to decorate iron founders' mass-produced goods (D). The second revolutionized the concept of a work of art. The division of labor still existed, but not in the painter's own studio. Turner could always get 25 guineas for what be himself called a scribble to be engraved as a title piece or column breaker in a ladies' magazine. Painters such as Fildes made large sums of money by illustrating novels or by working for picture magazines such as "The Graphic," or "L'Illustration," or "Harpers". The demand brought about the final breakdown of any studio system. Other contributory factors were the mass-production of artists' materials themselves, relieving the artist of studio assistants, and the change in marketing methods. The Impressionists almost entirely worked for professional dealers rather than individual patrons.

The change in training methods meant that what formerly had been part of practical training on the job became an academic study. Students were still kept copying sculpture as an exercise in simply developing manual skill, not because they would use this language of form in their own work but by tradition. Generally, because of the perpetuation of certain training maxims which had lost their purpose, the word academic became a derogatory term, although, of course, each modern movement generally had its own academic phases.

One completely new problem arises out of modern methods of reproducing works of art. Strictly speaking certain techniques are indisputably methods of reproduction—etching, lithography, and other forms of printing, and the taking of a number of bronzes from one masterwork by a sculptor. In lithography and etching, it is reasonable to suppose that the artist himself has had a hand both in preparing the printing plate or stone and in the printing, but this is not necessarily so. Secondly, the print of a print may be made and reproduced in numbers mechanically. Sometimes these reproductions are almost undetectable as mechanical reprints. Is there any virtue except to an investor in possessing an "original" print as against a "facsimile" reproduction? (p. 158, A, D).

With sculpture too the problem exists. Again, largely because of the breakdown of the workshop system of training, the use of stone by sculptors is on the decline, and even such a confirmed carver as Henry Moore tends

A

B

C

(A) REMBRANDT VAN RYN The Entombment (etching) about 1659 *London, B. M.*

(B) HONORÉ DAUMIER A True Smoker (lithograph)

(C) AUGUSTE RODIN Gustav Mahler (bronze) *Paris, Mus. Rodin*

(D) HENRY MOORE The Family Group (bronze) 1949 *London, Tate*

(E) KENNETH ARMITAGE People in a Wind (bronze) 1960 *London, Tate*

D

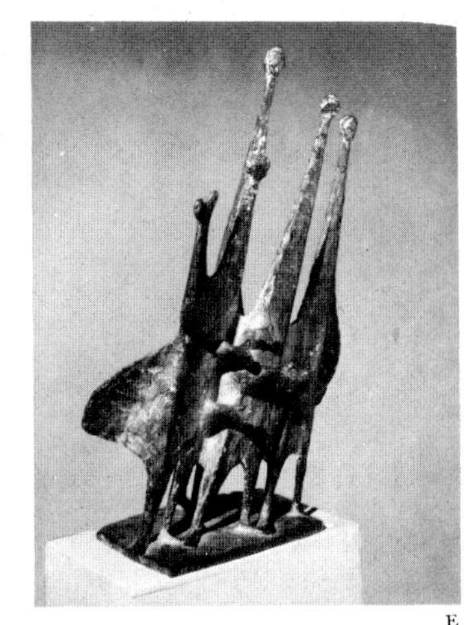

E

to work more often in wax or clay from which a craftsman will produce a bronze casting (C-E). The sculptor works much more empirically as a result, often using plaster of paris in a direct manner as a painter uses paint, altering and adjusting drastically as he goes along. As casting techniques improve, the limit to the number of copies indistinguishable from the original may rest only with the artist's own wishes. Does multiplication reduce aesthetic as well as monetary value?

Finally, not only are shops now flooded with colored reproductions of paintings from cave art to the present day, but with certain hard-edged forms of abstract painting there seems to be no reason why the pictures themselves should not be accurately copied indefinitely. Indeed, certain pure forms of abstract painting might well be drawn on graph paper and handed to, say, a skilled workman in an enameling factory to be carried out on sheet metal (p. 189).

The application of industrial techniques to the production of painting and sculpture has not really yet begun. It may have certain advantages. At the moment there is a danger that the good color reproduction may become a substitute for the real thing. It seems to be quite a good idea to hang, say, *Sunflowers* by van Gogh in a schoolroom, but by familiarity it may debase the idea of painting as an individual view of the world, and discourage people from bothering to look at the real thing. If so, it would be better to hang pictures by the children themselves. The answer might be to hang pictures intended to be made in quantity as originals, as engravings were once used. The engraving was never a substitute for the original picture, but a "work of art" in its own right.

CHAPTER 17

Fine Arts and Graphic Design

THE distinction between *fine* art and *commercial* art works well enough at extreme ends of each scale, but there is an important area where the two merge. The terminology itself is unhappy; is a portrait painter who sells very well any less "commercial" than a painter who also designs posters? Also, is a bad portrait or landscape still *fine* art, and therefore superior to a well-designed poster which is *commercial*? A poster designer works to order, but does he do so any less than the average and anonymous 14th-century painter of altarpieces? Clearly the distinction does not lie in the aesthetic approach but rather in the way each work is used and where it appears. The artist who also designs posters, or puts his ability to public use in some other way, is very important as an influence because of the wide audience he reaches. His gallery is the poster hoarding or magazine page. He does not rely on chance visitors to galleries or the interest of the connoisseur; he has a captive ready-made audience.

For *fine* artists to be involved in what might be better called graphic design (from the French *graphisme*) rather than commercial art is nothing new. Roman mosaics were also used as shop signs, floor decoration, or simply as a warning notice such as "Beware of the Dog" (A). Painters such as Hogarth were not above designing shopkeepers' cards (B), bill heads, or shop signs. One of the most moving of Watteau's works is *The Signboard for the Shop of the Art Dealer Gersaint* (C). Painted just before the artist's early death, it includes a comment on changing fashion. A bystander lounges against the shop wall, looking on at two men who are unpacking a portrait of Louis XIV from a straw-lined crate. It is being put up for sale.

However, the real collaboration between artist and merchant got under way in the 1860's. Literacy could be taken for granted among urban populations with money to spend. Mass-production meant that the products had to have mass distribution. Wares were no longer made locally in small quantities and sold within a limited area in specialized shops. Products were nationally advertised and the customer had to be encouraged to ask for a name of a brand rather than just the commodity itself.

Both Daumier and Manet were designing posters at this time. The use of lithography for printing meant that drawing was freed from the limitation of having to be engraved on metal or cut in wood, and that the artist could draw directly onto the stone. The stone could also be quite large, certainly much larger than the small block or plate used in engravings, and large enough to print fair-sized sheets that could be used in multiples to form very large posters (p. 160 A).

(A) Pompeii mosaic: Cave Canem (Beware of the Dog) *Naples, Mus. Naz.* (B) WILLIAM HOGARTH Goldsmith's trade card
(C) JEAN ANTOINE WATTEAU The Signboard for the Shop of the Art Dealer Gersaint, 1720 *West Berlin, Staatl. Mus.*

A

B

C

Daumier's manner in particular had been disciplined by years of drawing for lithographic printing, and as a result he had a ready-made, bold, and simplified technique very suitable for poster design. The movement reached its first peak in the 1880's. Théophile Alexandre Steinlen carried the Daumier and Gavarni style to its peak. He worked on a far larger scale than his predecessors and developed the use of color and texture. Like his predecessors, his modeling is three-dimensional and his scenes pictorial. Unlike them, they are far more vignetted, that is to say that the space they occupy is not firmly framed. The omissions become as important as the stated facts (B).

But it was Toulouse-Lautrec who changed the whole concept of the poster. His enthusiasm for the Japanese woodcut amounted to worship. Not blind worship or copying, but worship that led to an absolute understanding of the technique of simplified form, of the use of outline not as a boundary between changes of form but as a positive thing in itself, and of the use of flat planes of color and simple overprinting of these planes to suggest convincingly depth and modeling. The Japanese woodcut's fluid line has to be carefully contrived. It is a copy of a free brush stroke into a hard relief cut into a plank of wood with a knife (C, D).

In Lautrec's lithographed posters he was free to draw directly onto the stone. He worked, of course, in collaboration with skilled printers, who could produce the color separations on the various stones from his free drawings. But Lautrec learned his medium thoroughly,

(A) ÉDOUARD MANET Poster, 1868

(B) THÉOPHILE ALEXANDRE STEINLEN Poster, 1894
Paris. Bibl. des Arts Décoratifs. Exposition Cent Ans d'Affiches La Belle Époque

(C) HENRI DE TOULOUSE-LAUTREC Poster, 1892
London, V. and A.

(D) KUNIYOSHI Japanese woodcut
London, B. M.

(E) PIERRE BONNARD Poster, 1894
Paris, Bibl. Nat.

(F) ALPHONSE MUCHA Poster, 1895
Paris, Bibl. des Arts Décoratifs Exposition Cent Ans d'Affiches La Belle Époque

(G) FÉLIX ÉDOUARD VALLOTON Poster, 1895
Paris, Bibl. des Arts Décoratifs. Exposition Cents Ans d'Affiches La Belle Époque

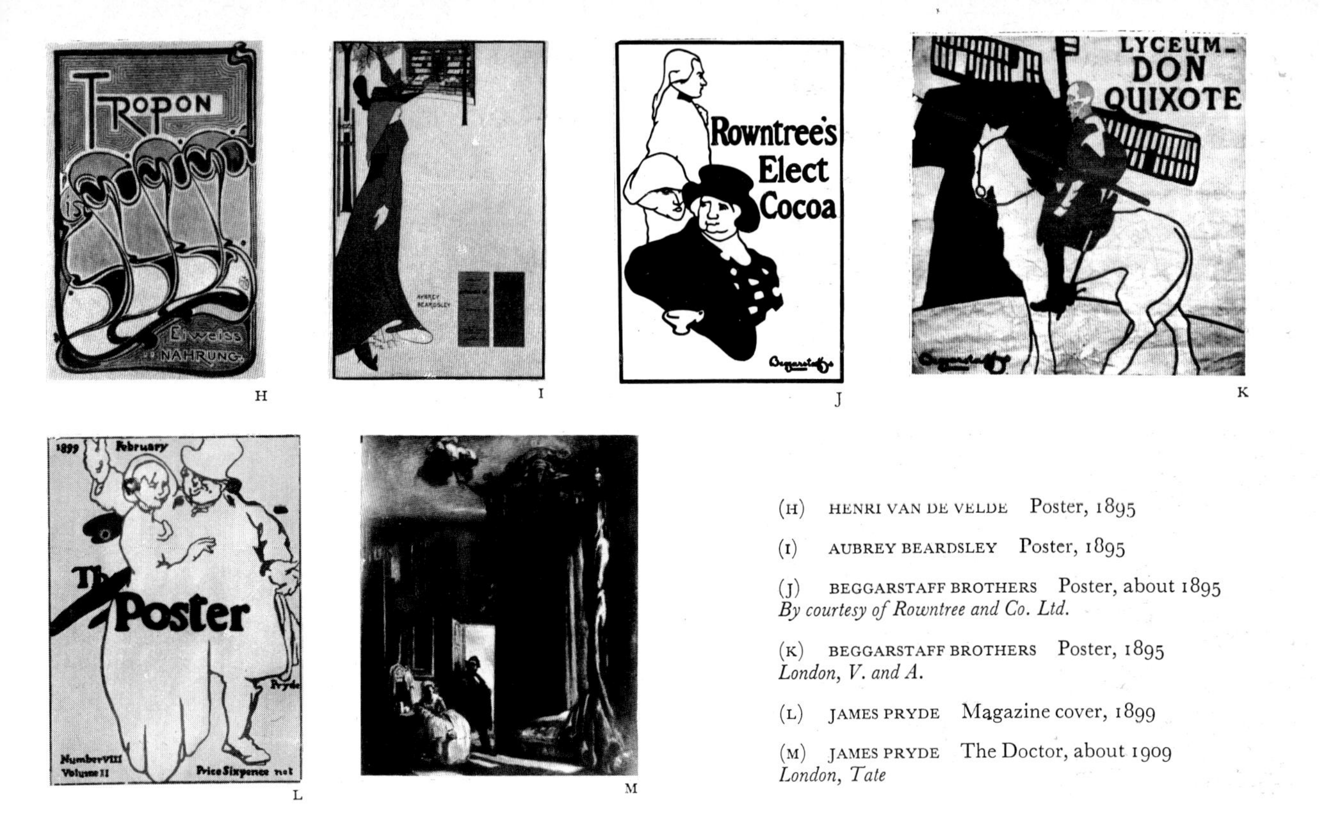

(H) HENRI VAN DE VELDE Poster, 1895

(I) AUBREY BEARDSLEY Poster, 1895

(J) BEGGARSTAFF BROTHERS Poster, about 1895
By courtesy of Rowntree and Co. Ltd.

(K) BEGGARSTAFF BROTHERS Poster, 1895
London, V. and A.

(L) JAMES PRYDE Magazine cover, 1899

(M) JAMES PRYDE The Doctor, about 1909
London, Tate

to the point of being able to predict and control printing effects, and would put the final touches to the stones themselves in the printer's workshop.

Above all, Lautrec freed the poster from the necessity of portraying natural local color. The sky can be bright red, the floor of the Moulin Rouge gamboge yellow, outlines thickly drawn in any half-tone, neutral or bright red. He spattered in stipple ink spots with a tooth brush, the lithographer's technique known as *crachis*.

The Paris hoardings blossomed with brilliant color. Félix Vallotton and Pierre Bonnard were among the painters designing posters. Particularly fine is Bonnard's work for the magazine "La Revue Blanche." Alphonse Mucha designed fascinating *Art Nouveau* posters in bright stenciled color for the theatre, especially for the Sarah Bernhardt productions. Van de Velde, the Belgian, an *Art Nouveau* architect, also designed a very pure abstract series of lettered posters. (E, F, G, H)

In England Aubrey Beardsley epitomizes the *Art Nouveau* movement in the graphic arts. Beardsley was not only the prolific illustrator of the "Yellow Book," a literary periodical of the 1890's, but designed booksellers' posters and bills. Beardsley, lank, pale, and sickly, an invalid all his short life, managed to insinuate an enervating decadence into practically every single line he drew. This was often done deliberately to shock the respectable and delight the followers of aesthetic cult of the time, but even in his designs for children's book posters the weird touch is still there. (I)

As important but unfortunately not so fruitful as Lautrec's contribution, was the work of the Beggarstaff Brothers. This pseudonym stood for the collaboration of an English and a Scots painter, William Nicholson and James Pryde. They took the elimination of all irrelevant detail to its extreme (J, K, L). Carefully singled-out details spaced with marvelous judgment are used to imply the whole form. The poster was divided into a few silhouettes and flat-toned surfaces. The outlines are bold, but discontinuous. All form is a suggestion, the statements are finished by the spectator's imagination. All texture is eliminated, all areas are flat. The Beggarstaffs were really the pioneers of their time; that is to say, their

A B C D E F G

(A) J. B. MAIER Café poster

(B) LEO EIBL Concert poster

(C) LUDWIG HOHLWEIN Tailor's poster, 1908

(D) WILLIAM BRADLEY Magazine cover, 1895

(E) EDWARD PENFIELD Magazine cover, 1907

(F) CHRISTOPHER NEVINSON Poster
London, Imperial War Mus.

(G) WILLIAM ROBERTS Poster
By courtesy of Heal and Son Ltd.

vision is what one would have expected in art only under the development of *De Stijl*. There was such a gap between their work and the prevailing taste that their output was severely limited. In his own painting Nicholson was an Impressionist in the "gray" Velázquez tradition, and now and again he approached the simplicity of his graphic work in a portrait. He also produced alphabet and other picture books with large woodcut illustrations that were as far advanced as the posters. It was really his son Ben Nicholson who, much later, in his own painting took the way pointed out in the Beggarstaffs' work and followed it to its logical conclusion of complete abstraction. Pryde, Nicholson's brother-in-law, died prematurely. His painting is highly romantic and morbid, something of Beardsley translated into solid form and dark tones (p. 161, M).

The Munich school of poster artists—J. B. Maier, Leo Eibl, and Ludwig Hohlwein—was strongly influenced by the Beggarstaffs and their principles of omission. Bold patterns of checks and stripes are carried flat across the form of figures, and background colors are deliberately chosen to be the same as some part of the main figure itself. Munich was an important local center for the beginning of the modern movement in art, the home of the Secession. Here in the early 1900's the new form was much more acceptable than in London, and the modern poster was firmly established (A, B, C).

Important contributions were also made in America by the work of William Bradley and Edward Penfield. Bradley worked for "The Chap-Book," Penfield for "Collier's," and their work reached a peak in simplicity, color, and pattern that has not been equaled since in American periodical publication (D, E).

After the war of 1914-18, the influence of Cubism was strongly felt among the poster designers. There was a tendency, as in painting, to call anything new *Cubistic* or *Futuristic* without any understanding of Cubism or Futurism; the best graphic artists however were not merely copying Cubism because it was new, but *using* Cubist form (F, G).

E. McKnight Kauffer's poster for the English "Daily Herald" newspaper of 1918 was another major break-through in design (H). The "Early Birds" were pure abstraction and counterchange of tone used in a way that only a handful of English painters, such as Edward Wadsworth or Wyndham Lewis, William Roberts (G) or

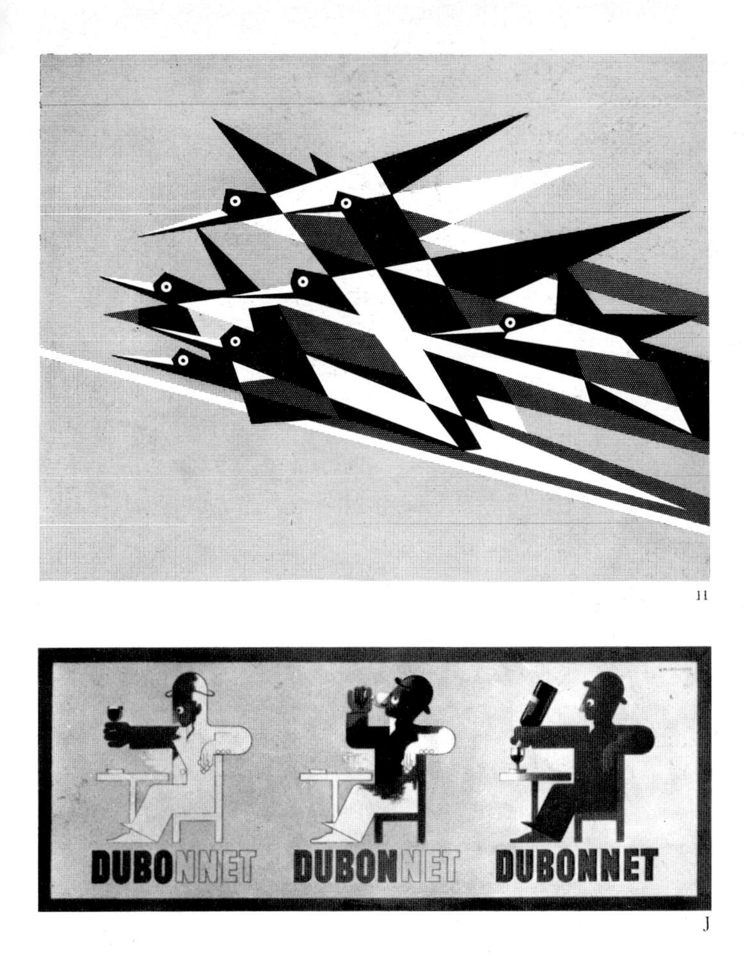

H

J

(H) E. MCKNIGHT KAUFFER Newspaper poster: "The Early Birds," 1918

(I) A. M. CASSANDRE Newspaper poster, 1925

(J) A. M. CASSANDRE Poster, 1936
Paris, Bibl. Nat.

(K) A. M. CASSANDRE Railway poster, 1928

I

K

Christopher Nevinson (F), would have been capable of understanding at the time. All these painters were also successful poster designers, but none was so direct and simple as Kauffer. The latter's work was mainly for the London Underground (p. 190) and the Shell Oil Company. The Underground in particular is an example of modern corporate patronage at its best, commissioning door handles, light fixtures, and other fittings from architects, and even fabric designs from modern painters.

A. M. Cassandre worked both in England and France, and was also strongly Cubist in his designs. His posters for "L'Intransigeant" newspaper, for Dubonnet or for French or British railways, show a degree of stylization of form that would have been unacceptable to the general public of the 1920's and 1930's in small-scale painting, and yet were enjoyed by them on a giant scale unthinkable to the mural decorator (I, J, K).

Consequently there has arisen a strong public feeling that somehow Cubist still-lifes are like posters, and one sometimes hears the complaint that modern artists are too much like "commercial" artists.

This understandable misconception has simply arisen out of the fact that *modern art* has been completely accepted in public life far more quickly than in private life. It may also be safely said that at this period there were far more so-called commercial artists with a true understanding of what had happened in painting, and the relationship of form, color, and design, and above all an architectural feeling for these elements, than there were pure painters who were following the real tradition of painting.

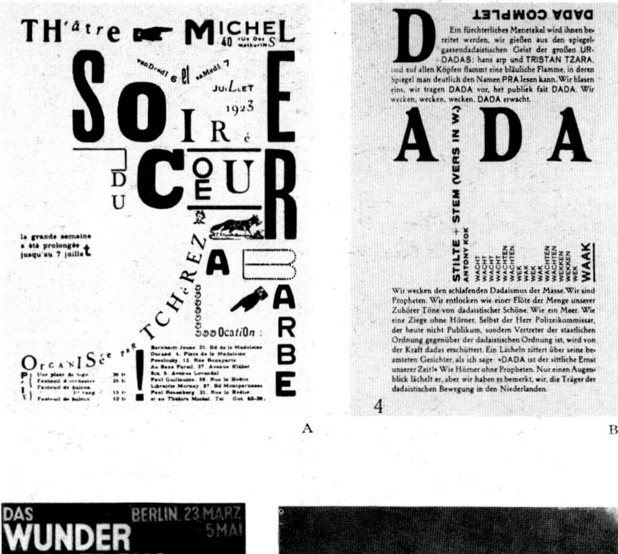

A B

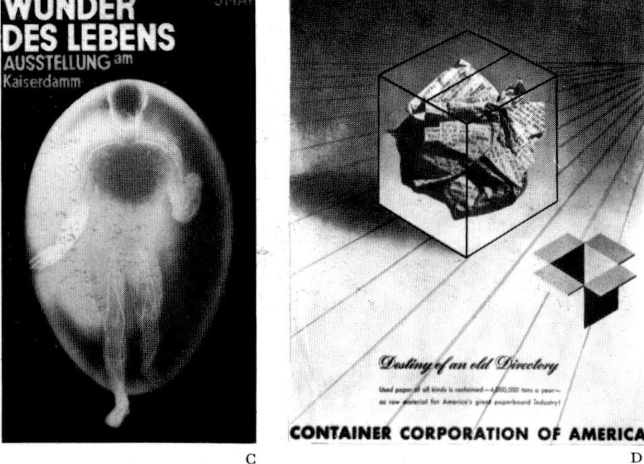

C D

E

Parallel to the Cubist-poster marriage, and not so obvious, was the effect of the Dada movement. Dada was an anti-movement. It was the expression of disgust and disillusion felt by certain painters, sculptors, and poets at what was in their eyes the over-all betrayal of mankind in World War I. They were unlike their political counterpart in that they believed that the solution did not lie in reason, for reason had joined in the betrayal. The aim of the movement, which spread from its headquarters in Switzerland, from the outset was to provoke and shock. The targets were not only unthinking philistines but also those people who prided themselves on their feelings for the arts. Everything was absurd. One of Dada's chief weapons was bad commercial advertising. The artists publicized meetings by imitating the technique of the give-away leaflet advertising silk stockings or patent medicines. They ransacked the typographers' cabinets for "bad" 19th-century typefaces and electrotypes. They deliberately tried to break all the rules of good taste in typography, and printed on the cheapest and most porous papers they could find (A, B).

Here lay a paradox. In the first place it was the hypersensitivity of the Dadaists that engendered their revolt. Consequently, however blatant and vulgarly insulting they tried to be, they were incapable of achieving the accidental banality of what they were trying to imitate. They could not help but *design* their pamphlets and posters. Above all they enjoyed what they were doing. The Dada movement mainly split into two: a Surrealist group and a radical political group, merging either with the Surrealists or social revolutionary painters and poets. What remains of the movement is something that has had a greater influence on graphic design than any other since Cubism. The work of Dadaists like Francis Picabia and Tristan Tzara suddenly made designers take a new fresh look at the 19th century. In particular they were a strong influence at the Bauhaus school of design in Weimar and Dessau, which in its short life from 1919 to 1933 was to set the pattern for design schools in Europe and America.

In particular Herbert Bayer has been one of the most important individual and influential designers in America since his Bauhaus student days. Bayer made full use of juxtaposition of electrotypes, engravings, and woodcuts against photographs and type, a complete and thorough assimilation of the idea of collage (C, D).

In Holland Hendrik Werkman combined painting and graphic design into an inseparable whole, using the whole armory of techniques that the Dadaists had released.

With such a full collaboration between the fine arts and graphic design one might expect to see reverse influences too.

The Cubist collages had made use very early of newspaper titles and headlines, and lettering and typefaces became an important part of the painter's repertoire. Fernand Léger in particular used giant letter forms as an intrinsic part of composition.

It was after World War II that young American painters, such as Robert Rauschenberg and Larry Rivers, followed Stuart Davis's example and turned to graphic design, the world of the poster and billboard, the street sign and destination board, the jukebox, the ball-game machine and coffee machine, for material. Parallel to this movement, a little behind it but not entirely derivative, are the so-called *pop*—popular—art painters. Larry Rivers in New York, and Peter Blake in London (E, F, G), seem to have taken hesitant, cautious steps in this direction when compared to the sudden burst of both adherents to and output of the pop movement. Blake's preoccupation was mainly with the figure. His self-portraits and portraits of children—for they are portraits, even when the composition is given a literary title—are painted with meticulous care for detail. Loving attention is lavished on incidentals, articles of clothing, ties, the enamelled metal disc-pin badges the figures wear, the comics and magazines they read or carry, and the sweet or cigarette cartons scattered about them. The pictures are as much about these cereal packet masks and matchbox tops as about the

F

G

(A) TRISTAN TZARA Invitation card, 1923

(B) KURT SCHWITTERS Leaflet, 1923

(C) HERBERT BAYER Exhibition poster, 1934

(D) HERBERT BAYER Press advertisement, 1941

(E) LARRY RIVERS The Vocabulary Lesson: Parts of the Face, 1961
London, Tate

(F) PETER BLAKE On the Balcony, 1955-57
London, Tate

(G) PETER BLAKE John Bull, magazine cover, 1961
By permission of "The Sunday Times"

(A) DAVID HOCKNEY Marriage of Styles II: On a Sofa, 1962-63
London, Contemporary Art Society

(B) PETER PHILLIPS For Men Only: Starring MM and BB, 1961
London, Calouste Gulbenkian Foundation

(C) R. B. KITAJ Junta, 1962
London, Marlborough Fine Art Ltd.

figures that are the vehicle for them. The true pop painters—Peter Phillips and David Hockney are two of the most competent and typical—enlarged these labels and wrappers to enormous poster size, as had Stuart Davis with his Lucky Strike packet in the twenties (p. 191). A great deal of their raw material is imported from America by way of magazines and films, enough to make them appear followers of the American movement, perhaps rather unfairly (A, B).

An interesting variation, and perhaps the most important of the new movement, is R. B. Kitaj, an American painter living in London. Kitaj paints serial pictures with a high story-telling content, rather like intellectual strip cartoons. His technique is a very interesting rediscovery of the technique of the Beggarstaffs and the Munich school (C).

The pop movement with its greedy assault on graphic design has only just begun, and one cannot forecast its future or the repercussion on the graphic world itself.

The real debt of *pure* painting to graphic design lies in the putting before the public the elements of modern art with, in the best examples, no dilution or debasement. Through it we have learned to accept painting freed from the bondage of *real* color of things, less emphasis on local realism and anecdotes in art, simplified form, dualistic punning forms, a return to symbolism and large-scale color and, above all, the cultivation of a public taste for design.

CHAPTER 18

Abstract Art

(A) JEAN BAPTISTE CAMILLE COROT La Route de Sin-le-Noble (detail) *Paris, Louvre*

ABSTRACTION is a term used as loosely in talking about modern painting and sculpture as Cubism or Futurism. All art without a recognizable subject is called abstract, but so is any with a subject that has undergone a certain degree of distortion, simplification, or stylization. The word is often used by artists themselves to describe certain qualities in works of art which are formal and more concerned with how the work is carried out than what it is about.

As far as stylization itself goes, all art of any kind must have certain of its elements inherent in it. However like a real landscape a painting might seem, we know that those rainwashed leaves are really dabs of paint (A). However realistic flesh and blood might seem in a figure by Titian or Rubens, we know that this is paint smeared on canvas. As for the form of, say, an eye in a late Rembrandt portrait, it is very difficult to say just why these coruscations really do appear as a human eye with all its dewy, liquid, and translucent qualities.

The degree of formality is high in Egyptian painting and in a work by Piero della Francesca (B, and p. 45). In the former we may see the same formal approach to a head that gives us the duality of Braque and Picasso, the superimposition of full and profile views (C). In the latter we see a strong geometrical element that later, divorced from Piero's subject matter and use of human and natural forms, gives us "pure" geometrical abstraction. These parallel links are more technical than philosophical. Although they are evident to the eye, this does not mean that they result from similar intentions.

This formal element was strong in all the arts while a classical tradition persisted. It was one of the techniques of organizing a work of art and was an important part of teaching. When the tradition decayed two things happened. On one hand those who thought that they were carrying the tradition on were merely repeating clichés without understanding, and so the formal element became neglected in their work. Whatever we may think of much 19th-century "official" art—portraits of politicians, academics in their robes, or royal families—as painting, we must agree that knowledge of the rules of composition or classical form is not the strong point of its practitioners. Whatever else the present-day academics might be, they are not academic in their teaching.

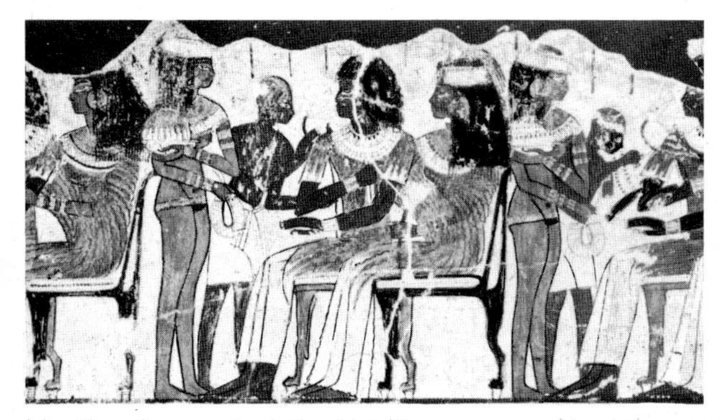

(B) Egyptian mural painting (detail). From a tomb at Thebes, about 1500 B.C. *London, B.M.*

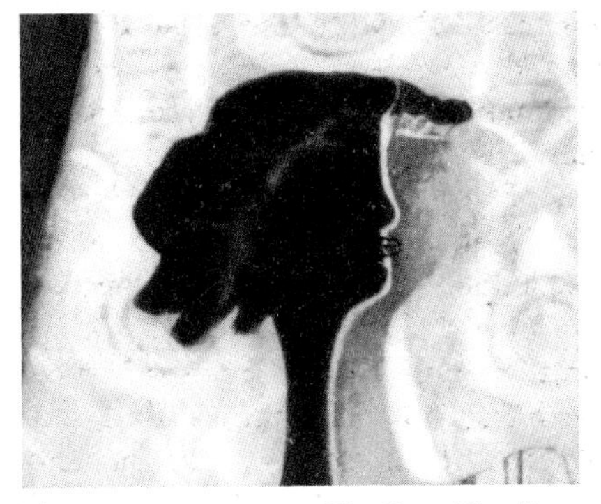

(C) GEORGES BRAQUE The Duet (detail) 1937 *Paris, Mus. d'Art Moderne*

(A) HENRI DE TOULOUSE-LAUTREC Jane Avril Dancing, 1892 *Paris, Mus. de l'Impressionnisme*

(B) PIERRE BONNARD The Table, 1925 *London, Tate*

On the other hand those who reacted against a dying system, the Impressionists, tried, as painters have done at no other time since the cave painters, to become unprejudiced recorders of nature with no preconceived ideas of form or composition to filter and change their vision. Their form of abstraction is the conversion of intangible light into solid paint, but they abandoned all formal ideas of composition. Indeed in so doing they came very close to inventing another set of rules for informal composition based on the snapshot photograph. The frame cuts across bodies and scenes at deliberately chosen awkward angles to give the picture an accidental appearance of on-the-spot reportage (A, B).

When Seurat tried to break from the limitations of Impressionist technique by painting with color spots, he was discovering his own formal, academic, synthetic, and abstract method of painting. Naturally we would presume that this sort of color analysis and reconstruction was a slow technique, depending on care and patience, and essentially a method for the studio, away from nature. Since so much care had to be taken over choosing color spots in the various changing areas of the painting, we should also expect the areas themselves, their outline and relative positions, to be as much the subject of great deliberation. A highly analytical method of portraying form generally means a highly organized method of composition as well. A good artist will apply his whole mind to all the problems he finds in his work. If his mind is one that by nature calls for order, then we will find this ordered scheme in all that he does, not in one element alone such as form or color or composition.

Seurat started to use geometry to compose his pictures. He turned in fact to a system of proportion that has been used and re-used in all periods, and that latterly has become important in the study of biological form. The system is the Golden Mean, and its use ensures that all parts of a form are related to each other in the same way as to the whole. The important thing is that Seurat began pictures by using geometry at all. This meant that no matter, say, where the entertainers outside a booth really stood, or where the factory chimneys really occurred in actual life, when he put them on to his canvas he adjusted their position to fit in with an abstract scheme of proportion that was preconceived and imposed upon nature.

Thus the figures, or trees, or chimneys, or masts of boats in his pictures become just as important, if not more so, as divisions upon a rectangular plane as familiar objects in a picture. A picture by Seurat is at least as much about the theory of color and proportion as it is about a promenade by a river. The scene is almost an excuse for telling us about color and proportion—the next step is to remove all excuse and apology and just use color and geometry alone (p. 113 F, and p. 152).

This is not to say categorically that this is how abstract or, more accurately speaking, non-figurative painting came about. There must be a psychological necessity for producing non-figurative works of art. Nevertheless, the technical revolution came about through struggling with paint itself, not by painters sitting down and thinking out schemes of painting which would spring fully

(C) KASIMIR MALEVICH
The Woodcutter, 1911
Amsterdam, Stedelijk Mus.

(D) KASIMIR MALEVICH
Oblique White Lines on White, 1918
Amsterdam, Stedelijk Mus.

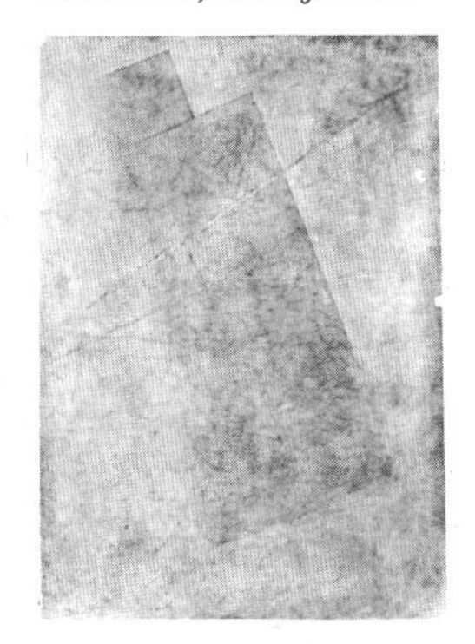

PIET MONDRIAN
(E) Still-life with Ginger Pot I, 1911
(F) Still-life with Ginger Pot II, 1911
The Hague, Gemeentemus., S. B. Slijper Loan
(G) Trees in Blossom
The Hague, Gal. Nova Spectra

E

F

and mature from their heads in the manner that Jupiter gave birth to Minerva.

Seurat's immediate influence was as limited as his own *pointilliste* technique. Cubism was wider, more universal, and a generation later. It was Cubism that influenced Kasimir Malevich and Piet Mondrian, the two pioneer non-figurative painters. Malevich was born in 1878 in Kiev. He studied at the Kiev School of Art and his early work tends toward the more Germanic form of Impressionism. He went to Moscow in the early 1900's when the magazine "World of Art" was at its height. This was financed by a group of wealthy merchants, collectors of modern painting, and edited by the impresario Serge Diaghilev. Malevich was attracted by the work of Post-Impressionists and Cézanne. He combined brilliant prismatic color with hard Cubism (C). The progress from this phase, to classical monochromatic Cubism, to Suprematism, is not recorded and not at all clear. However, it is sensible to suppose a gradual process of elimination of the subject, gradual in its working but manifested by sudden changes. The first exhibition of Suprematist work was in 1915, although Malevich may have been preparing for it over the previous two years. He exhibited a black square on a white ground. He said himself: "In my desperate attempt to free art from the ballast of the objective world I fled to the form of the square..." The critics complained, and with them the public. "Everything we have loved, we have lost... before us stands a black square on a white ground."

After having reached the essence of purity with his simple square, Malevich continued with a series of completely non-figurative pictures of simple geometrical shapes in plain colors (p. 192) culminating in the "white on white" paintings of 1918. Here the evidence of change of form is barely tangible and only indicated by transition from matt to shiny surfaces (D).

G

A parallel development is more clearly recorded in the work of Mondrian. He was born in Holland in 1872, and was first influenced by van Gogh and romantic Expressionism. In 1911 Mondrian went to Paris, was immediately affected by Picasso and Léger and became a Cubist. His Cubist paintings, conventional to begin with, develop in the most interesting manner. In paintings of landscapes with trees, of the sea, of still-lifes with books, boxes, ginger jars, and other studio objects, we see Mondrian becoming more concerned with the co-ordinate points of intersecting planes and forms than the things themselves. The pictures dissolve into something like those Cézanne watercolors that are taken no further than the plotting of a few salient points on paper, and emerge as a series of simple "plus and minus" compositions. The color is very subdued, black, white, pale blues, pinks, and ochers, very much in the classical Cubist tradition (E, F, G).

In particular there is an important series of drawings of an apple tree. Before our eyes, as in a series of cinema stills, the traditional tree becomes co-ordinate points until these latter become the picture itself. It is Seurat's approach to composition freeing itself from the subject.

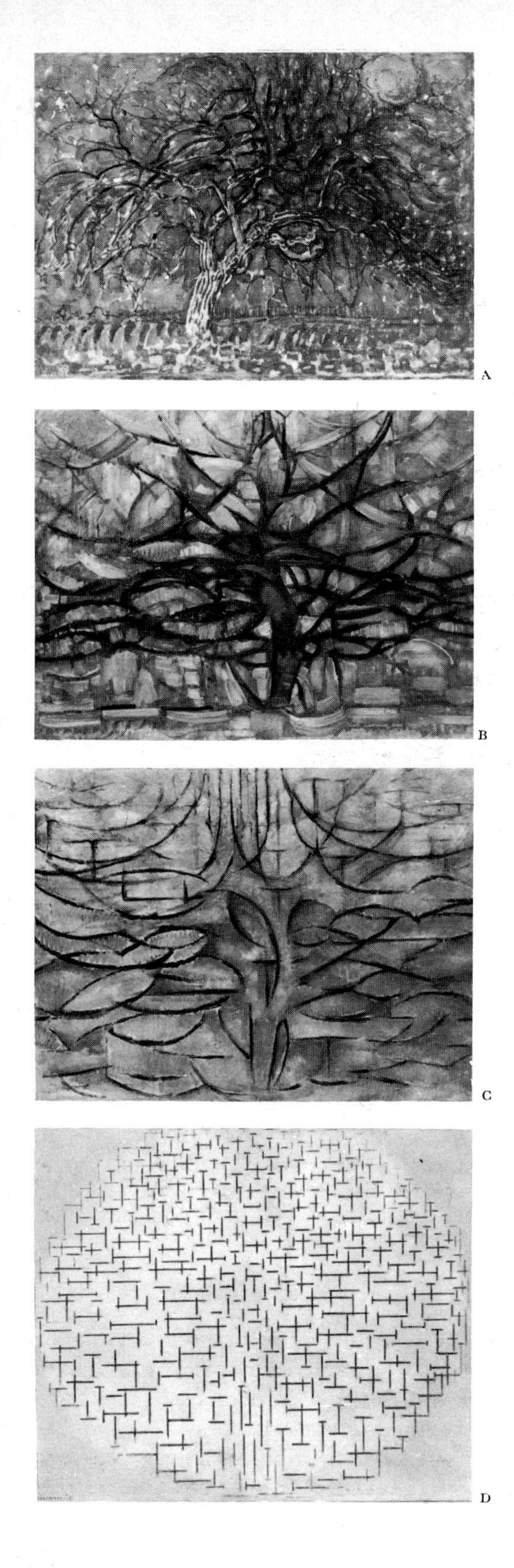

The plus and minus pictures harden. The points become longer lines. The pale colors become a combination of flat black lines, white spaces, the prismatic red, yellow, and blue, and a neutral gray for relief (A, B, C, D).

The year 1917 saw the foundation of the movement *De Stijl* (The Style) with which Mondrian will always be associated.

The growth of non-representational art is clear. To answer *why* must always be a series of half-guesses, half-deductions. Almost certainly the impetus was revolutionary, in a social and moral sense as well as aesthetic. Malevich was strongly in the cultural van of the Russian revolution until the revolution itself "killed" him as a painter. *De Stijl* as a movement concerned itself with revolution and social consciousness. Theo van Doesburg, abstract painter, poet, and the propagandist of the movement, also associated himself with the more outspoken Dadaists.

The non-representational painters thought that they were heralding the building of a new world. Their paintings were to be the rallying banners. The word "building" applies in a literal sense, for Malevich turned his abstract drawings into architectural combinations of solid blocks, and *De Stijl* was closely associated with modern architecture and saw its principles put into practice in actual buildings. Theo van Doesburg applied *De Stijl* principles of composition and color to architecture with the architects Jacobus Oud and Gerrit Thomas Rietveld, who even designed *De Stijl* furniture. Oud's Café de Unie façade is lettered in typography taken from the cover of the *De Stijl* magazine (E, F, G).

The Bauhaus school at Weimar was under *De Stijl* influence as early as 1919 in architecture, typography, and painting. Here Laszlo Moholy-Nagy painted his non-figurative pictures, which often present the illusion of receding planes hovering in space (H). The coupling of geometrical painting with machine aesthetics had a particular appeal to the scientific optimism of the time. The artists who produce paintings and sculpture that

(A) PIET MONDRIAN The Red Tree, 1910
The Hague, Gemeentemus.

(B) PIET MONDRIAN The Gray Tree, 1911
The Hague, Gemeentemus., S. B. Slijper Loan

(C) PIET MONDRIAN Apple Tree in Blossom, 1912
The Hague, Gemeentemus.

(D) PIET MONDRIAN Composition No. 10, 1915
Otterlo, Holland, Kröller-Müller

E

F

G

H

I

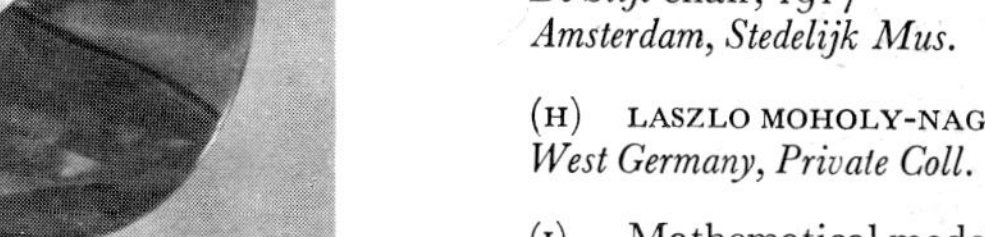

J

(E) Cover of De Stijl catalogue No. 81

(F) JACOBUS OUD Café De Unie façade
Amsterdam, Stedelijk Mus.

(G) GERRIT THOMAS RIETVELD
De Stijl chair, 1917
Amsterdam, Stedelijk Mus.

(H) LASZLO MOHOLY-NAGY AM2, 1925
West Germany, Private Coll.

(I) Mathematical model
London, Science Mus. (Crown Copyright)

(J) MAX BILL Endless Loop I, 1947-49
New York, Joseph H. Hirshhorn Coll.

look like a mathematician's models and graphs are propagandists for their idea of a cleaned-up, rational, emotionally hygienic world. Together with the founders of modern architecture they believe that a clean rational environment produces a similar society. The movement is no less emotional for this, for it is based on feelings about society. The paintings and sculpture are still only *like* mathematical structures. They are an emotional use of the language of scientists, engineers, and mathematicians in a highly poetic way (I, J).

Mondrian became a pessimist. He died in New York having produced a remarkable series of paintings given

A

(A) ANTHONY HILL Relief Construction, 1963
London, coll. the Artist

(B) BART VAN DER LECK The Rider, 1918
Otterlo, Holland, Kröller-Müller

(C) VICTOR VASARELY Super Nou AE, 1959-61
London, Tate

B

C

boogie-woogie titles, named after the popular eight-beat piano music. They can only be described as a Baroque development of his pure style. Of the *De Stijl* movement, Bart van der Leck is the most persistent, but he allows a modicum of figurative element in his work. The social propaganda has now been taken up by the new young Constructivists, of whom there is a strong active element in Britain and Scandinavia. Anthony Hill is the spokesman for the group (A, B).

The abstract painters were also concerned with color illusion. In pure geometrical painting certain colors appear to advance and others to recede (p. 189). Thus the two-dimensional picture always has a certain inherent three-dimensional quality that cannot be avoided. Color, even when limited to the primaries—red, yellow, and blue (p. 193)—also has its emotional effect. At the most obvious level red appears "warm" and blue "cold," yellow "gay" and blue "sad."

The veteran French painter Auguste Herbin has produced an elaborate philosophy based on the emotional impact of pure shape and pure color which he applies to his painting (p. 189). Max Bill, the Swiss, has also treated his painting as color experiments comparable to musical variations, the equivalent of the figure and canon. He has produced highly mathematical sculpture too. In Switzerland there are other younger painters who are purely non-objective to form and movement. Victor Vasarely in France exploits the optical illusion of three-dimensional planes in two-dimensional painting, sometimes of an architectural scale (C).

The essence of non-objective non-figurative painting lies in its architectural associations, not simply as mural decoration or the suggestion of color schemes, but as a research laboratory for pure form and its effect on environment. This is really the next stage for consolidation of the movement.

CHAPTER 19

Expression and Abstraction

(B) GEORGES SEURAT
The Circus, 1891
Paris, Mus. de l'Impressionnisme

THE limitations that painters felt in Impressionism brought about two reactions. One was a search for a new discipline, felt to be a necessity by painters such as Seurat and Cézanne. The other was for a more expressive form, such as in the work of Gauguin and van Gogh. The former has geometry as its foundation, the latter color. The psychology and symbolism of color is a complex field of special study. What must be remembered is that this sort of analysis is always made after the event, as a result of looking at pictures and taking them apart. The sort of color analysis that the painter uses to help him is much more straightforward and mechanical. He wants to know how to control his colors, to be able to produce soothing harmonies or violent discords at will. The Impressionists and Post-Impressionists used the color circle derived from Newton's spectrum to help them, and van Gogh, for all the *violence* on the surface of his late pictures, carefully calculated his color effects in advance. Gauguin too disciplined his color, and as far as color goes can be considered a pupil of van Gogh. But Gauguin attempted to match color and mood still further in his direct allegorical paintings. Van Gogh's feelings are implied in a landscape or still-life taken from nature, whereas Gauguin tried to show his feelings by choosing dramatic subjects from the Bible or Edgar Allan Poe, and heavily underlining them with motto-like titles (A). In the paintings of both, it must be noticed that however bright they appear to be, the colors are in fact always modified and subdued. They are nearly always mixed, rarely used straight from the tube, and their brilliance depends upon their juxtaposition and relative effect on one another.

It was Seurat who used pure color to produce apparent mixtures; it was from Seurat that the *wild beast* painters or Fauves drew their color technique in the first place (B,C). Henri Matisse was using a modified *pointilliste* technique in about 1900, together with André Derain and Maurice Vlaminck. Seurat's own work called for a great deal of painstaking patience. Naturally enough,

(A) PAUL GAUGUIN Nevermore, 1897
London, Courtauld Inst. Gall.

(C) HENRI MATISSE
Luxe, Calme, et Volupté, 1904 *Paris, Private Coll.*

A B

the painters who seized on his use of pure color because they wished above all to express their exuberance would have found his laborious technique irksome. The pin-point spots became large dabs of pure color rather energetically applied. Here we find a fusion between Seurat and van Gogh. We might say that while van Gogh's painting looks violent, that of the Fauves is violent. It was their use of color that earned the Fauves their nickname of wild beasts and shocked the public and critics. Their form and subject are quite conventional and recognizable (A). There are no intellectual stylizations, distortions, or purely synthetic form as in Cubism. The subjects are portraits, river scenes, landscapes, or towns *en fête*. What struck their contemporaries as odd was the use of brilliant green as a neutral half-tone in a bright red and orange portrait by Matisse, or vermilion trees in a landscape by Vlaminck, or a picture of a river with blood-red water and orange sky.

When painters start painting green trees in vermilion or the flesh and blood of a head in green, it is all very well to analyze and intellectualize after the event, and say that of course red is the complementary color to green, and there is a natural relationship. What in effect happens is that color is being used free of association with a clearly recognizable object. The portrait might be a good portrait and the color scheme might also be very stimulating, but we are arriving at a similar point, as in geometrical non-figurative painting. What had been the structure of a picture becomes the picture itself without the *raison d'être* of a subject. Now color too is becoming the picture itself; freed from a subject. Forty years later, in his series of red interiors, Matisse again used strong color, but instead of violence the overall single tone produces a startling and profound restfulness (p. 194).

Wassily Kandinsky published his book, "Concerning the Spiritual in Art," in 1912 in Munich. It appeared in

(A) HENRI MATISSE Portrait with Green Stripe, 1905
Copenhagen, Statens Mus. for Kunst

(B) WASSILY KANDINSKY Composition 4, 1911
Paris, coll. Nina Kandinsky

(C) JACQUES VILLON The Soldiers, 1913
Paris, Mus. d'Art. Moderne

(D) FRANK KUPKA Disques Rouges et Bleus, 1911
New York, Mus. of Modern Art

(E) FRANK KUPKA Nocturne, 1910
Paris, coll. Gall. Louis Carré

(F) WASSILY KANDINSKY On Points, 1928
Paris, coll. Nina Kandinsky

(G) FRANK KUPKA Elementary Games, 1932
Paris, coll. Gall. Louis Carré

(H) HENRI MATISSE The Odalisque
Paris, Mus. d'Art Moderne

English translated from his Russian in 1914. It is a strange mixture of sound color theory and theosophy. The links with Gauguin are very strong, as M. T. H. Sadler, the translator, points out. The illustrations to the book are by Kandinsky himself. His paintings began as a series of brilliantly colored compositions. They look as if they were enameled or executed in stained glass. The figures, houses, and trees are heavily outlined in dark blue, black, or brown. The colors appear to be illuminated (p. 195). Very soon the outlined areas began to lose their identity as recognizable objects, and Kandinsky began to call his paintings by numbers, *Composition 1, 2,* and so on (B). The shapes themselves began to break up. In order to work more rapidly Kandinsky turned to watercolor and ink. These were completely free. Wash ran into wash, inks were splashed on or drawn in scored lines through wet color so that the grains of ink ran like the fronds in a moss agate (p. 196).

D E F G

H

Kandinsky laid strong emphasis on a kinship he claimed with eastern painting. By surrendering himself blindly to the moment, he attempted to find and realize subconscious depths only usually reached by carrying contemplation to the point of complete self-absorption. Whether this was possible or not, the emphasis on personality is highly important. It is the completely opposite point of view of that of the Cubists and Constructivists. They were seeking a new universal language of painting as anonymous as any of the great styles of the past, Egyptian, Greco-Roman, or medieval. This to a certain extent meant subordinating the personality to an idea. The emotional context of painting was left to take care of itself. The personality would automatically assert itself if simply left alone. The Fauves, and with them Kandinsky, the Czech Frank Kupka, and Robert and Sonia Delaunay, opposed this "cold" point of view and put the personality before all. Their philosophy of expressing emotion and individual feelings by pure form and color derives from the new discovery of the personality and the depths of the subconscious by Freud and his followers. Later the Surrealists were to do the same thing. Whereas the abstract painters sought to express the subconscious mind directly, untampered by symbolic form, the Surrealists used indirect means, relying on the psychologists' symbols to release emotions. Thus their painting is full of highly finished "solid" images, and the paint is subordinated to the form.

With this new assertion of the personality, one could expect to find a fresh individual approach to the handling of paint itself. Kandinsky relied on the accidents of flooding one wash into another. Frank Kupka was a competent late 19th-century academic painter when he arrived in Paris, where he met and was influenced by Jacques Villon (C). But color attracted him more than Cubism. His *Bathers* of 1905 shows the influence of the late Monet. Within a short time Kupka was producing pictures with such themes as *Violets Orchestre*, *Disques Rouges et Bleus* (D). The *Nocturne* of 1910 (E) is simply freely painted slabs of paint in the colors of the night.

The Delaunays were also among the pioneers of Abstract Expressionism. Robert Delaunay stated that it was during 1912-13 that he had the idea of developing painting concerned with pure color values and contrasts, and most important, capable of perception at a glance. The execution too was to be "simultaneous." He read Chevreul and used the theory of simultaneous contrasts. "I wished to play on color as if it were music, to write color fugues." Sonia, his wife, spoke of "the liberation of color, freeing it to speak for itself in its own language."

The Delaunays' paintings were prismatically brilliant. Paint was freely applied. Even the more disciplined *orphic* paintings of concentric circles are rough at the edges (p. 197).

(A) HAROLD E. EDGERTON
Stroboscopic photograph of tennis player

(B) JACKSON POLLOCK Painting, 1952
London, Tate

(C) JACKSON POLLOCK Detail of (B)
London, Tate

Towards the end of the 1920's all four painters, Kandinsky, Kupka, and the Delaunays, hardened their work into more rigid, sharp-edged, carefully painted abstracts (p. 175 F, G). The former Fauve painters had become less violent, were applying the color lesson they had learned to a relaxed, softer painting (p. 175 H). The *wild beast* painting, which had flourished mainly before World War I, was almost forgotten when, after the second war, Abstract Expressionism and action painting shocked public and critics as violently as any new departure in the modern movement had ever done. It was at least partly engendered by romanticism and pessimism. The new self-assertion was romantic. It was pessimistic in its deliberate turning away from logic and reason. The movement is very close to the 18th-century cult of the natural man, the noble savage, which expressed itself in a taste for wild landscape and picturesque ruins. The idea is that man is naturally whole but spoilt by civilization. Much Abstract Expressionism is calligraphic in appearance. The gesture itself is important. The painter seeks to find himself in an unguarded moment, and tries to capture this moment by abandoning himself to a sweep of the arm. This is frozen forever by the trail of paint left by his brush on his canvas. The painters themselves are often, as Kandinsky was, interested in the technique of eastern philosophy, particularly in the Zen form of Buddhism. Traditionally this was taught through the practice of a craft of some sort, pottery, fencing, or archery, or the art of writing—calligraphy. The craft is a physical way to concentration. By completely losing oneself in the absorption of doing a particular thing, one finds oneself. The expert archer is completely unselfconscious when taking aim. The painter tries to achieve a similar state.

The next step from sweeping a brush across the canvas is the throwing of paint from the brush without actually touching the canvas. The splashes and spots follow each other in a line and register the acceleration and deceleration of a sweep of the arm. This is very similar to the successive images on the plate of a camera taken with a series of stroboscopic flashes in an effort to freeze and analyze the action of a dancer, a tennis player, or a golfer as in the well-known photographs of Professor Harold Edgerton (A). The painter finally abandons all control by laying a canvas flat and pouring paint over it. The canvas is tilted this way and that so that the paint runs and dribbles. The patches of wet paint swirl and mingle, spreading like fingered branches or tributaries of rivers. All this may be on a very large scale. At first glance it would appear that the painter has completely abdicated all responsibility. The beauty of an action painting would appear to be of the same order as a sunset or bird song, an accident of nature. One aim is indeed to capture and take advantage of the happy accident, cultivating a deliberately haphazard set of conditions within the four sides of the canvas in which contours, lakes, puddles, trails, ridges, can all form as in a landscape. On a second appraisal the action painter's world is more subtle than may be realized (B, C).

The late Jackson Pollock, the first master of action painting, chose his colors with great care. He often used subtle violets, grays, and pure silver. The effect is sometimes quite *chic*. He often dribbled an "advancing" color such as yellow over his canvas in an elaborate tangled skein. Over this he would dribble another net of a "receding" color such as a misty blue-violet. The advancing color appears to be trying to fight its way out. The dramatic tension that results reminds one of a wild animal caught in a net or trapped behind the bars of a cage (p. 198).

The paintings of Sam Francis, in common with the scrawly Pollock's, are concerned with effects of space and light. Pollock's work is dynamic and agitated, that of Francis calm and contemplative (p. 199). The paintings most quoted as precedent for the North American school are the late Monet *Nympheas*, the series of lily-pond pictures of floating leaves and flowers which become blobs of light and color (p. 112 C). Undoubtedly the main American contribution to painting is in the post-war action school. The output is tremendous and tends to make the European equivalent seem small-scale and derivative. In Paris Georges Mathieu is the most calligraphic of action painters (p. 200). His gesticulations are like an unreadable oriental script. He sees them himself as blazons and banners of medieval armies. Mathieu attacks his canvas like a fencer. In Holland Karel Appel attacks his as if with a slashing sabre. Appel paints as if paint were a weapon and canvas a bitterly hated enemy (p. 85 F). Alan Davie is the most important English action painter, and again shows his own national characteristics. The canvases are comparatively small in scale, the imagery, though intangible, is romantic; the paintings are related to that war-time phase of English painting when English painters, cut off from all European developments, rediscovered Blake, Fuseli, and Samuel Palmer and their mixture of wild dreams and pastoral imagery.

The movement has its sculptured equivalent too. We can generally say that the cool Constructivists tend to work in highly finished materials suggestive of engineering and architecture, in brass, copper, aluminium, in glass and perspex; they make full use of machine extruded sections of metals. Their work looks like miniature architecture, scientific instruments, or hygienic fittings.

Action sculptors tend to work directly in plaster, a much faster method than carving or modeling in clay or wax. The plaster is thrown and dribbled. The force of gravity is allowed its share in creating the work. All accidents of form are left. Sculptors today manufacture fragments that look like archeologists' finds from unknown civilizations. Figures are eroded, decayed, and mutilated. Some look like the maimed victims of modern warfare returned to haunt and accuse the living. Devoid of light and color the sculpture tends to be more pessimistic than the painting (D).

The early Kandinsky gouaches were very much an act of defiance, and this is still the main banner under which the action artists march. There is open defiance in pouring oneself out on to a canvas and then waiting for the resulting attack. If the attack does not come, then the painter returns to provocation with added aggressive energy. The movement depends on this sort of energy, the physical energy of the gesticulation, the apparent energy contained in juxtaposition of colors. Generally, these are pictures and sculptures with teeth in them that bite the spectator.

The movement can be dangerous. It can attract the immature and impatient, those who want natural forces to take over because they have none of their own. It attracts those who think that very bright color is easy to achieve by relying on the color manufacturer rather than their own imagination. Its sensational element attracts those who think that it is easier to shock than to build, or those who believe that to build is useless in any case because to do so is to invite destruction. Action painting seems so deceptively easy that more have fallen into its trap than in any other branch of the modern movement. The result has been a dilution of its aims and consequent refusal by the public to take the school seriously as a sign of a very important philosophical condition of the post-war 20th century.

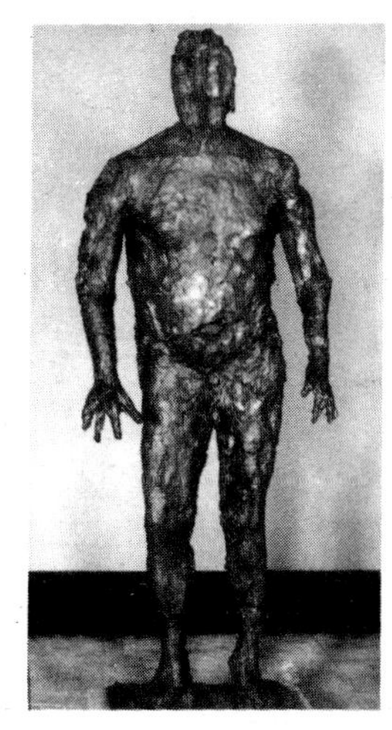

(D) GERMAINE RICHIER
The Storm, 1947-48
Paris, Mus. d'Art Moderne

CHAPTER 20

Art and Us

(A) Propeller of R.M.S. Queen Mary
Photo lent to Science Mus., London
by J. Stone and Co., London

ANY work of art is ultimately a great mystery. In the last resort all verbal interpretation is inadequate. The painting or sculpture, poetry or music, architecture or piece of furniture must itself in the end have the last word, and all explanation and description, however much it may help toward understanding, dies away. Finally we are left face to face with the work itself and our feelings. Today more is written about art than ever before, and more and more picture books with evermore accurate illustrations are being published. Although this means that we can have our own private gallery or museum on our bookshelves, we must guard against the facility becoming a substitute for the real thing and the real experience. It often requires considerable effort to enable us just to see one or two original works of art, but the time and trouble we take are worth more than a great deal of reading. These are firsthand experience. All else, no matter how well written or presented, can only be at secondhand. This is worth mentioning only to restore our sense of proportion, not in any way to diminish the value of the properly used book. In fact the latter is of increasing importance because it may help in our understanding of art and free us from the handicap of prejudice and ready-made likes and dislikes.

Art is with us everywhere, not only good art but bad art. We must recognize this fact while trying to find the best in art. Everything made has something of art in it. Like the city dweller who has lost sight of the fact that the food he eats is the result of someone's hard struggle with the land, and who has forgotten the earth that lies under the sidewalk that he treads, we forget that everything we use is made. We think of things as being bought rather than made.

In an age when we hear traditional critics say that no one draws any more and that accurate drawing is dead, we forget that everything that is manufactured began its existence as a drawing—an idea—the houses we live in, our place of work, the pens we write with, machines, ploughs, vehicles, the chair we sit on, all were drawn. Even if we live in a shack of corrugated iron, the material itself was made on a machine and someone somewhere made a drawing. Plastic toys, inane furniture for caged birds, can labels, all the lettering we read, all need a drawing in order to be made. Thus art is everywhere, and the standard of accuracy is greater than ever before.

It is beside the point that most of these things might be "bad" and that good design is only a minority quality. The potential is there. If a drawing has to be made at all, then this could be good. It is unlikely that the whole of our environment will ever be a first-rate work of art but it is not impossible. Every time something new is made, the choice is there, the chance to decide anew.

In the field of machine production, drawing as a craft is of as high a standard as ever. Machines themselves read and work directly from drawings. The draftsman can correct and alter as he goes along. The machine must have all the information it needs, as the object is to be made with no margin for error. This order of unfumbled accuracy of declaring one's intention is a direct

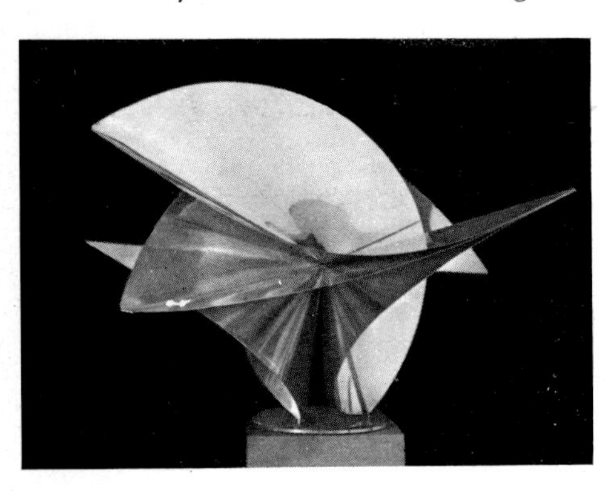

(B) STEPHEN GILBERT Structure 14c, 1961 *London, Tate*

return to the super-accurate type of art we see in Egyptian times, and there is a strong parallel in the timeless, anonymous, mass-produced quality of both kinds of art.

Thus the intermingling of art and ideas in everyday life continues in a subtle unconscious way, slowly influencing the way we see and think, often without our knowing what is happening to us. Sometimes the connections are obvious, as in the way in which modern painting and modern advertising art have mutually affected one another, or the way in which modern sculpture was influenced by the new machine forms of the ship, the airplane, and the mathematician's laboratory (A, B). More recently this process has been reversed, and now articles in common use, light fittings, furniture, automobile bodies, may tend to look like modern sculpture.

During the 1920's and 1930's there was a strong tendency for fashion drawings and the wax shop-window models to look like works by Modigliani or Brancusi sculptures (C, D, E). Furnishing textiles are sometimes designed under the influence of modern painters. Anni Albers' woven rugs are among the best examples (F). In England, painters Eric Ravilious and Paul Nash designed hard-wearing upholstery for London's underground railway. But apart from direct commissions of this sort, designers are always using the results of the painters' exploration of texture, color, and the language of drawing. The recent practice of painting walls in different colors is a direct heritage of *De Stijl*.

In entertainment, of course, the contribution of the fine artist has been as important as in poster design and book illustration. Serge Diaghilev's patronage of modern painters as ballet designers immediately after World War I did more to popularize both Fauves and Cubists than any number of gallery exhibitions and explanatory publications (G). Since then the theater, freed from indiscriminating naturalism in the same way as modern painting and sculpture, has borrowed freely from painters and sculptors as well as making direct use of their services. Films too use the fine arts as a laboratory of

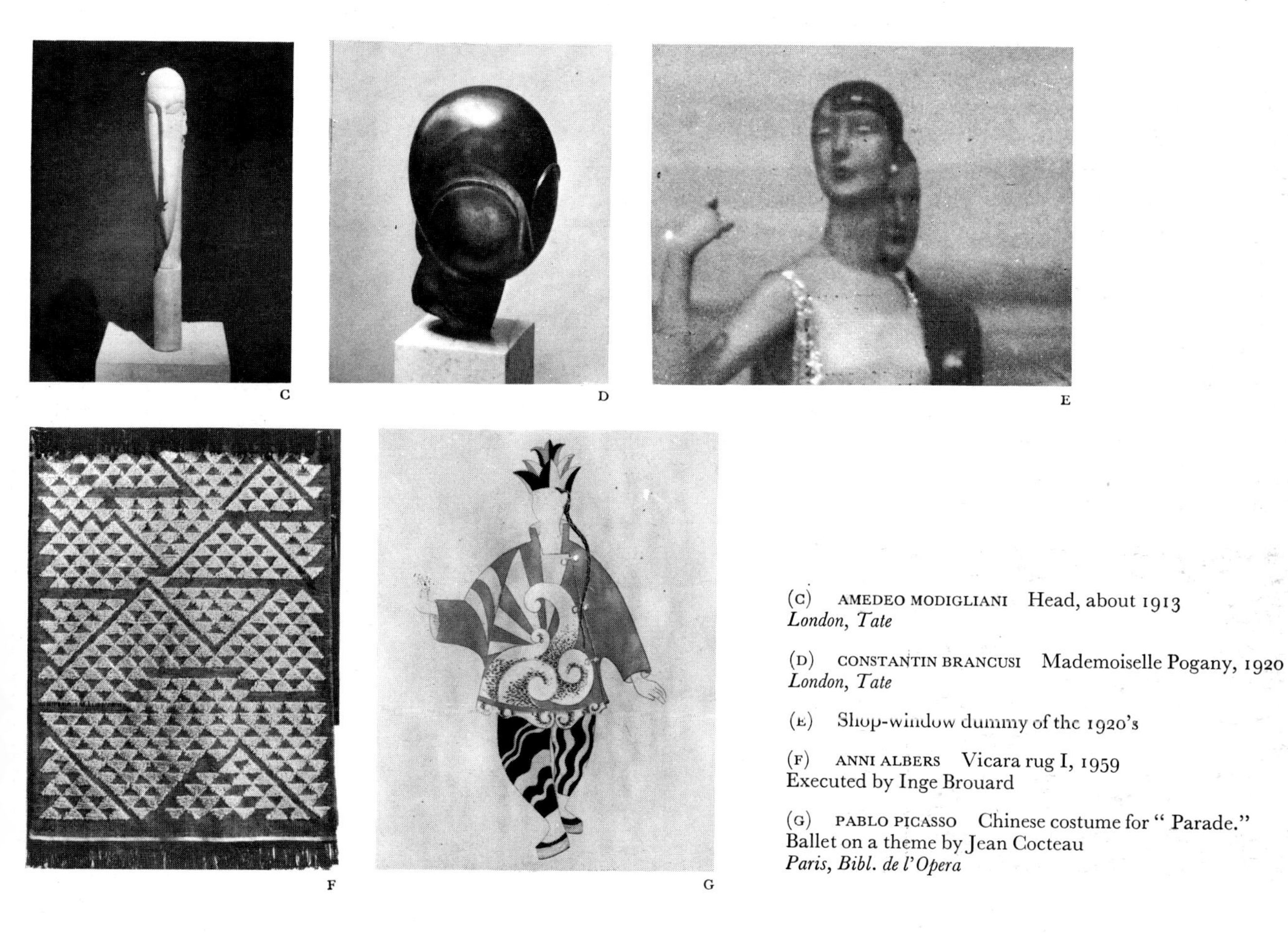

C D E F G

(C) AMEDEO MODIGLIANI Head, about 1913
London, Tate

(D) CONSTANTIN BRANCUSI Mademoiselle Pogany, 1920
London, Tate

(E) Shop-window dummy of the 1920's

(F) ANNI ALBERS Vicara rug I, 1959
Executed by Inge Brouard

(G) PABLO PICASSO Chinese costume for "Parade."
Ballet on a theme by Jean Cocteau
Paris, Bibl. de l'Opera

(A) DIEGO RIVERA
The Workers' Revolution (detail) 1929-35
Mexico City, Palacio Nac.

(B) BARBARA HEPWORTH
Cantate Domino, 1958
edition of six

vision. The modern costume epic is the direct successor to the 19th-century battle scene or that of romanticized classical Greco-Roman life. The film director Serge Eisenstein used painting freely as reference material. In the coronation scene of "Ivan the Terrible," the close shots of the various European ambassadors are all visual quotations from his knowledge of painting.

Sometimes the designer uses his borrowed material intelligently and with understanding. More often, the result is a nasty, misunderstood, garbled travesty of the real thing. What is important is that, good or bad, this pervasive influence of the artist penetrates deeply into all that we see in everyday life, to our can labels, magazines, and the season's fashionable colors in coats and dresses.

There is a deeper, less obvious influence than all this. Since the beginning of the Renaissance there has been an increasing tendency to set fine art apart from everyday life, to use it as a cultural buffer against a very tough outside world. The voluptuous and sensual pictures of the High Renaissance were housed in palaces built like fortresses, ever ready against instant attack. In the 18th century, painting was almost entirely escapist and presupposed an educated clientele. In the 19th century, the arts were supposed to provide an antidote of ideal beauty to the often brutal effects of the Industrial Revolution. Since then the attitude of the painter and sculptor has changed. Generally speaking they have become less servile and more aggressive. The element of stylization present in nearly all modern painting and sculpture shows an inclination on the part of artists to take the natural world by the scruff of its neck, to push it and pull it about and turn it into something else. It is true that from time to time certain modern painters have closely allied themselves politically. The Futurists and Dadaists issued revolutionary manifestos. Modern art in Latin America almost became synonymous with political revolution (A). On the other hand in the Communist countries the artist is definitely discouraged from taking liberties with the natural world, while in the west some of the wildest work has been produced by the most bourgeois and respectable painters.

This attitude toward nature of command and control is only the reflection of the physicist's domination of natural forces or the biologist's ever-increasing hold over life itself. As man gains more and more mastery over his environment and dictates his own living conditions, so the tendency is for the artist to make objects that are part of the environment rather than comments on it or reflections of it. Paintings are no longer pictures of things but things to live with. Sculpture is not of figures but stands in its own right like a figure or a rock or a tree (B). The artist no longer wants to be a decorator of buildings, he wants to have a say in their design. His work has left the picture frame and the niche and spread over the walls and out of doors into the streets. Like the modern architect, he believes not only in serving the world but in changing it. The prince, the statesman, is gradually losing his power and control of events to the scientist. In the world of art he has almost entirely lost control. He no longer tells the artist what he wants, he takes what the artist gives him. The artist is now master and not the servant, but while gaining the master's responsibility he has lost the servant's security.

So today the artist no longer works for an enlightened

patron who asks him to do a particular job. He works in semi-seclusion. Only a few friends are usually aware of what he is doing and thinking. When he goes out into the world it is to receive stimulus and ideas, to live another part of his life to which and on which his creative working life will react and feed. He then relies on a sympathetic dealer to take a collection of his work and find buyers for it. The private patron usually buys his work indirectly from the artist, and it is the artist who arouses his interest, not the reverse.

It is not only the private individual who buys the artist's work. He hopes to sell to the large public galleries as well. Here the buyer is usually a committee, but the money comes from the state and therefore ultimately from the public funds. In this way everyone is a patron indirectly. And not only in this way. Very few artists train their own assistants and pupils; private art schools are almost as rare. Most artists get their training at a publicly owned and financed school. This presupposes some sort of control, not only of funds that have to be accounted for, but by measuring in some sort of way the output of the school. Attempts are made to measure the standard of work produced by examination. This for better or worse has replaced the apprentice's "masterpiece" by which he was judged at the end of his training. At least two positive benefits come from the system. It provides students with somewhere to live and with a place to work and meet other students and artists. It provides practicing artists with the means of livelihood while they are preparing their collections of pictures for sale, a hazardous business full of the risk of failure and involving a large capital outlay. At its worst it produces students who are judged by their examination results rather than their work, and shelter for indifferent teachers. Generally the most forward-looking work from schools seems to be in spite of the schools, for the public resents its money being spent on work that it does not understand. Schools which are forward-looking tend to be regarded with a certain amount of criticism and suspicion, and considered to be revolutionary, full of students whose ambition is to shock, and generally encouraged to do so by their masters.

The system also attracts those who want to be artists rather than those who want to paint pictures or make sculpture. The artist's life seems to be the last stronghold of individual freedom of action, the last kind of heroic life. Even armies today require more technicians than hot-headed men of action. At one time the great romantic ambition was to be a poet, a writer. Today it is to

(C) Painted porcelain plate, about 1760
London, V. and A.

be an artist. It attracts those who would be non-conformists, whether they have talent or not. It is also becoming one of the last fields of study where the student has time to think and read without pressures both of time and of an academic nature.

The world of the artist is heroic to a certain extent. He can work on an architectural scale with a freedom that the architect no longer enjoys, with the sense of a mission to influence, attack, and change the public mind and public life, with the strong element of gambling including extraordinary reversals of fortune, with the exciting international element of the artist's world. From behind his barricade of security the average man tends to exaggerate this view of the artist's life, and envies him his excitement while ignorant of the far larger numbers of unknown and disillusioned failures.

For the artist's world tends to be one of all or nothing. In the past there was a steady demand for the minor artist. All past periods have their wide range of anonymous average work—the Egyptian paintings, the Greek tombstones and painted pottery, the Italian chests and altarpieces, the 19th-century topographical paintings, engravings, lithographs (C, and p. 182 A, B, C). None of the artists had to be original; they all had a talent for drawing and enjoyed both their work and a modest but secure standard of living. Today we expect our artist to be a genius, at least completely original, and sometimes an infant prodigy. If he is none of these he may go into an advertising agency or an industrial design firm. To take up *applied* art still carries a stigma of failure. But advertising art or industrial design is still an art, although different from painting and sculpture. It has its own standards in its own right and to fail to impress the authorities or galleries as a painter is no recommendation for success in producing books, posters,

(A) Egyptian mural: Men feeding oryxes, about B.C. 1500 *London, B.M.*

(B) Greek tombstone, 4th century B.C. *Athens, Nat. Mus.*

(C) Kilsby Tunnel working shaft: from "The London and Birmingham Railway" by John C. Bourne, 1837

fabrics, or furniture. The so-called applied arts have suffered very much from a negative attitude. A work of art is a work of art in its own right in its own category.

Both topographical painting and portrait painting are said to have been killed by photography and the growing excellence of mechanical reproduction. This is only true as long as one believes it to be. Landscape painting, together with still-life painting, is a necessary art form minor only in scale. Few houses are large enough or suitable for holding polemic paintings, important though these are. At the moment when we look for pictures to hang on our walls mechanical reproduction dominates the market. These are printed from plates made by means of photography. Anything and everything is photographed and reproduced, no matter how unsuitable. There is no consideration of scale, subject, or texture. These are often an important part of a painting and impossible to reproduce. Instead of having badly colored reproductions of old masters on our walls it would be far better to have works made expressly for this purpose by modern artists, reproduced by a more sympathetic means such as engraving, lithography, or screen printing, or even made especially for mechanical half-tone reproduction. These, however, can never supersede the unique vision of the artist's view of the world about us in his original creation.

Portrait painting was not killed by photography but by confusing the prototype portrait of the Renaissance with the technique of the latter half of the 19th century. It is the forcing of solid, opaque, and overworked paint into a superficial resemblance of a portrait by Reynolds that has brought the academic portrait into disrepute and killed it, for there is nothing more dead than these muddy semblances of public figures. Either the classical technique of portrait painting must be given a new lease of life and coupled to a new vision, or else the painter must evolve a fresh view of the portrait to make full use of Impressionist and Post-Impressionist technique.

It is dangerous to generalize. Sweeping statements are always being made about figurative painting being finished, and that from now on only abstract painting is significant, or vice versa. We are bound to be proved wrong by an artist simply ignoring the critics' taste and rules and producing vital and valid work. The fight between feelings and emotion on one hand and reason on the other is not new. Plato backed one and opposed the other; the public of that time obviously thought otherwise. Later on the battle was labeled Romanticism versus Classicism. It is a battle that goes on in all of us in our personal lives, and always will as long as men both feel and think. To choose one and not the other as a means of producing works of art is not right or wrong as long as one recognizes and comes to terms with the opposite. The problems confronting the artist when face to face with his block of stone, pile of clay, or blank canvas have not changed fundamentally since the beginning, although his language is always changing. Constant though they are, the problems are never finally solved, and are born afresh with each generation as though the previous had never existed.

CAMILLE PISSARRO The Pilot's Jetty, Le Havre, Morning, Cloudy and Misty Weather, 1903 *oil on canvas* $25\frac{5}{8} \times 32$ *in.*
London, Tate Gallery

SEE PAGE 114

CLAUDE MONET London, Houses of Parliament, Sun Coming through Fog, 1904 *oil on canvas* *32×36 in.* SEE PAGE 115
Paris, Musée de l'Impressionnisme

GEORGES BRAQUE Coffee Pot and Pitcher, 1908 *oil on canvas* *18½ × 15 in.* SEE PAGE 119
Stuttgart, Württembergische Staatsgalerie

PABLO PICASSO Les Demoiselles d'Avignon, 1907 *oil on canvas 96 × 92 in.*
New York, Museum of Modern Art, Lillie P. Bliss Bequest

SEE PAGE 119

Mask from the Ibo, Southern Nigeria
London, British Museum

SEE PAGE 119

GEORGES BRAQUE The Portuguese, 1911 *oil on canvas* *$46 \times 32\frac{1}{8}$ in.* SEE PAGE 119
Basel, Öffentliche Kunstsammlung, Raoul La Roche Bequest

AUGUSTE HERBIN Shelter, 1958 *oil on canvas*
Paris, collection the Artist

SEE PAGES 158 AND 172

E. McKNIGHT KAUFFER Poster, 1928
London, Victoria and Albert Museum

SEE PAGE 163

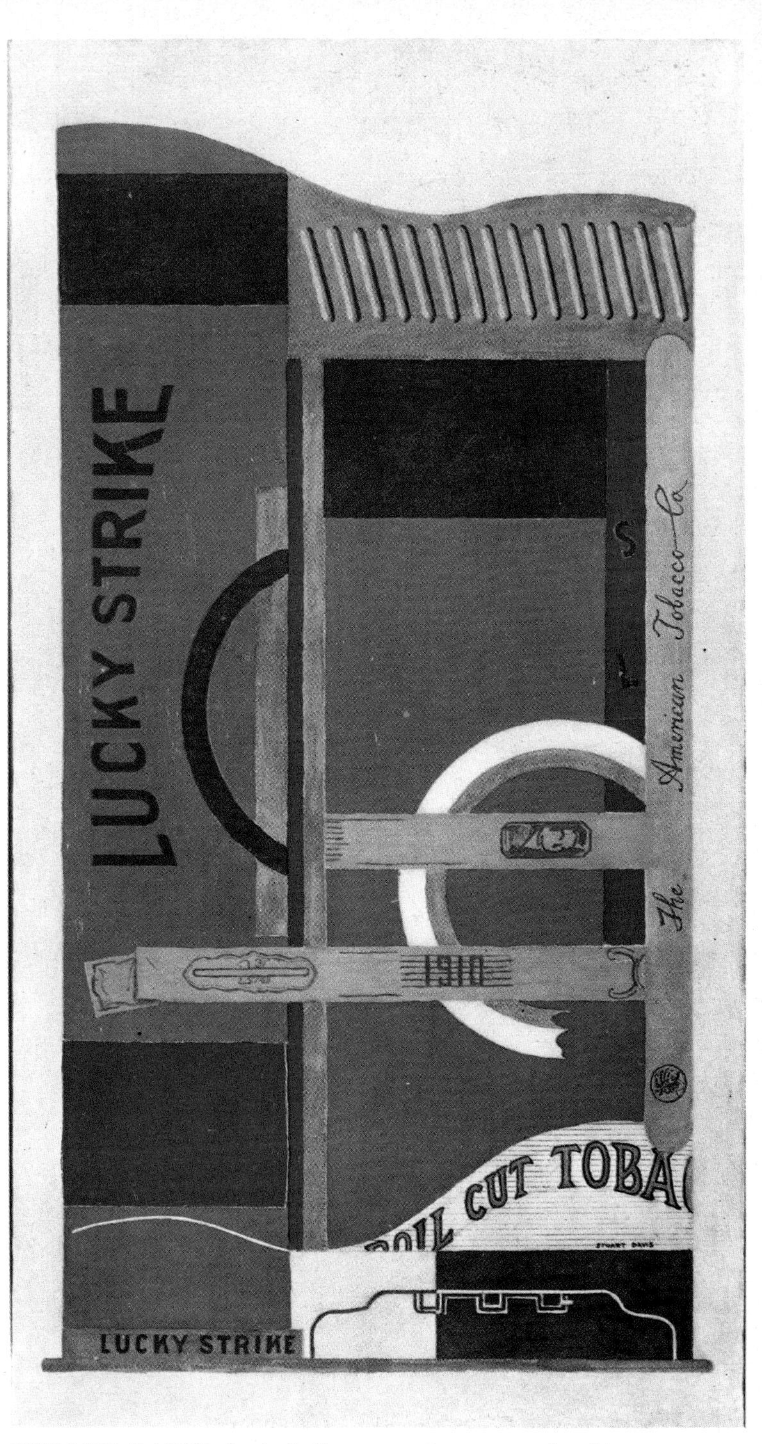

STUART DAVIS Lucky Strike, 1921 *oil on canvas* $33\frac{1}{4} \times 18$ *in.*
New York, Museum of Modern Art, Gift of the American Tobacco Company, Inc.

SEE PAGE 166

KASIMIR MALEVICH Yellow-Orange-Green, 1915 *oil on canvas* $17\frac{3}{8} \times 11\frac{3}{4}$ *in.* SEE PAGE 169
Amsterdam, Stedelijk Museum

PIET MONDRIAN Composition with Red, Yellow, and Blue, 1939-42 *oil on canvas* *28⅜ × 27¼ in.*
London, Tate Gallery

SEE PAGE 172

HENRI MATISSE Large Interior in Red, 1948 *oil on canvas* $57\frac{1}{2} \times 22\frac{1}{2}$ *in.*
Paris, Musée d'Art Moderne

SEE PAGE 174

WASSILY KANDINSKY Landscape at Murnau, 1909 *oil on paper* *27½ × 40 in.*
Düsseldorf, Kunstmuseum

SEE PAGE 174

WASSILY KANDINSKY Dreamy Improvisation, 1913 *oil on canvas* $51\frac{1}{8} \times 51\frac{1}{8}$ *in.*
Munich, collection Frau Ida Bichert

SEE PAGE 17

ROBERT DELAUNAY Homage to Blériot, 1914 *oil on canvas* $98\frac{1}{2} \times 98\frac{1}{2}$ *in.*
Paris, collection Gazel

SEE PAGE 175

JACKSON POLLOCK Number 1, 1948 *oil on canvas 68 × 104 in.*
New York, Museum of Modern Art, Purchase

SEE PAGE 177

SAM FRANCIS Composition, 1960 *oil on canvas* $63\frac{3}{4} \times 51\frac{1}{2}$ *in.*
London, collection Mr. and Mrs. Charles Gimpel

SEE PAGE 177

GEORGES MATHIEU Homage to Maréchal de Turenne, 1952 *oil on canvas* $78\frac{3}{4} \times 157\frac{1}{2}$ *in.* SEE PAGE 177
Paris, collection the Artist

General Glossary

abacus
In architecture, the flat upper portion of the capital of a column.

abstract art
A term used to cover a number of forms of non-naturalistic art in which the subject, in varying degrees, gives way to considerations of color, line, volume, composition, pattern, and paint quality; pure abstract art is independent of subject and the artist exploits only the values inherent in these. Qualities of abstraction are commonly found in primitive art, and at various points in all later stages. The advent of the camera has perhaps led 20th-century artists to explore widely the possibilities of non-representational art, so that abstraction, far from being a mere movement or phase, has come to be an important concept in both modern painting and sculpture.

Abstract Expressionism
A term first applied to the work of a number of abstract painters in New York after World War II. In Abstract Expressionist art the act of painting itself is of prime importance. Color is strong and applied vigorously to large canvases, sometimes with action painting techniques. Jackson Pollock and Mark Rothko in the United States, and Hans Hartung and Alfred Wols in Europe, are among those associated with this style. See also **action painting.**

Abstraction-Création
The Abstraction-Création group was formed in Paris in 1932 by Antoine Pevsner and his brother Naum Gabo.

The group held regular exhibitions of abstract painting and sculpture, and published a yearly almanac. Membership reached 400 at times in the 1930's, so that the group became a vital cohesive force. Its function was to consolidate the position of the abstract artist rather than to pioneer any dramatic new development.

Artists associated with the group included Kandinsky and Mondrian.

academy
The term "academy" derives from Academia, a park and gymnasium near Athens, where Plato founded a society about 387 B.C. for the purpose of teaching and discussing philosophy. In 15th-century Italy, the name was revived by groups of humanists who met informally to discuss and exchange views on cultural matters, the group associated with Lorenzo de' Medici in Florence being one of the most famous. In art, from the 16th century, academy denoted the studio academy, which was the workshop of a master painter where other artists gathered to sketch or sculpt from the same live model. Bandinelli's academy, 1531, is one of the earliest known of this type. The academy as studio and school saw its most important realization in 19th-century France, where it was particularly advocated by David. The term also denotes the official academy, which sought to raise the artist, who was a craftsman, subservient to the guilds, and make him at least equal to the writer, poet, or musician. Vasari' Accademia del Disegno, founded in 1563, was the first of this type, which because of its need for powerful protection often had the monarch or other ruler as patron. Subsequently the adherents of the official academy found themselves subjected to the dictates and service of the state, as in France during the reign of Louis XIV, when art took its shape and impetus from the precepts and doctrines of Colbert's Académie Royale de Peinture et de Sculpture.

The 18th century saw an increase in the number of academies in all countries. One of the most famous was the Royal Academy, London, founded in 1768, which provided teaching facilities for young artists. With the changing social conditions of the 19th century the academies, by their insistence on a grand art more compatible with an autocratic than a democratic society, acquired a dogmatic and stultifying aura. The ensuing schism between the progressive painter eager to try new ideas and the academy with its wealth of artistic tradition and heritage, has been to the detriment of all art and artists.

acanthus
A Mediterranean plant that inspired the stylized leaf forms used in the decoration of Corinthian and Composite capitals, as well as for other decorative motifs.

ACANTHUS

action painting
The production of a painting by means other than the orthodox painters' tools. These methods include splashing, trickling, or even throwing on the paint, and may also involve the use of implements such as sticks or trowels. The technique, initiated by Jackson Pollock in 1947, was devised so that the artist should "feel nearer, more a part of the painting." The term "tachisme" is virtually synonymous.

aerial perspective
See **perspective.**

aisle
In a basilican church or hall, the area which runs parallel to the nave and separates it from the lateral walls. See also **ambulatory.**

alla prima
Italian: "at first." The technique of finishing a painting at one sitting in colors that are opaque enough to cover any preliminary sketch drawn or painted on the canvas. Seldom used before the 19th century, the practice has since become general. *Au premier coup* is the French term for such painting.

altarpiece
A sculpture or painting set above or behind an altar. See also **diptych, triptych, polyptych.**

ambulatory
The extension of the nave aisle to form a walk around the east end of a church behind the altar. The term also applies to the open or closed arcaded passageway of a cloister.

(A) AMPHITHEATER

(B) ART-BRUT

(C) ART NOUVEAU

(A) The Amphitheater, 290 A.D.
Verona, Italy

(B) KAREL APPEL
Amorous Dance, 1955
London, Tate Gallery

(C) JAN TOOROP
Delftsche Slaolie, 1895
Amsterdam, Stedelijk Museum

amorino (pl. amorini)
Italian: "little love." A small winged putto or cupid. See also **putto.**

amphitheater
A Roman building constructed for entertainment purposes. It was oval or elliptical in shape, and had seats in tiers surrounding the central arena where athletic and gladiatorial contests took place. The arena could be flooded for aquatic displays. The structure was unroofed; however, covering was provided by a movable awning (*velarium*) when required. Many Roman towns possessed an amphitheater, the most famous being the Colosseum, Rome.

Analytical Cubism
The primary phase in the development of Cubism, lasting from 1906 to 1909. See **Cubism.**

anamorphosis
The representation of an object or scene so that it appears distorted when viewed directly, but regains its natural aspect when seen from one particular viewpoint or by means of special apparatus (such as a polyhedron).

anthemion
A floral decorative motif used in the embellishment of Greek and Roman architecture. It can take a variety of forms, all of which appear to derive from the flower and leaves of a plant resembling the honeysuckle. The anthemion is similar to the palmette.

ANTHEMION

apse
In basilican and later churches, a vaulted or domed semi-circular projection terminating the aisle or choir.

aquatint
An etching technique, developed in the late 18th century, that produces effects similar to watercolor. See **engraving.**

arabesque
From French: "in the Arab manner." A linear surface decoration of rhythmic interweaving patterns, usually of foliage or scroll-forms, although animal, bird, or human forms also occur. The Moorish decoration from which the Western arabesque has indirectly derived is more purely geometric, and does not include representation of the human figure.

arch
A curved structure of brick or stone built over a doorway, gateway, or other opening, supported at the sides and designed to transform the downward pressure of the weight above into a lateral thrust. The center brick or stone, without which the arch would collapse, is called the keystone.

archivolt
The molding or architrave attached to the face of an arch following its contour. It can also be on the soffit or underside of the arch.

armature
A rigid framework, made of metal, used by sculptors in modeling to take the weight of the clay and prevent distortion.

Armory Show
An exhibition staged from February to March, 1913, in the Armory of the 69th Infantry Regiment in New York. It contained a representative collection of works illustrating the various phases in European painting during the 19th and early 20th centuries. This revelation to Americans of modern work, such as that of the Cubists, met with great public disapproval and hostility. The exhibition was nevertheless a success and went also to Chicago and Boston. It is important historically as the first real introduction of advanced painting to the United States.

arras
Franco-Flemish high-warp tapestry produced at Arras, a town of northern France. The finest tapestries were produced from the late 14th to the mid-15th century.

art-brut
French: "raw art." An approach to art that has emerged in the 20th century, in which Western conventions are rejected in favor of an unadulterated and direct pictorial language, comparable to that found in primitive and archaic art, child art, and the art of madmen. Among its exponents are Jean Dubuffet, Karel Appel, and the Cobra group of artists from Denmark, Holland, and Belgium.

art engagé
French: "committed art." A term that could be freely translated as "art committed to a purpose." It is particularly used of French art between 1820 and 1850 that commented on contemporary social and political history. It included the depiction of actual events, such as Géricault's *Raft of the Medusa*; political allegory, as in David's works; and social comment, as in Daumier's graphic art.

Art Nouveau
A style that spread over Europe and the United States during the 1890's and the

1910's. It was known as Art Nouveau in Britain and America, as Stile Liberty or Floreal in Italy, as Style Guimard in France, and as Jugendstil in Germany.

The style was particularly suited to interior decoration, and although Art Nouveau tendencies can be detected in contemporary painting, its influence was most felt in the applied arts. Its characteristic forms, which derive from animal and plant life, twist and move sinuously with excessive elongation and an emphasis on the asymmetrical, but with an over-all sense of delicacy and sophistication. Its origins are debatable, but the graphic work of Mackmurdo, the linearism in the painting of Edvard Munch or Jan Toorop, and Japanese prints, all contributed to the formation of the style. The various aspects of Art Nouveau are best exemplified by Aubrey Beardsley, with his brilliant black and white drawings; Louis Sullivan, in his Auditorium Building, Chicago, 1888; Victor Horta, in his interiors in the Rue Paul Émile Janson, Brussels, 1892-93; Hector Guimard, with his Paris Métro station designs of 1900; the work of Charles Mackintosh in Glasgow; and Antonio Gaudi, whose highly individual creations are in Barcelona. See also **Jugendstil, Stile Liberty, Style Guimard.**

Ash Can School
A depreciatory name given to a group of American realist artists who preferred as their subject matter the venal and often depressing aspects of contemporary city life. They were first active in Philadelphia during the 1890's, but moved to New York by the turn of the century. In 1908, they formed themselves into a group known as The Eight, the members being:

Arthur B. Davies (1862-1928); George Luks (1867-1933); Everett Shinn (1876-1953); John Sloan (1871-1951); Robert Henri (1865-1929); William Glacken (1870-1938); Maurice Prendergast (1859-1924); Ernest Lawson (1873-1939).

Of later followers, George Bellows (1882-1925) is perhaps the best known. The group took part in the Armory Show.

asymmetry
In art, the rejection of the precepts of formal symmetry and balance.

atelier
French: "workshop; studio." An artist's studio. The *ateliers libres*, providing studio facilities for a fee, but no supervision or instruction, were particularly important to the development of painting in 19th-century France. The best known, the Atelier Suisse, was established in Paris in the 1820's. It was used by Courbet and Delacroix, and later by many of the Impressionists.

au premier coup
See **alla prima.**

automatism
A technique in which the artist creates lines and forms not under the control of the conscious will, but at the dictates of the subconscious; "doodling" is a simple example. Some of the more complex manifestations of automatism can be seen in Surrealism.

avant garde
French: "vanguard." The pioneering minority responsible for innovations in the fine arts and other spheres, and whose ideas are in advance of those currently and generally accepted.

bacchanalia
A scene of drunken revelry. It was a subject painted and sculpted frequently in the 16th, 17th, and 18th centuries.

baldachin (baldacchino, baldaquin)
An architectural canopy supported by columns, suspended from the roof, or projecting from the wall, placed over an altar or throne.

bambocciata
An Italian word that has a variety of meanings, the most common perhaps being "something created for amusement." In art, the name is applied to the popular, low-life peasant or genre scenes, usually on a small scale, which were favored by Dutch and Flemish artists working in Italy in the 17th century. At that time, this kind of work was thought trivial in comparison to more noble subjects, such as history painting. The word is sometimes written as *bambocciade.*

baptistery
A part of a church or a detached structure housing the font used in the rite of baptism.

Barbizon School
A French school of landscape painters taking its name from the village of Barbizon in the Forest of Fontainebleau, where the artists were centered. These painters set a precedent for open-air painting. They depicted in unsentimental terms the local forest scenery and the life of the peasants. This choice of subject matter, the freedom with which they handled paint, and their rendering of atmospheric conditions, place them among the precursors of Impressionism. Théodore Rousseau, Millet, and Diaz de la Peña were Barbizon painters; Corot was also associated with the school.

Barochetto
A style associated with Naples in the first half of the 18th century, which involved an unorthodox use of forms in a decorative and often frivolous spirit. It is seen in the work of the architects Nauclerio and Vaccano, and particularly in Sanfelice, with his ingenious staircase designs. The term is also applied to an ornate style of furniture of similar date and provenance.

(D) ASH CAN SCHOOL

(E) BACCHANALIA

(F) BARBIZON SCHOOL

(D) JOHN SLOAN
Backyards, Greenwich Village, 1914
New York, Whitney Museum of American Art

(E) NICOLAS POUSSIN
Bacchanal
London, National Gallery

(F) THÉODORE ROUSSEAU
A Group of Oak Trees, Apremont, 1852
Paris, Louvre

(A) BAS-RELIEF

(B) BISTRE

(A) LORENZO GHIBERTI
Detail from the East Doors, 1425-52
Florence, Baptistery

(B) REMBRANDT VAN RYN
Hendrickje Stoffels Sleeping, about 1660-69
London, British Museum

Baroque
A term of disputed origin applied to European art and architecture from the early years of the 17th century to the middle of the 18th century. The zenith of the style, the High Baroque, was reached in the art of Rome from about 1630 to 1680. From here it spread to North Italy and other parts of Europe, finding particular favor in Roman Catholic countries.

The Baroque style was conditioned by the militant and fervent spirit of the Catholic Counter-Reformation, but its immense possibilities were also seen and utilized by secular authorities. It represented a new fusion of architecture, painting, and sculpture, all subordinated to the *concetto*, or theme, deliberately calculated to evoke an emotional response in the spectator, and to involve him spiritually in the subject. In spite of a sometimes theatrical illusionism, Baroque art in the hands of its greatest exponents, such as Bernini, Borromini, Pietro da Cortona, and Lanfranco, achieved a new integral unity of the arts, an exciting harnessing of space, and, by original experiment with forms, captured rippling movement in static structures.

Outside Italy, the Baroque was modified by national tastes and traditions. In France, its manifestations were stylistically more pompous and designed to glorify the state. Baroque features also appeared, but in a more restrained form, in the arts of the Protestant North—in the churches of Sir Christopher Wren, for example, and in the painting of Rembrandt. The true development from Italian High Baroque was in the Late Baroque and Rococo interior decoration of 18th-century South Germany and Austria, where the style reached new heights of extravagance and richness of form and color, and was imbued with a new, secular gaiety.

basilica
Originally a large, aisled hall used by the Romans for public administration. The term was later applied to similarly constructed churches.

bas-relief
Low relief. Sculpture that projects slightly from background. It has the least projection of all relief sculpture, and is nearest in intention and effect to painting.

Bâteau-Lavoir, Groupe du
The name of a group of artists and writers. It derives from a cluster of ramshackle artists' studios in Montmartre, said to resemble the *bâteaux-lavoir* or laundry boats of the Seine, because of their creaking and unstable condition. Between 1908 and 1914, it became an increasingly important artistic center, the most illustrious of the day finding their way there sooner or later for an interchange of ideas and the evolvement of new doctrines and formulas such as Cubism. Picasso and Juan Gris were among the Bâteau-Lavoir's most renowned tenants.

batik printing
A method of dyeing fabrics, commonly used in Indonesia, Malaysia, and the Philippines. Various parts of the design on the material are impregnated with wax, so that they remain uncolored during any of successive dippings in dye. Finally, the wax is removed from the cloth by boiling or by the application of a hot iron.

Bauhaus
An artistic institution founded by the architect Walter Gropius, which began at Weimar in 1919, moved to Dessau in 1925, and was finally closed with the advent of the Hitler régime in 1933. Its aim was to promote a fusion of all aspects of the arts, including architecture, to create the integral and consummate perfection of "the great building." In practical terms it consisted of a collaboration of the artist and technician to fulfill the demands of modern industry, which had the added advantage of orientating the student to the type of work he would eventually be called upon to do. Its scope was virtually limitless, and among its educators of architects, painters, sculptors, craftsmen, and technicians, are to be found distinguished names such as Oskar Schlemmer, Paul Klee, Wassily Kandinsky, and Lászlo Moholy-Nagy. The Bauhaus played a leading part in the formulation of the modern style in Europe and its influences were felt much further afield in, for example, the United States.

Berliner Sezession
German: "Berlin Secession." A group of painters headed by Max Liebermann who broke away from the official academic *Verein Berliner Künstler* (Association of Berlin Artists) in 1899, when controversy arose over the exhibition of work by Edvard Munch. See also **Sezession.**

biomorphic art
Abstract art with forms derived from organic life, in contrast to the more usual geometric ones.

bistre
A brown pigment made from soot or charred wood, used to obtain monochrome effects. It is prepared as an ink or chalk. In the 17th century bistre was frequently used in watercolor as a dark wash.

bitumen
A compound deriving from asphaltum used in a variety of processes, including Egyptian mummification, glazing, printing, and etching, but most usually as a pigment in painting. It is brown in color and easy to handle, but as an oil paint it has the supreme disadvantage of never drying completely. Consequently, many of the works of the 18th and 19th centuries, when it was widely used, have deteriorated badly through cracking and discoloration.

Blaue Reiter, Der
German: "The Blue Rider." An artistic movement initiated by Franz Marc and Wassily Kandinsky in Munich in 1911, whose purpose was to bring together the many and diverse forms of modern painting. The mouthpiece of the group was to have been a magazine also called "Der Blaue Reiter," but only one copy of this appeared, in 1912. More important was the group's series of exhibitions in which all similarly minded artists, whether German or foreign, took part. World War I virtually brought about the end of the movement, several of its members, including Franz Marc and Auguste Macke, losing their lives, but its purpose, that of establishing modern art in Germany, had been achieved.

blot drawing
A method of composing landscape and other subjects, using shapes suggested by random blots as a starting point. Alexander Cozens used this principle to encourage his students to compose more freely. About 1785 he described the technique in his pamphlet, "A New Method of Assisting the Invention in Drawing Original Compositions of Landscape."

bodegón
Spanish: "tavern; eating place." A type of genre painting in which the main emphasis is placed on still-life arrangements of articles of food and kitchen utensils. Outstanding painters of the bodegón, a popular theme with Spanish artists, include Alejandro de Loarte, Luis Melendez, and Velázquez.

body color
Watercolor mixed with white, giving the paint an opaque effect and hence more "body." Synonymous with **gouache.**

bottega
Italian: "shop; work place." The studio or workshop of a master artist, particularly during the ascendancy of the guilds. An apprentice system was applied, as in other trades and crafts, with communal living and the gradual integration of the young artist into the method of picture production then practiced. See also **workshop production.**

broken color
Color applied in small strokes of different colors that blend in the eye of the viewer.

bronze
An easily handled metal comprised of an alloy of copper and tin, which has been used by man for both domestic and artistic purposes from prehistoric times. Its use in sculpture was revived in Italy in the 15th century and by the Renaissance it had become common. Bronze acquires a green patina through the years. It is quite usual in modern times to achieve something of this effect by chemical means. "Bronze" can also mean a work cast in bronze. See also **casting.**

Brücke, Die
German: "The Bridge." A group of artists led by Ernst Ludwig Kirchner, Karl Schmidt-Rottluff, Fritz Bleyl, and Erich Heckel, who came together in Dresden in 1905 for the purpose of promoting and sustaining interest in advanced art. They are often linked to the contemporary French Fauves and exhibit certain comparable traits, although the German work has more violent social and political undertones. Die Brücke had no one particular style or program, although each member could be said to belong to one or other category of the Expressionists, and most of the early work shows a similarity in the use of loud and often harsh colors, jagged contours, and in fervent dramatic power. The group, which moved to Berlin in 1910 and was finally dispersed in 1913, had a great importance, together with Der Blaue Reiter, in establishing modern painting in Germany. Its influence was felt also in sculpture, graphic art, and most other fields of design.

brushwork
The personal manner in which the pigment is handled in painting, particularly in oil painting. The differing textures give the paint surface an aesthetic value of its own, and also indicate the artist's temperament and methods.

In 20th-century painting, particularly since van Gogh, brushwork has assumed a greater intrinsic value and has become a key compositional factor.

Byzantine Art
The art of Byzantium, the Eastern Roman Empire centered at Constantinople from 324 A.D.; important development in this art also took place at Ravenna. The first phase of Byzantine art ended with the Iconoclast Age, from 730 to 787, and 815 to 843, after which it entered on a new and prolific era of more than 300 years. In the early 13th century another revitalization occurred.

Byzantine art drew on both Oriental and Western sources. It was always strictly subordinated to the requirements of religious doctrine, so that a sense of overpowering majesty and monumentality is created, for example, in the image of Christ, but there is no attempt at life-like characterization. There is a high degree of stylization in paintings as well as mosaics.

cabinet picture
An easel painting, of small dimensions, rarely more than three feet wide, usually painted for display in a private house. With the rise of middle-class prosperity in 17th-century Holland, the demand for this type of work increased, and some of the finest examples of the genre were created for the Dutch market.

(C) DER BLAUE REITER

(D) DIE BRÜCKE

(C) WASSILY KANDINSKY
White Clouds, 1903
London, Marlborough Fine Art, Ltd.

(D) ERNST LUDWIG KIRCHNER
Title-page, Chronicle of Die Brücke, 1913
Hanover, Kestner-Museum

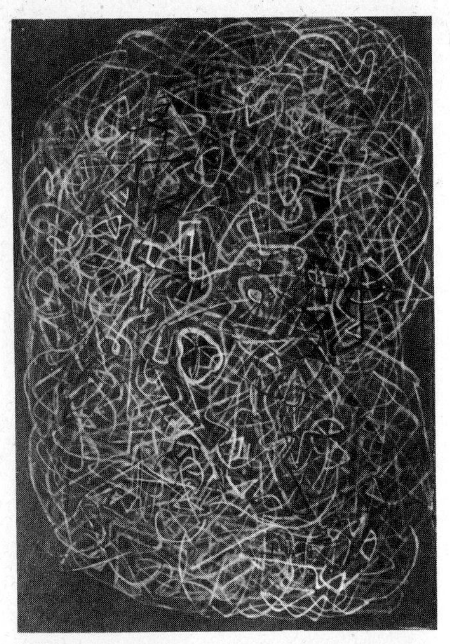

(A) CALLIGRAPHY

(B) CAMPANILE

(A) MARK TOBEY
Calligraphy in White, 1957
Seattle, Wash., collection Otto S. Seligman

(B) Campanile
Florence, Cathedral

calligraphy
Beautiful or elegant writing with a pen or brush on paper or similar material. With the growth of Oriental influence on Western art, the adjective "calligraphic" has been increasingly used in reference to linear patterns or free, rhythmic brushwork.

Camden Town Group
After the first Post-Impressionist Exhibition in London in 1910, the ranks of the New English Art Club became divided and the first rival group formed was the Camden Town Group. It was founded by Walter Sickert and Spencer Gore in 1911, the latter artist becoming its first president. The Group numbered 16 to begin with, including Henry Lamb, Wyndham Lewis, Lucien Pissarro, and Harold Gilman; Duncan Grant was a later member. The Camden Town Group amalgamated with the Cumberland Market and Nineteen Fitzroy Street Groups, and by 1913 all had merged to form part of the London Group. See also **N.E.A.C.**

camera obscura
A 16th-century device, created as an aid to accuracy in drawing, which reflects the subject onto a surface so that its contours can be easily traced by the artist. The "camera obscura," which is composed of lenses and mirrors assembled in a darkened box, was superseded in the middle of the 19th century by the "camera lucida," a more advanced invention that utilized the prism.

campanile
Italian: "bell tower." A bell tower, one built separate from a church or main building. Many are in Italy, for example, Giotto's Campanile in the Florence Cathedral complex, and the renowned Leaning Tower of Pisa.

canopy
A decorative covering constructed over an altar, pulpit, tomb, or throne. The term is also applied to such external architectural features as a projection hooding a niche or doorway, or one which runs continuously along a building forming a shelter. See also **baldachin.**

cantoria
A choir gallery. Elaborately carved and decorated cantorias were frequently made for Italian churches during the Renaissance. Notable examples are those by Donatello and Lucca della Robbia in Florence.

canvas
Primarily, a coarse cloth of hemp, cotton, or flax, on which an artist paints his picture. "Canvas" can designate the picture itself. Although painting on cloth was known from ancient times, canvas has only really been favored since the 16th century. The weave and texture of canvas can vary tremendously.

capital
The uppermost section of a column, placed above the shaft and supporting the entablature. Capitals are usually carved and decorated according to the main orders of architecture.

CAPITAL

capriccio
A type of painting particularly popular in the 18th century, in which realistically depicted architectural features or buildings are juxtaposed in fantastic order.

cartoon
From Italian *cartone*: "a big sheet of paper." In current usage, the word cartoon signifies a drawing intended as a comical or satirical comment on contemporary events or personalities. Formerly it described a full-size drawing, usually complete in all details, carried out as the final stage before embarking upon an actual painting. From the cartoon the composition could be transferred to the wall, canvas, or panel for which it was intended. The back of the cartoon was rubbed with chalk, and the main lines were transferred by drawing over them with a stylus, or pricked with a series of small holes so that charcoal dust could be puffed through onto the painting surface.

cartouche
A decorative form, shaped like a roll of vellum, found in all types of fine and applied arts from the 16th century onwards.

cassone
Italian: "coffer; chest." Carved chests, often painted with mythological scenes, popular in Italy from the 14th to 16th centuries. Outstanding examples were painted by Uccello and Botticelli, but usually they are the work of lesser artists.

casting
In sculpture, the process whereby a clay or wax model is reproduced in metal or plaster. For making bronzes the two main methods are sand casting and the *cire perdue* (French: "lost wax") process. In the former, a mold of the original sculpture is made in damp sand and a core inserted; the space between these is

filled with the molten bronze. In the cire perdue method, a clay model slightly smaller than the required bronze is covered with wax and enclosed in a shell of clay mixed with ashes or other material. Vent pipes are fixed top and bottom. The clay having set, molten bronze is poured in through the top vent, replacing the wax that has run out at the bottom. In plaster casting liquid plaster is poured into a mold, and when this is set, the mold is chipped away. An inner layer of tinted plaster used in the making of the mold serves as a guide to prevent damage to the cast.

catacomb
A subterranean burial place, usually in the form of passageways with niches in the walls for the remains of the dead. Though the burial chambers under the early Christian basilica of S. Sebastiano, Rome, appear to be the origin of the present concept of the term, the Etruscans had similar ideas of burial.

Cercle et Carré
French: "Circle and Square." The name of a group of artists and a magazine devoted to pure abstraction in art. The group was founded by the Uruguayan painter Joaquin Torrés Garcia (1874-1949) in 1930, when he was working in Paris. In April of that year, a large exhibition of the same name was held in Paris in which all the leading abstract painters, including Kandinsky, Mondrian, Pevsner, and Le Corbusier, took part. The Parisian review "Cercle et Carré" was edited by Michel Seuphor. Three issues were distributed. Torrés Garcia returned to Montevideo in 1932, opened an art school there and continued himself to issue the magazine under the title "Circulo y Cuadrado." It became concerned with the activities of the school, however, and did not remain a vital mouthpiece for abstract art.

charcoal
A dark carbon substance used for drawing. It is produced by charring willow or vine wood in a kiln from which air has been excluded. Charcoal is easily erased and is therefore useful for preparatory drawings which may need numerous corrections. Charcoal drawings are sometimes treated with a fixative to prevent their being smudged. Charcoal was frequently used by 16th-century Venetian painters, such as Tintoretto and Titian, who combined it with white heightening. Charcoal has also been used with oil to give it a more lasting quality.

chiaroscuro
Italian: "light-dark." The science of dealing with light and shade in painting; the use of strongly contrasting tones; the skill with which the painter is able to combine strong lighting and shadow effects. The term is used particularly of 17th-century painters, such as Caravaggio and Rembrandt.

chinoiserie
From French *chinois*: "Chinese." A term which was evolved in the 18th century to describe works of art emanating from China, Japan, and the Indies, and also European products taking their design and embellishment from them. Chinoiserie decoration is consequently closely linked with the Rococo style in architecture and interior design. In Europe the taste spread rapidly into all types of decorative art, the original forms becoming debased and fantastic, owing very little to the native products. The fashion, which was at its height in the mid-18th century, lasted until the 19th century and spread to America.

chuban
See **kakemono-ye**

churrigueresque
An architectural style that takes its name from José de Churriguera (1650-1723) and his family, whose work abounds in Salamanca. As often happens, the originators of this rather florid Spanish Baroque style were much less exuberant in their handling of details and architectural decoration than their followers, notably Pedro de Ribera and Narciso Tomé. The style, which spread to Andalusia, became a feature of Spanish colonial architecture in America in the 18th century.

Circle, The
A book published in London in 1937 with the subtitle "International Survey of Constructive Art." Its co-editors were J. L. Martin, Ben Nicholson, and Naum Gabo. It put forward the modern point of view on paintings, sculpture, architecture, and art education. Distinguished contributors included Piet Mondrian, Le Corbusier, Henry Moore, Barbara Hepworth, and Walter Gropius.

cire perdue
See **casting.**

classic
A description applied to any work of art of any period which is perfect of its kind; a phase in which a particular style is at its zenith.

Classical
Appertaining to the art of ancient Greece and Rome or to later works which embody its inherent qualities of harmony, symmetry, and balance.

classical abstraction
A non-spontaneous facet of abstract art in which the forms and colors are a result of rigid intellectual application and selection. The mature work of Piet Mondrian is perhaps the most renowned of this genre.

Classicism
A rather dogmatic insistence on the forms and principles derived from classical art, with subsequent restriction of the artist's individuality

(C) CHIAROSCURO

(D) CHURRIGUERESQUE

(C) CARAVAGGIO
The Supper at Emmaus, about 1600
London, National Gallery

(D) JOSÉ DE CHURRIGUERA
High Altar, 1693
Salamanca, Spain, S. Esteban

(A) CLOISONNISM

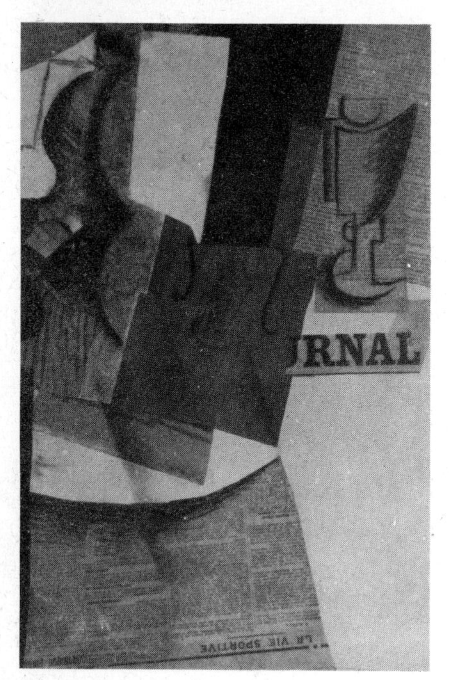

(B) COLLAGE

(A) PAUL GAUGUIN
The Vision after the Sermon—Jacob Wrestling with the Angel, 1888
Edinburgh, National Gallery of Scotland

(B) PABLO PICASSO
Detail from: The Violin, 1913
Philadelphia, Pa., Museum of Art, A. E. Gallatin Collection

and free expression. From about the mid-18th century this attitude is usually known as Neoclassicism. See also **Neoclassicism.**

Claude glass
A type of reducing glass said to have been used by Claude Lorraine. Black in color and convex in shape, it reflected the image of the sitter in miniature, simplifying appreciably the task of the artist.

Cloisonnism
From French *cloison:* "partition or wall." A style of painting evolved by Gauguin, Émile Bernard, and other painters working in Pont-Aven, Brittany, in the early 1890's. The name derives from "cloisonné" enamels. The style relinquishes effects of naturalism in favor of large areas of flat, vibrant color separated by black lines, and this, together with its two-dimensional method of painting figures, naturally stresses the importance of the decorative plane. Synthesism is closely allied to Cloisonnism. Both are linked with the Symbolist movement in painting, which in its turn is associated with the Symbolist movement in literature.

collage
From French *coller*: "to stick." A technique in which paper and other miscellaneous materials are applied to a canvas, paper, or panel to form part of or an entire picture. Picasso and other Cubists made extensive use of this technique, particularly favoring newspaper fragments. The Dadaists also used the medium. Matisse in his last years evolved a technique of composing pictures that are entirely built up of cut-out shapes of colored paper.

color circle
A circular key or color guide in which the colors of the spectrum are arranged as segments and divided into areas of warm and cool colors with the complementary colors placed opposite each other. When the circle is rotated at speed an illusion of white is obtained, white being the composite color of all the divisions of the spectrum.

columbarium
Vault constructed with recesses for cinerary urns, as in Roman catacombs. The literal meaning of the word is "dovecot" or "pigeon house," and the term was used in this sense in Roman antiquity.

commedia dell'arte
Italian comedy originating in the medieval period in which the actors improvised their dialogue within the framework of a given plot. The leading stock characters, such as Harlequin, Columbine, Pantaloon, and the Captain, have been frequently used by artists as subjects for paintings, especially during the 18th century. In later art, particularly in the late 19th and early 20th century, the emotional potential of the characters has been emphasized rather than their picturesque qualities and romanticism.

complementary colors
Two colors which when mixed in the proper proportion produce gray. The complement of one of the three primary colors (red, yellow, blue) is obtained by mixing the other two. Thus, green is the complement of red, violet the complement of yellow, and orange the complement of blue.

Constructivism
A movement that developed in Russia in the early years of the 20th century. Vladimir Tatlin was one of its chief exponents, and the movement in its Russian phase is alternatively known as Tatlinism.

The Constructivists created sculpture, relief constructions, and architectural schemes in such new materials as transparent plastic, metal tubing, sheet metal, wire, and glass. They were equally concerned with spatial conceptions and solids, the visual interaction of form and space. The use of welding in sculpture derives from this group. In 1920 there was a large Constructivist exhibition, and Antoine Pevsner and his brother Naum Gabo published their "Realistic Manifesto," which restated the Futurist claim that the important element in art is movement in space. The movement ended, for political reasons, in Russia by 1921, but some Constructivists, including Pevsner and Gabo, continued working in Western Europe.

continuous representation
A method of composition in painting in which several episodes of a story are shown together in one picture. It was a very popular form in medieval painting, being particularly suited to illustrations of the life of a saint. Although some Mannerist artists revived it, the method had virtually died with the coming of the Renaissance.

contour
The outline in drawing or painting made to indicate change of direction, variations in volume, qualities of surface, and textural differences. Contour, consequently, implies more than a simple outline, for the line itself is used to suggest these compositional factors in addition to indicating the boundary between different planes and colors. This range of uses of line in drawing is best illustrated in the work of Ingres, where contours describe intricacies of volume.

contrapposto
Italian: "opposite; antithesis." A term used to describe a posture of the body in which the hips and legs face in one direction and the torso in the opposite direction, giving an extreme twist to the pose. The device was frequently used by the Mannerists, sometimes to excess, giving an overcomplicated descrip-

tion of a comparatively straightforward movement.

conversation piece
An informally arranged painting of a genre type, consisting of several portraits of people, often in domestic surroundings and representing members of the same family. In the 18th century these paintings were sometimes large, and the term was used of informal groups. The first extensive use of the form was in 17th-century Holland, and it became particularly popular there in the 18th century.

copper engraving
See **engraving.**

Cosmati
The family name of several generations of mosaic workers, architects, and sculptors active in and around Rome in the 13th and early 14th centuries. Brightly colored, geometric types of mosaic decoration of tombs, pulpits, or cloisters are known as Cosmati work whether executed by the Cosmati family or not.

couillarde
Cézanne's *facture couillarde* denoted a manner of painting, especially in portraiture, which was first evident in his work about 1863 in a portrait of his father. It involves the use of paint in a thick, impasto style, applied to the canvas by the palette knife. The technique is to some extent derived from Courbet, but Cézanne's use and range of color is original.

Cubism
Cubism was evolved by Braque and Picasso in Paris, where a group of young painters soon adhered to the movement. These painters, taking Cézanne as their point of departure, attempted a revaluation of volume and spatial relationships in a picture as opposed to the representational values predominant in the work of the Impressionists.

Landscapes by Braque were the first Cubist paintings. Primitive art, and in particular African masks and Iberian sculpture, were a strong influence on Picasso when he painted *Les Demoiselles d'Avignon*, 1907. This picture marks a turning point in 20th-century art.

In landscape, still-life, and portraiture the Cubists attempted a detailed examination of the subject, breaking it up into facets and fragmenting it in order to give an all-round impression. Several views were thus combined and superimposed. The first Cubist exhibition took place in 1907 and was greeted with considerable public scorn.

The movement may be divided into three phases: the first phase of Analytical Cubism between 1906 and 1909; a second phase of "High" Analytical Cubism between 1909 and 1912; and a period of Synthetic Cubism between 1912 and 1914. In this last phase the image became more complex, the painters attempting to build up the picture in an intensive organization of faceted planes rather than breaking down or analyzing the subject in its multiple aspects.

cuneiform
The wedge-shaped characters used in ancient Persian, Babylonian, and Assyrian inscriptions. These characters were impressed into soft clay tablets.

cupola
A small rounded structure built on top of a roof or the roof of a lantern. See also **dome.**

Dada Movement
French: "hobby horse." A movement started in Zurich in 1916 by refugee writers and artists. Its name was chosen at random from a dictionary. Behind it lay the emotional upheaval of World War I and current theories on the substitution of an illogical order for the established, logical one, so that new truths could emerge. Dada upheld the absurd, the immediate, and the fortuitous. Tristan Tzara the poet, Jean (Hans) Arp, Frances Picabia, and Marcel Duchamp were among the leaders of this movement, which successfully set out to shock the public with nihilistic ideas of "anti-art." Dada exhibitions included ready-made objects and assemblages of unusual or incongruous materials. At a show held in Cologne in 1920, spectators were invited to smash up the exhibits, an invitation that was accepted. Dada, which lasted until about 1921, was important in paving the way for Surrealism.

Decorated Style
A phase in English Gothic architecture between about 1290 and 1350. It is typified by the decorative forms of the window tracery that became increasingly varied, with spiky network patterns and a marked curvilinear tendency. The convex/concave ogee arch is also characteristic of the Decorated Style. See also **Gothic.**

design
Either the composition (the disposition of line, mass, and other formal elements) of a finished work, or a preliminary sketch, outline, or model of it. See also **disegno.**

diablerie
From French *diable*: "devil." A picture of Hell, its demons and inmates.

diptych
A picture, often an altarpiece, consisting of two hinged panels. In 15th-century Flanders the custom arose of portraying the owner or donor on one panel looking reverently toward the Madonna on the other.

disegno
Italian: "drawing; design." When used in the latter sense, the word may have a wider implication than a purely visual one. It referred,

(C) CUBISM

(D) DECORATED STYLE

(C) PABLO PICASSO
Detail from: Les Demoiselles d'Avignon, 1907
New York, Museum of Modern Art, Lillie P. Bliss Bequest

(D) The Percy Tomb
Beverley, England, Minster

(A) DOME

(B) WOODCUT (see ENGRAVING)

(A) FILIPPO BRUNELLESCHI
The Dome, 1420-36
Florence, Cathedral

(B) ALBRECHT DÜRER
St. Jerome, 1492

particularly in the 16th century, to the Neo-Platonic idea of *disegno interno*, the perfect concept of an object, implanted by God in the artist's mind, that he endeavors to re-create.

divisionism
See **pointillism.**

dome
A vault of round or polygonal form constructed over the whole or part of a building. The external shape may be hemispherical, as in the Pantheon in Rome, or elongated, as in Florence Cathedral. The term cupola is often used synonymously for dome. See also **vault.**

drawing
The representation of an image by pen, pencil, chalk, crayon, or paint, characteristically with an emphasis on line. A drawing is usually a quick, spontaneous record of an image or emotion. It may be a preliminary step toward the production of a finished work, or a finished work in itself.

drypoint
See **engraving.**

Early English Style
The first phase of English Gothic architecture. It lasted from the latter years of the 12th century until just after 1300. This phase represents the Gothic style in its purest and simplest forms, with untraceried lancet windows, simple moldings, pointed arches, and rib vaults. See also **Gothic.**

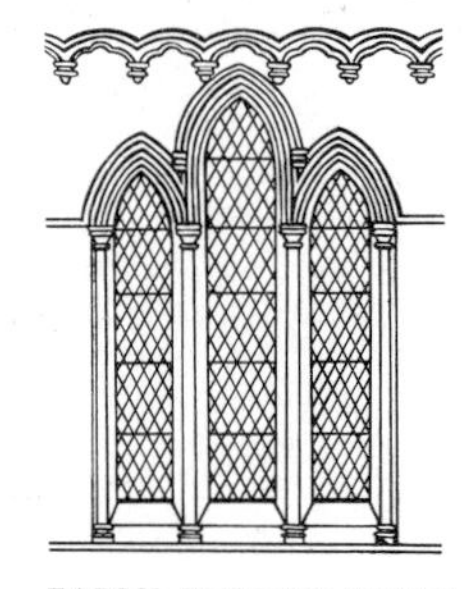

EARLY ENGLISH STYLE

earth colors
Pigments from earth containing metallic oxides. These include ocher, umber, Venetian red, and terre verte.

easel painting
A picture painted on an easel. This type of painting developed during the Renaissance, and was popularized in the 17th century as the middle-class demand for moderate sized, movable pictures increased.

eclectic
An adjective used to describe an artist who selects forms and ideas from earlier or contemporary artists, or from classical antiquity or other periods, and combines them to produce a harmonious whole. The word is now slightly derogatory.

The Eight
See **Ash Can School**

Elementarism
Theo van Doesburg began to formulate the ideas of Elementarism in 1924, but the term itself was not used until two years later, in a review in "De Stijl." It represented a divergence from Mondrian's perpendicular-horizontal Neo-Plasticism; inclined planes and diagonals were introduced in a deliberate attempt to invoke instability and surprise.

emulsion
In painting, a medium formed by a combination of oil and water, mixed by adding wax, albumen, casein, or other emulsifying agents.

encaustic painting
A technique of painting with wax on walls and other surfaces practiced in the classical world. Pigments were probably mixed with melted wax, applied to the surface, and then driven in by heating with irons. Unsuccessful attempts at reviving this technique were made in the Renaissance and again in the 19th century.

engraving
A term that properly applies only to the production of prints by intaglio processes, but is commonly extended to relief techniques. The purpose of engraving is to enable the artist to print numerous copies of a work. Each type of engraving demands a special method of printing.

Relief

This includes woodcuts and wood engravings and, in more recent times, linocuts. In the woodcut, a technique dating from the late 14th century, the block is cut with the grain. The parts intended to print white are cut away, and the remaining raised parts receive the ink. Color prints require a block for each color and a key block that shows the entire design. In wood engraving, introduced in the 18th century, the wood block is cut across the grain.

Intaglio

This type of engraving involves the use of a metal plate, generally copper. Line, or copper, engraving was the earliest intaglio technique, dating from the mid-15th century. A line of V-shaped section is cut into the metal plate with a graver. In the drypoint technique, the design is drawn on the plate with a steel stylus. The burr that turns up above the furrow adds to the textural variety of the print but is not very durable. Drypoint is sometimes combined with engraving and etching. In etching, the copper plate is covered with resin. The line is drawn on the plate with a needle, exposing the copper; the exposed parts are the ones that print. The plate is immersed in an acid bath, and the acid eats into the exposed parts. After the first brief immersion, lines required to print faintly are covered with protective varnish, and the plate is re-immersed. This process is repeated until the required range of depth of line has been achieved. Etching techniques were brought to perfection in the 17th century, especially in the hands of such masters as Rembrandt.

Mezzotints were invented in the 17th century. In this technique the plate is scratched all over with small dots. To achieve half-tones, the burrs left by the implement are scraped off, and highlights are produced by smoothing with a burnisher. The mezzotint process was the most extensively used method of reproduction in the 18th century, especially in England, where the most popular works of art were copied and circulated in large quantities. The process is now virtually extinct, its reproductive role having been taken over by mechanical photographic techniques.

Aquatint is a form of etching carried out on a ground that is porous, so that acid can be used to eat away numerous small dots of metal. The variations of depth are stopped out in the same way as in a true etching. A variety of textures can be achieved by using sulfur or sugar in the ground.

Stipple engraving is achieved by cutting dots on the surface of the prepared plate with an etching needle or with a tool (mattoir) that produces a grained effect.

In all types of intaglio the plate is inked, and then wiped off, leaving the ink in the cut-out lines. The paper is damped and placed on the plate, and great pressure is used in the process of printing.

entablature
The upper section of a classical order in architecture, made up of cornice, frieze, and architrave, and resting on columns, piers, or walls.

estipite
A pedestal or shaft in the shape of an inverted, truncated obelisk or pyramid, found particularly in decorative types of architecture in Latin America, such as Mexican churrigueresque.

etching
See **engraving**

Euston Road School
A group of painters taking their name from a London street, who worked together between 1937 and 1939. Members included Graham Bell, Victor Pasmore, William Coldstream, and Claude Rogers. They were concerned with producing a realistic type of art that ran contrary to both current abstract and Surrealist fashion.

Expressionism
In Expressionist art form, line, and color are governed by the need to express emotion; it is characterized therefore by distortion and exaggeration of form combined with marked simplification of line and strong color. Expressionistic features can be seen, for example, in German Gothic painting and sculpture.

As a movement in modern art, Expressionism dates from the early years of the 20th century and is mainly a Northern European phenomenon. Formative influences were the passionate art of van Gogh and to some extent that of the Fauves; African art, brought to European notice in the late 19th century; and the work of the Norwegian Munch. The latter's interest in graphic art in general and the woodcut in particular, and his concern with social comment, are reflected in the work of the German Expressionists. These artists formed two main groups, Die Brücke and Der Blaue Reiter. Outside Germany, Expressionist artists included the Belgian Ensor, the Russian Soutine, and the Frenchman Rouault. See also **Blaue Reiter, Der; Brücke, Die.**

faience
A general term used to describe fine, glazed earthenware whether or not it originates from Faenza, Italy, whence the name derives. It is also applied to the type of porcelain used in architectural decoration.

Fauves, Les
French: "wild beasts." A depreciatory name applied to a group of artists who first exhibited together at the Paris Salon d'Automne of 1905. The artists, who included Vlaminck, Derain, Marquet, Rouault, and Matisse, were of varied background, training, and inspiration. They never formed a really organized group, although Matisse came to be regarded as their leader. Common qualities such as strident colors, linear surface patterning, and a disregard for formal academic qualities of proportion and composition are individually interpreted. The Fauves also show affinities with German Expressionism. Other artists such as Dufy, Braque, and Metzinger later exhibited with them, but by 1908 the group was breaking up. The Fauves, with their exploitation of pure color and anti-academic precepts, hold an important place in the development of 20th-century painting.

fête champêtre
French: "rustic feast, festival or festivity." As a subject, fête champêtre can have widely differing interpretations from the homely village gatherings of Bruegel to the exotic mythological scenes of Giorgione, where the subject is used as an attractive setting for classically inspired nude figures. Watteau is another famous exponent of the theme, using it as a highly elegant and picturesque excuse for grouping together beautifully dressed people in sylvan settings.

(C) WOOD ENGRAVING (see ENGRAVING)

(D) ETCHING (see ENGRAVING)

(C) THOMAS BEWICK
Detail from: The Egret, from "Water Birds," 1804

(D) REMBRANDT VAN RYN
Detail from: Christ between the Two Thieves, 1653
London, British Museum, et al.

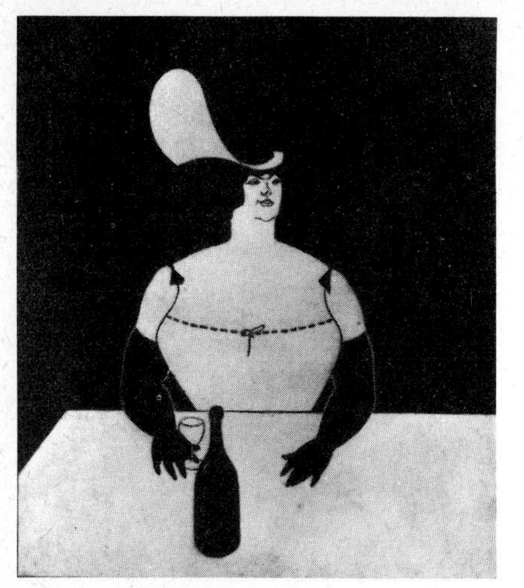

(A) FIN DE SIÈCLE

(B) SCHOOL OF FONTAINEBLEAU

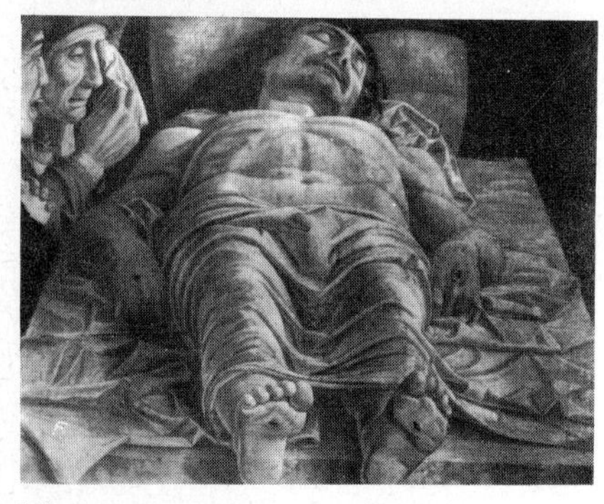

(C) FORESHORTENING

(A) AUBREY BEARDSLEY
The Fat Woman, 1894
London, Tate Gallery

(B) SCHOOL OF FONTAINEBLEAU
Danaë
Fontainebleau, Palace, Francis I Gallery

(C) ANDREA MANTEGNA
The Dead Christ, about 1506
Milan, Brera

fête galante
A genre popular in the 18th century, particularly in France, its greatest exponent being Antoine Watteau. The term applies to a variety of scenes, including concert parties, dancing, courtship, and play acting in idyllic garden or rural surroundings.

fin de siècle
French: "end of the century." A term applied to the last years of the 19th century. When used in connection with art, it evokes the highly stylized, over-sophisticated, slightly decadent atmosphere manifested in such works as the black and white drawings of Aubrey Beardsley, to which the term was applied somewhat derisively.

fixative
A varnish applied to drawings in various media to protect them from smudging.

Flamboyant Style
From Old French *flambe*: "flame." The last phase in French Gothic architecture, evident from about the middle of the 15th century. It is characterized by highly decorative, curvilinear forms, particularly in window tracery, where flame-like shapes evolve with little heed to rationality or the basic shape of the window itself. See also **Gothic.**

School of Fontainebleau
Decoration that was executed at the royal palace of Fontainebleau for Francis I from the 1530's provided the foundation for the School of Fontainebleau. This decorative system, a new fusion of painting, stucco sculpture, and architecture, is seen at its best in the Francis I Gallery at Fontainebleau. Rosso, Primaticcio, and Niccolò dell'Abbate, Italian painters called to France, were responsible for its creation, and Primaticcio was its perpetuator although his masterpiece, the Ulysses Gallery, is lost. This elegant and sophisticated style came to an end in the 1560's with the religious wars in France. The so-called second School of Fontainebleau, from about 1595, again arose out of decorative schemes which were principally in the hands of Toussaint Dubreuil (1561-1602), Ambroise Dubois (1542-3-1614), and Martin Fréminet (1567-1619). Little of their work remains, but the vault of the Chapelle de la Trinité, painted by Fréminet, 1606-14, displays decorative qualities of high order.

foreshortening
The application of perspective to a single object or figure in order to achieve a complete illusion of depth. The device was exploited from the Renaissance onwards.

found object
In Surrealist thought, some natural object found haphazardly, such as a pebble or a shell, are held to contain the aesthetic potential of a work of art, and have been exhibited, untouched, as such. If the artist intervenes and adds his skill they are known as "found objects composed" or "interpreted." The term is a translation of the French *objet trouvé.*

fresco
Italian: "fresh." Painting on wall or ceiling using a medium similar to watercolors, directly applied to the plaster. In "fresco secco," often used for details or touching up, the colors are applied to dry plaster and tend to flake off quickly. In "buon" (or "true") fresco, the colors, being painted onto damp plaster, are absorbed into the plaster or ceiling itself and remain fresh and permanent. For climatic reasons, fresco paintings deteriorate badly in Northern Europe. They are seen at their best in Italy, where they were in favor from the 14th century on, although the process dates back beyond classical antiquity. Fresco painting reached its heights in the hands of artists such as Michelangelo, Raphael, and Veronese.

frottage
From French *frotter*: "to rub." This term, meaning a rubbing, is particularly used in connection with collage pictures. The rubbing, usually made by black lead on a piece of paper placed over a textured surface such as wood or fabric, is introduced into the picture and a composition built up around it.

Futurism
An Italian art movement that attempted to evolve an art compatible with the speed of the machine age and to place the spectator in the heart of the picture. The poet Filippo Marinetti first published a Futurist Manifesto in February, 1909. During the next year, his ideas, with the help of Carlo Carrà, Umberto Boccioni, and Luigi Russolo, were applied to painting, and a general manifesto was issued. In the search for "the perpetuation of dynamic sensation," devices such as the multiplication and interpenetration of figures in movement, and dynamic diagonal lines were used. In color, the Neo-Impressionist palette is seen, as well as the gray tonalities of Cubism. The most gifted members of the movement, which virtually ended in 1915, were Gino Severini and Boccioni.

genre painting
French: "sort; variety." A type of small-scale painting showing scenes from everyday life, rather than idealized or exalted themes. Some of the ingredients of genre painting appeared in 14th and 15th-century Italian and Flemish works. It emerged as a distinct art form in the 17th century, when Dutch and Flemish masters, such as van Ostade, Brouwer, Steen, and de Hooch, painted peasant revels and domestic interiors for middle-class patrons. The tradition was continued in the 18th

century by Chardin in France, Longhi in Italy, and by Hogarth, Morland, and Gainsborough in England, and persists in many Impressionist and Post-Impressionist works. The term is also used as a synonym for "sort" or "type."

gesso
The chalk or gypsum ground used for tempera painting and for some oil painting. The absorbency of gesso being high, it was usual to prepare the surface with several layers of gesso mixed with size. Next were added numerous coats of plaster of Paris, previously soaked in water over a period to reduce its setting qualities and then tempered with size. The resulting surface was brilliantly white, smooth, and not too absorbent.

gilding
In painting, the application of gold to the surface of a picture. This was particularly popular in medieval panel painting, giving not only a sumptuous effect but also having sacred connotations. The process was to affix gold leaf to a slightly sticky surface. After setting this could be either embellished by tooling or burnished. In mordant gilding, colors were painted on top of the gold-leaf background and portions of this top paint scraped away to reveal the gold underneath. Some of the finest gilding is to be found in Sienese painting.

glaze
A translucent layer of color applied over solid oil or tempera color to give a subtle luminous effect. This technique was most widely practiced in the 16th and 17th centuries. It is seen, for example, in the works of Titian and Veronese.

Gobelins
Originally the Gobelin family of clothmakers and dyers who settled in the Faubourg Saint-Marcel, Paris, in the 15th century. Their workshop was loaned to Henry IV in 1601 for the production of tapestries. In 1662, Colbert purchased the works on behalf of Louis XIV, and under the leadership of Lebrun, the Gobelins produced not only tapestries but furniture, carpets, furnishings, and metalware. During the French Revolution, the Gobelins were closed, but were re-established by Napoleon.

Golden Mean (Golden Section)
A system of proportion formulated by Vitruvius, the Roman architect. It was considered to symbolize a universal harmony, and to possess an intrinsic aesthetic virtue. The Golden Mean often occurs as a purely instinctive proportion in works of art, but it has been consciously adhered to in periods when artists have turned to Antiquity for inspiration, as during the Renaissance. It is best represented as a line divided in such a way that the smaller part is to the larger as the larger is to the whole.

Gothic
Originally a derogatory word used during the Renaissance to describe the non-classical painting, sculpture, and architecture that had prevailed in Western Europe from the 12th to the 16th centuries, and was anachronistically described as the work of the Goths, in other words as barbaric.

Gothic art was largely dedicated to religious purposes. It is characterized by an elongation of forms that express intense religious feeling, and by brilliant color (statuary was polychromed).

Gothic architecture flourished in France, England, Germany, and neighboring countries between the 12th and 16th centuries. In each country its common characteristics were subject to local variation, but pointed arches, rib vaulting, tracery, intricately carved decoration, and a strong vertical emphasis are general. See also **Decorated Style, Early English Style, Flamboyant Style, Perpendicular Style.**

Gothic Revival
An architectural fashion much in evidence throughout the 19th century, particularly in England. It can be said to have started with Horace Walpole's house at Strawberry Hill, Middlesex, 1755, but until the 19th century, the style was mainly reserved for garden architecture and sham ruins. Gradually, Gothic features appeared in every type of private or public building, sometimes completely disguising their function. Mostly, architects would undertake commissions in the Gothic, Classic, or any other manner required by their clients, but men such as Pugin in England, Viollet-le-Duc in France, and Schinkel in Germany showed a serious and often emotional approach to the subject. Perhaps the finest example of the Gothic Revival is the Houses of Parliament, London, begun by Pugin and Charles Barry in 1836.

gouache
Watercolor mixed with white, giving the paint an opaque effect and more "body."

graffito (pl. graffiti)
Italian: "scratching." An ancient technique that became particularly popular for decorating stuccoed walls in 16th-century Italy. A coating of plaster was applied over a layer of a different color, and a design was then scratched on the top layer, revealing the color underneath. This technique is also used in decorating pottery.

Grand Manner
A manner having its origins in the High Renaissance and centered on the representation of the human figure in noble and exalted themes. The Grand Manner of painting was prescribed by the academies: the French Academy, under Lebrun, codified types of painting in order of importance, placing history painting first, and devised rules for depicting sentiments and passions.

(D) FUTURISM

(E) GOTHIC

(D) GIACOMO BALLA
Mercury Passing before the Sun as Seen through a Telescope, 1914
Milan, collection Dr. Giovanni Mattioli

(E) West Front
Amiens, France, Cathedral

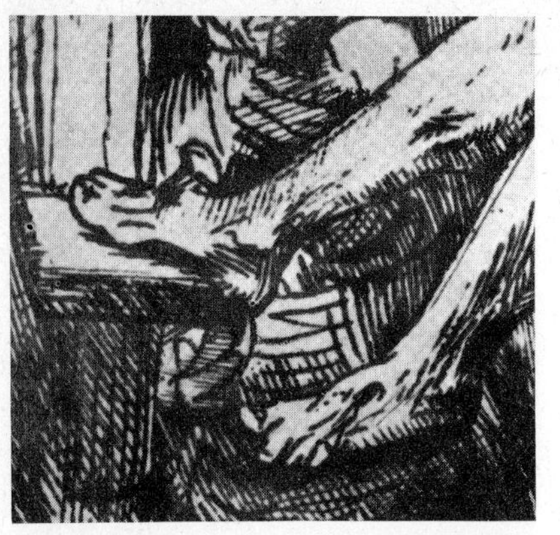

(A) HATCHING

(B) HUDSON RIVER SCHOOL

(C) ILLUSIONISM

(A) REMBRANDT VAN RYN
Detail from: The Descent from the Cross
London, British Museum, et al.

(B) THOMAS COLE
In the Catskills, 1837
New York, Metropolitan Museum of Art, Gift in memory of Jonathan Sturges

(C) GIOVANNI BATTISTA TIEPOLO
Justice and Peace
Venice, Labbia Palace

grisaille
From French *gris*: "gray." A monochrome painting in shades of gray. It was sometimes used as a preliminary to an oil painting, and also as an imitation of relief sculpture. See also **monochrome.**

grotesque
From Italian *grottesche.* A type of ornament that originated in ancient Roman grottoes. Grotesques consist of graceful, linear, scroll-like forms, often surrounding fantastic human, animal, or flower shapes. This ornamental form has continued in use since its revival in decorative work on the Vatican loggie by Raphael and his school, who were inspired by Roman examples found during excavations.

ground
The primed surface on which a painting is carried out. Canvas is sized and then generally given a coating of white lead in oil, or white lead and zinc. Gesso is used on panels. See also **gesso.**

guild
A society of tradesmen or craftsmen organized particularly for the regulation of practice and apprenticeship. Guilds were at their most powerful in the Middle Ages, when artists, being regarded as craftsmen, were normally required to join one.

hatching
Shading in drawing composed of parallel lines. Cross-hatching consists of such lines crossed by others at a right or acute angle.

highlight
Bright or intense areas of color in a painting or drawing used to model or to give emphasis to particular parts of the composition.

history painting
The representation of scenes from ancient history, or from mythology or Christian history, that portray intellectual concepts or the human passions. It was thought the highest form of painting from the Renaissance until the breakdown of the academic tradition in the 19th century. Not until the 18th century were scenes from contemporary history admitted.

hortus conclusus
Latin: "enclosed garden." A popular subject in 15th-century painting in which the Madonna and Child are seated in an enclosed paradise garden in full flower. The subject is well represented in International Gothic painting, particularly in its German manifestations.

Hudson River School
A group of American landscape painters that first concentrated its efforts on reproducing scenery around the Hudson River. The group, active from about 1825, included Thomas Cole (1801-48), Thomas Doughty (1793-1856), Asher B. Durand (1796-1886), and John W. Casilear (1811-1893). Although taking its tradition from Italian landscape artists, the group sought to capture and glorify the essence of the American landscape. The orientation of the school doubtless came from the earlier work of Washington Allston (1779-1843) and John Vanderlyn (1776-1852).

Humanism
A philosophy that places man in a central and key position. In art, from the Renaissance onwards, it is manifested in classical principles of symmetry, balance, and emotional unity, expressed in forms derived from Roman and Greek Antiquity.

icon
From Greek *ikon*: "portrait; image." Originally a panel painting of Christ or an incident from His life, or a saint. The conventions of icon painting developed early in the history of the Greek Orthodox church and remained practically unchanged for centuries.

iconoclasm
The breaking of religious images. The word originated with the controversies of the 8th and 9th centuries A.D. that sharply divided the Byzantine world on the question of images. From 730 to 787, and from 815 to 843, the representation of the figures of Christ or the saints was forbidden by law.

ideal art
Art that is concerned with the representation of material objects, not as they are perceived by the senses but as they are ideally conceived in the mind. The underlying principle is Platonic: only ideas are real, and objects seen in the natural world are no more than their imperfect images. This has led artists to attempt to realize their ideal concepts, particularly of the human figure, by selection and refinement. To this end, systems of ideal proportion were evolved in Classical Antiquity, and artists of the Renaissance and subsequent classical-inspired periods have been much concerned with these aspirations.

illumination
The decoration of manuscripts with embellished initials, patterns, or illustrations of the text. The art dates back at least to classical antiquity. It was greatly developed in 7th-century monasteries, and persisted throughout the Middle Ages in Europe, declining and dying out with the decay of monastic life and the invention of printing. Illumination was carried out on vellum.

illusionism
In art, painting in which the element of optical illusion is exploited. In a limited way, it is found in late antique Roman painting. The Renaissance saw its real emergence, how-

ever, and during the 17th and 18th centuries illusionism was at its most popular. Painted surfaces can be made to represent costly materials such as marble or onyx; false architecture, especially colonnades, can appear to extend the space of a room. Ceilings in which the vault appears to be removed and the sky to show through or lifelike figures which people the imaginary spaces, are examples of illusionism in art brought about by skillful use of perspective, foreshortening, light, and color. Illusionistic painting applied to still-life objects is usually known as *trompe l'œil*. See also **trompe l'œil.**

impasto
Italian: "mixture; thick color." Paint applied thickly to a canvas or panel, often with palette knife rather than a brush.

Impressionism
The most important art movement in the 19th century. It represented the final development of Realism in France and provided a starting point for modern art. Impressionism grew out of a desire to paint things as they are actually seen, and to record the effects of light and atmosphere on an object. The work of Constable, the Barbizon School, of Delacroix, Courbet, Boudin, Jongkind, and Manet inspired the young painters who created this style. The color theories of Delacroix and of the scientist Chevreul stimulated the Impressionists' interest in color and their investigation of the properties of shadows, of light on water or snow. To achieve the shimmering effects of light they applied paint in small dashes of pure color; they eliminated blacks and browns from their palette. Their rejection of the conventional line drawn round objects, and the freedom with which they drew forms, aroused violent criticism and opposition from the public and most critics.

In 1874 Monet, Pissarro, Sisley, Renoir, Cézanne, Degas, Morisot, and others held their first group exhibition. The name Impressionism, used derisively by the critics, was derived from the title of Monet's *Impression: Sunrise*. Six other group shows were held between 1876 and 1886. Degas and Cézanne were never Impressionists in the strict sense of the word, and Manet, although associated with them, did not participate in the shows.

India (or Indian) ink
An ink from the Far East which is comprised of a mixture of lamp black and gum. It has the advantage of being waterproof. It is mostly found in calligraphic work or in pen drawing.

indigo
A deep, intense blue dye obtained from various *indigofera* plants. It was used both as a pigment for painting and as a fabric dye from the 16th century, but has latterly tended to be replaced by synthetic dyes. Its great drawback, particularly in the oil medium, is that it is not entirely stable.

intaglio
Engraving processes in which the lines are cut into the printing surface. See **engraving.**

International Gothic
A painting style that spread through much of Europe toward the end of the 14th century. It combined a new realism in the treatment of details, such as landscape, costume, and everyday objects, with the essentially nonrealistic Gothic principles of form, design, and composition. The style first appeared at the courts of Burgundy and France; in Italy it was practiced simultaneously with the new realism of Masaccio.

Intimisme
Vuillard and Bonnard, with certain other Nabis, reacted against a type of neoclassical mysticism advocated by Sérusier, and developed Intimisme, a type of Impressionism applied to quiet, domestic genre scenes. See also **Nabis, Les.**

Italianate
In the style of the Italian masters. The adjective is applied particularly to artists of Northern Europe who, during the Renaissance and the 17th century, picked up and used Italian motifs and methods in their work without necessarily understanding the true principles of Italian painting.

Jugendstil
German :"Youth Style." A term derived from a magazine "Jugend" founded in Munich in January, 1896. It was the name given to the German and Austrian version of the Art Nouveau movement that swept Europe in the late 19th century. This essentially decorative style, which found its best expression and application in architecture and interior decoration, was based on curvilinear forms from naturalistic sources such as plants, trees, flowers, and animals. Jugendstil was a sophisticated manner which perhaps found its best outlet in prosperous, cosmopolitan Vienna at the turn of the century, where its leader, Gustav Klimt (1862-1918), displayed the new style in his decoration of the university from 1900 to 1903. The rhythmic linear patterning and forms can easily be discerned also in the early work of Munch, Hodler, and Kokoschka. See also **Art Nouveau.**

kakemono
A Japanese word for pictures in the form of a scroll. They have a small stick at top and bottom and can be hung from the wall, or rolled up when not in use.

(D) IMPRESSIONISM

(E) INTERNATIONAL GOTHIC

(D) CLAUDE MONET
Rouen Cathedral, 1894
Paris, Musée de l'Impressionnisme

(E) THE LIMBOURG BROTHERS
April: from the Très Riches Heures du Duc de Berri, begun 1415
Chantilly, France, Musée Condé

(A) LITHOGRAPHY

(B) MAESTÀ

(A) PABLO PICASSO
Face, 1928

(B) CIMABUE
Maestà (upper portion)
Florence, Uffizi

kakemono-ye
Japanese wood-block prints of approximately 28 × 10 in. with vertical compositions. For those with horizontal compositions, the term *makemono* is used. Smaller vertical prints, roughly 11 × 8 in. are known as *chuban.* A still smaller variety, about 8 × 7 in., again read vertically, is termed *kōban.*

Kitchen Sink School
The modern school of realistic painting which sees, as A. Clutton-Brock put it, "the casual and even repellent circumstances of everyday life as a fit theme for painting." No object is too humble as a subject for painting, even the kitchen sink itself, and it is a challenge to endow such "arid products of a modern mechanical process" with a life and dynamism of their own. John Bratby is the most successful exponent of this type of art.

kōban
See **kakemono-ye.**

kouros (pl. kouroi)
Figures of young men in archaic Greek sculpture or architectural decoration.

kwacho
A Japanese picture having as its subject matter birds and flowers.

landscape
The date of the earliest independent landscape painting is debated, although an awareness of landscape, and the desire to reproduce it in art as a background, goes back at least as far as the Greek civilization. Throughout the Middle Ages, landscape remained a background to other themes. Although Leonardo gave great importance to the study of natural features and the depiction of aerial perspective, it is not until the time of the Dutch 17th-century landscape painters that it really emerges as an independent subject. Since then on, many theories and techniques have been evolved to capture natural features in the ever-changing conditions of air, light, or weather.

Les XX (Les Vingt)
French: "The Twenty." In 1883, a group of 20 young Belgian painters and sculptors, whose work had been refused for official exhibitions, joined together under the leadership of a Belgian lawyer and art critic, Octave Maus. From 1884, they held annual exhibitions in Brussels of their own and foreign artists' work, and they were a vital force in putting avant-garde art before the public. Rodin, Whistler, Gauguin, van Gogh, Toulouse-Lautrec, Cézanne, Redon, and Ensor are a few of the famous artists who exhibited with them. The group, which lasted until 1893, had as its mouthpiece the review "L'Art Moderne," edited by Maus.

limning
Miniature painting, particularly portraiture. An archaic term that has been revived.

linear perspective
See **perspective.**

lithography
A printing process in which the design is drawn on to stone or metal with a crayon or greasy chalk. Water is applied to the surface, dampening the blank areas, but not the crayoned design. Greasy ink is applied which adheres to the design only. Prints by this process, which was invented in the late 18th century, resemble pencil or crayon drawings.

local color
The basic color of an object uninfluenced by the changes that take place under varying conditions of light, atmosphere, distance, or reflection.

loggia (pl. loggie)
Italian: "gallery; lodge; balcony." A gallery, portico, balcony, or veranda that is open on at least one side.

London Group
A still-extant group that originated in 1913, representing an amalgamation of the Camden Town Group and others such as the Vorticists. Its scope is wide, embracing all forms of non-academic painting and sculpture, and having only quality as its criterion. Its exhibitions, in which non-members are allowed to take part, are held regularly in London. Famous names associated with the group have been Walter Sickert, Lucien Pissarro, Harold Gilman (the first president), Augustus John, Vanessa Bell, Paul Nash, and Jacob Epstein.

luminosity
In art, an effect often obtained by the painting of tinted glazes over lighter foundations, so that the surface thus treated has the quality of emitting light rather than reflecting or absorbing it.

lunette
A round or roundarched aperture in a vaulted ceiling, dome, or roof. It may be filled with glass or decorated with painting or sculpture.

Maestà
A representation of the Virgin and Child, seated in majesty upon a throne and surrounded by angels or saints. This subject was particularly favored in 13th and 14th-century Italian art.

makemono
See **kakemono-ye.**

malerisch
German: "painterly; in a painterly manner." A term first employed by the critic Wölffin to

indicate the type of painting which is concerned with expressing form by color and light rather than by outline, eliminating hard edges to objects and achieving a rhythmic and tonal unity. Rubens, Rembrandt, and Velázquez manifest this quality in their highly individual ways.

manichino
Italian: "little man." The lay figure or dummy used by artists to assist them in figure compositions. It is also applied to the strange, puppet-like figures in the work of the Metaphysical painters. See also **Pittura Metafisica.**

Mannerism
The name now applied to a style of art that flourished between the High Renaissance and the Baroque, from about 1520 to 1600. Seen in the early stages as a reaction against the classical rules of proportion, symmetry, and perspective implicit in High Renaissance art, Mannerism became, during the second half of the 16th century, a highly sophisticated, decorative art much favored by the courts. Its spread outside Italy was precipitated by Francis I of France who, in 1530, employed many Italian artists in the decoration of the Château of Fontainebleau, and by Flemish and Dutch artists who went to Florence, Rome, and Mantua (the primary centers of Mannerism) and took the style back with them to their own countries. Mannerist artists include Rosso, Primaticcio, Pontormo, Giulio Romano, Parmigianino, Cellini, Vasari, Tintoretto, El Greco, and, the greatest single influence of all in the style, Michelangelo.

medals
Although commemorative medals were much in favor in ancient Rome, their revival dates from the late 14th century. Some of the finest were created during the 15th century in Italy by Pisanello. About the middle of that century, a successful German school grew up to which Dürer later made important contributions. Gold, silver, bronze, copper, and alloys are all used for medals. Until the 16th century, medals were usually cast by the *cire perdue* method. Later they were struck from engraved dies; this process was used in antiquity.

medium
The liquid, such as egg yolk, linseed oil, or gum arabic, with which powdered pigments are mixed to form a paint; an addition to paint to make it flow more easily; the material employed by the artist, as for example oil, tempera, or watercolor medium.

memento mori
Latin: "remember you must die." A motif, such as a skull, hour-glass, or candle, allegorically used to emphasize the mortal condition of man. It is commonly seen in the art of Northern Europe, especially Germany, and was one of the sources from which still-life painting derived.

Merz
The purely chance name given by Kurt Schwitters in 1920 to a variant on Dadaism. It was applied to works of art that depended not upon form but upon the crowding together of diverse waste materials such as bus tickets, cardboard, nails and so on, in an attempt to create a new order of reality. Four years later, Schwitters extended his ideas to sculpture and produced constructions which he called *Merzbauten*. See also **Dada.**

mezzotint
See **engraving.**

miniature
A painting on a very small scale, generally a head and shoulder portrait but occasionally a full-length figure, that has its origins in medieval manuscript illumination. 16th-century miniatures were usually painted in watercolor pigment on parchment or on small pieces of playing cards. During the 18th century, ivory replaced parchment as the support; it could be left white or backed with silver or color. Although watercolor is most often used, miniatures are sometimes executed in oils, particularly when the support is metal.

mirror painting
Painting executed on the back of a mirror. The coating is scraped from the areas of the design, and the colors applied in the spaces left. Although many mirror paintings were produced in China, the technique was originally Western.

mobile
A form of movable sculpture invented by Alexander Calder in 1932, constructed from a wide variety of materials, including metal sheets, wire, rods, glass, and plastics. Mobiles consist of sculptured forms linked together, usually by wires or rods, which can be set in motion by a touch, or by currents of air.

modeling
In sculpture, the building-up of forms, usually in clay or wax, as distinct from carving. In painting, or low relief sculpture, the achievement of a three-dimensional solidity of forms by use of colors, light, mass, and void.

modello (modelletto)
Italian: "model." A small picture intended by the artist for his patron to give the latter an idea of the finished work. Some modelli, which often reach a high artistic standard, are invaluable historically, showing the original intention of the artist.

(C) MINIATURE

(D) MOBILE

(C) NICHOLAS HILLIARD
Self-portrait, 1577
London, Victoria and Albert Museum

(D) ALEXANDER CALDER
The Black Crescent, 1960
Toronto, Art Gallery, Gift of Mr. and Mrs. H. R. Jackman

(A) MOSÂIC

(A) Detail from: La Primavera
Rome, Museo Nazionale Romano

monochrome (monotone)
A painting in tones of one color only. See also **grisaille.**

monotype, monoprint
A single print taken from a copper plate on which a design has been painted in printer's ink or oil colors. By printing, the design acquires additional qualities of texture, but only one satisfactory impression can be taken.

montage
The placing of materials or pictures in overlapping or adjoining layers to form a new picture or design. When confined to photographs it is known as photomontage. See also **collage.**

monumental
A term used frequently in art criticism to indicate a work that, regardless of size or period, has a nobility and grandeur of conception, and the qualities of balance, simplicity, and permanence inherent in great architecture.

Moorish art
Moorish art, because of the complex origins of the Moors from Mauritania, the North Sudan, Morocco and elsewhere, takes its forms from various cultures, and is in itself a part of Muslim art. The Moorish conquest of Spain in the 11th century brought about the Hispano-Mauresque style which is the most important phase of the art. Its outstanding feature is overall decoration that takes complete precedence over structural form. Stone and brick are used in construction, but these are more generally patterned all over externally and internally. Walls are covered with stucco decoration and brilliantly colored designs, often composed of arabesque motifs. A dado of colored tiles is also usual. Other typical features include the horse-shoe shaped arch, often with cuspings; slender columns with very fine, complex carvings; and twin-opening windows. Wood carving in these intricate patternings is also found in Moorish art. The finest extant example is the 14th-century Alhambra Palace of Granada, Spain.

mosaic
A method of decoration used for walls, vaults, and floors from ancient times. It involves the use of tesserae, small cubes of colored glass, stone, marble, or enamel, set into cement. Mosaic design is essentially flat and linear with pronounced outlines. Animation is achieved by the play of light on the edges of the tesserae, which are deliberately set unevenly for this purpose.

mosque
The place for public Muslim worship corresponding to a Christian church. Its history as a building goes back to 622 A.D. when the Prophet Muhammad built the first example at Medina, Arabia. Mosques vary widely, but all must include an enclosed space for prayers which can be open or covered, a niche (*mihrab*) in one wall to indicate the direction of Mecca, and a minaret from which comes the summons to prayer.

motif
The theme or subject of a picture; in architecture, a recurrent or predominant form usually setting the design or style of the whole.

Mozarabic architecture
Church architecture of Northern Spain dating mainly from the 10th century, the work of Christian builders who had been influenced by Moorish practice. It has many manifestations, the most important being the basilicas found near the town of León. The style, which was much influenced by the architecture of the mosque at Cordova, includes such features as the horseshoe arch, horseshoe-shaped sanctuaries, and ribless "melon" domes.

The term Mudejar is applied to Moorish-influenced art and architecture in Northern Spain, the work of either Christian or Moorish artisans.

mural
The painted decoration of a wall, whether carried out directly on its surface or on panel or canvas and afterwards attached to the wall.

Musicalists
Founded by Henry Valensi in the 1920's, the "Association des Artistes Musicalistes" is a group that still holds exhibitions in Paris. The Musicalists' theory is that music can be translated into abstract painting by a co-ordination of color, line, and rhythm.

Nabis, Les
Derived from the Hebrew word for "prophet," the name given by the poet Cazalis to a group of painters active from about 1889 to 1899. In their painting, which was influenced by the flat, pure color technique of Gauguin, they sought to combine the distortion inherent in purely aesthetic, decorative, and color concepts, and the distortion of the personal perception of the artist. The scope of their work was wide, embracing book illustrations, posters, lithography, and stained glass, as well as both easel and tempera painting.

The Nabis were closely related to the Symbolist movement in literature and art, and their development was markedly in reaction to the naturalist approach of the Impressionist painters.

naga-ye
See **kakemono-ye.**

naturalism
A quality in painting in which objects are singled out and reproduced as closely as

possible to their actual form, that is, in contradiction to the visual form that they may *appear* to have, particularly in relation to their surroundings. The effect of such painting is likely to be less realistic than one in which the reality of the whole, rather than individual parts of it, has been sought. This quality is evident in 15th-century Flemish painting.

nave

In longitudinal churches, the main body of the church extending from the west wall to the crossing. In basilican churches, the nave is flanked by aisles, usually lower in height. Lighting is normally by clerestory windows. The nave has its origins in the Roman basilica hall.

Nazarenes, The

Two young German painters, Overbeck and Pforr, founded the *Lukasbrüder* (Brothers of St. Luke) in Vienna in 1809. The aim of this semireligious order was to emulate the earnestness of Dürer, Perugino, and the early Raphael, and thus achieve a spiritual renewal of German art. In 1810 they went to Rome, and a group of painters, including Cornelius, formed around them. They collaborated in the medieval manner on decorative schemes for the Casa Massimo. As a result of their activities they were dubbed *Nazarener* by their fellow-countrymen. The English Pre-Raphaelite Brotherhood was influenced by their ideals, and Ingres by their style.

N.E.A.C.

Abbreviation for the New English Art Club, a group founded in 1886 (and still extant) to oppose traditional theories and conventionalism as practiced by the Royal Academy. The artists, led by Sargent, had mostly studied and worked in Paris and were much influenced by contemporary French painting and practice. Other distinguished names associated with the Club include Sickert, Steer, and Whistler. From this foundation sprang forward-looking associations, such as the London Impressionists, the Camden Town Group, the Vorticists, and the London Group.

Neoclassicism

A style of art that consciously seeks to emulate the principles and forms of antique Classical art. It is particularly applied to the style that swept across Europe and the United States during the late 18th and early 19th centuries. This tendency was doubtless precipitated by excavations and discoveries of new works of antique art in Greece and Rome, which were then taking place with great frequency. Leading exponents include Canova, Thorvaldsen, David, Ingres, Flaxman, Mengs, and Powers.

Neo-Impressionism

A movement in painting which first appeared in Paris in 1884. Deriving its theories from the science of optics, the technique of "pointillism" was evolved. This consisted in the application of small dots of pure color to the canvas so that the final fusion takes place in the eye of the viewer. The strictly formal methods of composition used were equally scientific. The new style relates to Impressionism in that its theories involved a knowledge of and exploitation of complementary colors, and the dividing of colors into their components. Its scientific, formal approach and static composition have, however, little in common with the fleeting, transitory quality of Impressionism. The founder of the movement was Georges Seurat, who was quickly joined by Paul Signac and Camille Pissarro. Van Gogh, Gauguin, and Toulouse-Lautrec were among the artists influenced by Neo-Impressionism. Seurat's untimely death, in 1891, was probably responsible for the comparatively short life of the movement, although it was continued by followers such as Signac, Henri Edmond Cross, and Maximilien Luce.

Neo-Plasticism

A theory and practice of pure geometric-abstract painting that took its name from Piet Mondrian's "Le Néo-Plasticisme," published in Paris in 1920. An austere development of Cubism, Neo-Plasticism is characterized by rigid adherence to the primary colors of red, yellow, and blue combined with the so-called "noncolors," black, white, and gray; by geometric compositions based exclusively on the rectangle; by an insistence on two-dimensional painting. Theo van Doesburg was Mondrian's most gifted follower until 1924, when his deviation into Elementarism first began to be evident. The mouthpiece of the movement was the Dutch review "De Stijl." Mondrian continued with this doctrine of pure plastic art until his death in 1944. See also **Elementarism**; **Stijl, De.**

Neo-Romanticism

In general, tendencies in art related in some way to the Romantic movement which swept Europe in the early 19th century. The term does not indicate any one group or movement, but is applied freely to artists whose work expresses the feelings aroused in them by natural phenomena. Perhaps because of native temperament, Neo-Romanticism is applied most frequently to British painters of various styles and periods as, for example, Palmer, Paul Nash, Michael Ayrton, and Graham Sutherland.

Neue Sachlichkeit

A German phrase, best translated as "New Objectivity." A movement that arose in Germany in reaction against Expressionism about 1920. Objects which had, in Impressionist painting, tended to lose their real form were now given greater importance in themselves by detailed and realistic treatment. The intensity of mood of Expressionism was not les-

(B) NEO-IMPRESSIONISM

(C) NEO-ROMANTICISM

(B) GEORGES SEURAT
Detail from: The Seine at Courbevoie, about 1887
Brussels, Musées Royaux des Beaux-Arts

(C) GRAHAM SUTHERLAND
Entrance to a Lane, 1935
London, Tate Gallery

(A) NOCTURNE

(B) NORWICH SCHOOL

(C) ORPHISM

(A) JAMES ABBOT MCNEILL WHISTLER
Nocturne – Black and Gold: The Fire Wheel, about 1870
London, Tate Gallery

(B) JOHN SELL COTMAN
The Drop Gate, about 1828
London, Tate Gallery

(C) ROBERT DELAUNAY
Circular Forms, 1912
New York, Solomon R. Guggenheim Museum Collection

sened in the new movement, but found its outlet in almost clinical observation of detail rather than in emotion. Although New Objectivity did not have a long life, certain of its elements are to be seen in Surrealism. Otto Dix, Georg Grosz, and the early Max Beckmann are among the best-known exponents of the theory.

Neue Sezession
German: "New Secession." One of a number of Secession Movements in Germany and Austria during the late 19th and early 20th centuries. The Neue Sezession was a protest group led by Max Pechstein whose work had been refused for exhibition by the Berlin Sezession group in 1910. Its members held their own exhibitions, displaying a variety of post-Impressionistic styles. A number of important artists showed an interest in the Movement, for example, Kandinsky, Marc, and Jawlensky. Others included Klein, Berger, Melzer, Tappert, and the future Die Brücke, group members, Kirchner, Schmidt-Rottluff, Heckel, as well as Pechstein himself. When these latter members broke away in 1912, the Neue Sezession virtually came to an end. See also **Sezession.**

nocturne
The title given by Whistler to certain of his paintings in which an impression of an actual scene at night or in evening light was built up through a series of color harmonies. In using this type of title he was deliberately reacting against the Victorian taste for the predominance of subject matter in painting.

Norman Style
The name given to the Romanesque style in England, where it was introduced by the Norman conquerors after their invasion of 1066. The Normans built many great churches and cathedrals, often replacing earlier Anglo-Saxon work, and constructed castles. Characteristics of Norman architecture include rounded arches, massive supports and masonry, and plain or geometrically carved capitals. Many English cathedrals still have Norman parts, the most striking being that of Durham, which dates from 1093.

Norwich School
A school of painting centered around Norwich, England, that arose from the Norwich Society formed in 1803 by John Crome and his friends. The group began exhibiting in 1805, and two years later John Cotman became a leading member. The school is particularly famous for its fresh rendering of the rather flat East Anglian landscape, and innumerable examples of its painting exist in private and public collections in the area, particularly in Norwich Museum. Other artists associated with the Norwich School include Ladbrooke, Stannard, Vincent, Thirtle, and Stark.

ocher
One of the oldest pigments in painting (its use dates from prehistoric times) ocher is found in silica and clay mixtures containing iron oxide. In color it ranges from yellow, through russet, to brown, including countless gradations of these. The pigment is cheap to produce and stable and permanent.

oeuvre
French: "work; task; performance." The entire production of works achieved by a painter, sculptor, or architect during his lifetime.

oil paint
Paint in which the ground pigment is mixed with a binding agent of oil. The usual agents are linseed, poppy, or nut oil, or volatile oils extracted from mineral or plant substances, such as petroleum or turpentine. The earliest paintings executed entirely in oil paint date from the beginning of the 16th century.

Op art
A type of abstract art with flatly painted, carefully defined patterns that produce predetermined optical responses in the viewer. The name comes from the word "optical." Op art has a vibrant, pulsing effect. It emerged as a distinct type about 1964.

optical mixtures
Colors placed on the canvas so that they mix in the eye of the spectator. According to the theory of optical mixtures, a purer, brighter secondary color may be obtained by placing yellow and blue on the canvas than by mixing them on the palette. Optical mixtures were much used by the Impressionists and even more by the Neo-Impressionists.

orant
A praying figure with outstretched arms, common in classical and early Christian art.

orders
In architecture, the relative proportions of entablatures, capitals, columns, and bases; the five architectural orders, namely the original Greek, Doric, Ionic, and Corinthian, and the later Tuscan and Composite, whose use in conjunction with each other is governed by rules of relative positioning, proportion, and decoration.

Orphism (Orphic Cubism)
A facet of Cubism based on the theory of pure color as the most important factor in painting, thus negating the value of form. The poet Guillaume Apollinaire was responsible for the name. At a lecture he gave in 1912, he invoked the name of Orpheus and compared the games that delighted the god to the experiments of Robert Delaunay and Frank Kupka, the leaders of Orphism. Their ideas were fundamental to non-representational, abstract art.

outdoor painting
Painting out of doors was little practiced before the 17th century, although many features of landscape and natural objects in earlier works were based on direct observation, and brilliant outdoor scenes are found in the sketches of Dürer. John Constable (1776-1837), however, was the first artist to go out into the open air and deliberately try to capture the ever-changing aspect of scenery under out-of-door conditions of light, weather, and atmosphere, but even he adhered to the system of constructing in his studio the large, landscape picture based on his small, spontaneous oil sketches. The Impressionists on the whole worked in the open air. Inevitably, however, much work must be done in the studio, and a great deal of improvisation is necessary even when working out of doors, since the aspect of nature is in a state of perpetual change and motion. The feeling of the outdoor world is captured with passionate intensity in the work of van Gogh. See also **plein air.**

pagoda
A tower found in China, Japan, Burma, and other Asian countries, usually in Buddhist sanctuaries. Generally a shrine for sacred relics, it is built in the form of several diminishing stages, each with its own projecting roof. The structure is often lavishly carved, painted, and gilded. Buildings in pagoda style are sometimes used as garden architecture.

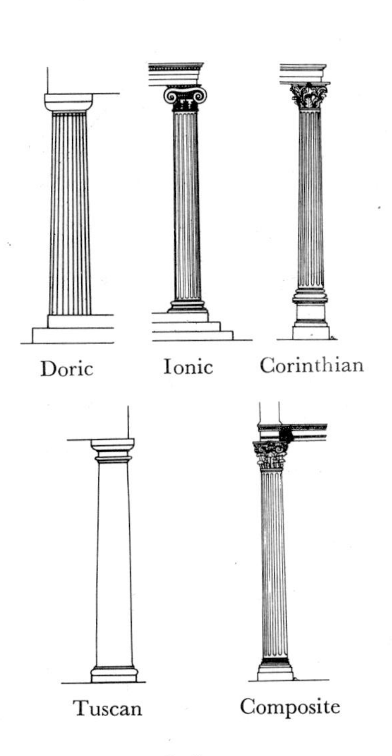

Orders

painterly
See **malerisch.**

palette
A piece of thin wood used by artists for setting out paints and mixing colors; the range of colors favored by a particular artist, group, or school.

panorama
A pictorial representation of a landscape or other extensive view in continuous form. This is most effectively achieved in a circular or cylindrical-shaped space with the spectator standing in the center, the circle varying from 60 to 130 feet in diameter. Carefully arranged lighting and the introduction of painted objects between the spectator and the scene assist this illusionistic art. Robert Barker actually produced the first example in Edinburgh in 1788. A century later it became popular in Europe. Varied scenes, especially of battles, were created. Artists well known in this field include Henri and Paul Philippoteaux, Ludwig Braun, and Anton von Werner.

Panoramists
A term sometimes applied to painters in the United States who, about the middle of the 19th century, began to produce very wide landscape pictures to convey the sweep and grandeur of Western scenery, especially the Rocky Mountains. The most renowned artists in this field were Albert Bierstadt (1830-1902), and Thomas Moran (1837-1926).

pantheon
A word of Greek origin meaning a temple dedicated to "all the gods." The most famous is at Rome, built by Hadrian in 120-124 A.D. on the site of an earlier temple. The form of its great rotunda and portico has attracted architects through the ages, and inspired various "pantheons." One example is the Panthéon, 1757-90, in Paris, built as Ste. Geneviève, secularized in 1791, and dedicated to the illustrious men of France.

papier collé
French: "pasted paper." A term applied to the later Cubist methods of pasting pieces of paper – newspaper, cardboard, colored paper, tickets – into a pictorial composition, sometimes linking them together by painting or drawing. See also **collage.**

pastels
Powdered pigments mixed with a small quantity of gum arabic, as a binder, and made up into small sticks. The colors are permanent, but unless the paper surface is treated with a fixative, it can easily become smudged. When used thickly, pastels give the effect of soft, velvety painting. They are equally effective when used for drawing, as in the manner of charcoal, for example. Works in this medium are themselves known as pastels. The word can also be used to describe pale, light colors.

(D) PAGODA

(E) PANORAMISTS

(D) The Shoay Dagone Pagoda
Rangoon, Burma

(E) ALBERT BIERSTADT
Thunderstorm in the Rocky Mountains
1859
Boston, Mass., Museum of Fine Arts

(A) PERSPECTIVE (LINEAR)

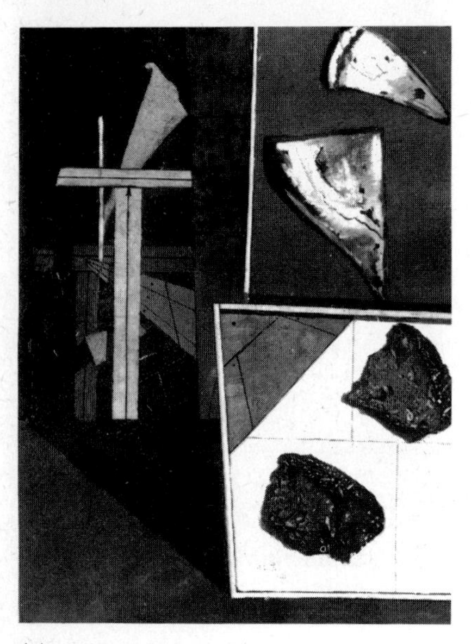

(B) PITTURA METAFISICA

(A) MEINDERT HOBBEMA
The Avenue at Middelharnis, 1689
(showing perspective lines)
London, National Gallery

(B) GIORGIO DE' CHIRICO
Metaphysical Interior, 1917
New York, collection William N. Copley

pastiche
French: "imitation; copy." A fake or imitation in which motifs are assembled from a number of a particular artist's works, and formed into a picture which purports to be an original creation by the master; a work of art in an acknowledgedly borrowed style. *Pasticcio* is an Italian word of similar meaning.

patina
A green film that forms on the surface of bronze after it has been exposed to the air for some time. By extension, the word has also come to signify atmospheric surface effects on other substances, such as marble or stone, and sometimes the old dirt and varnish on a painting.

pendentive
The triangular area of vaulting that forms the transition from the corners of a rectangular building to its rounded or polygonal dome.

Perpendicular Style
In England, the third and final phase of Gothic architecture that developed in the second half of the 14th century. It is characterized by a marked vertical stress, flattening of window arches, and by outside walls with an unprecedentedly large window area. See also **Gothic.**

perspective
A mechanical system of depicting objects in a three-dimensional fashion on a flat, two-dimensional surface. The ability to create an illusion of recession and depth beyond the picture plane was first scientifically formulated during the Renaissance, probably by Brunelleschi. During this period several perspective systems were evolved, and painters such as Uccello, Piero della Francesca, and Leonardo were concerned with extremely detailed aspects of the subject.

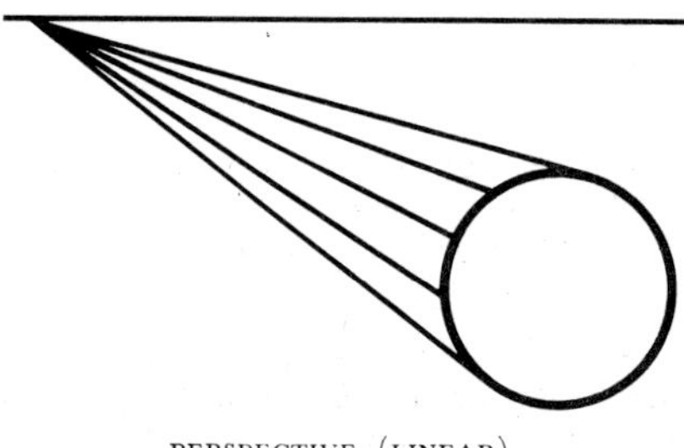

PERSPECTIVE (LINEAR)

Linear perspective is a form of radial projection, based on the cone of vision. It is used to show the appearance and apparent size of an object. All the rays of light that enter the eye from the viewed object are considered as forming a cone of which the eye is the vertex. The lines of natural objects parallel to the direct radial appear to meet at the center of vision, or vanishing point. The flat surface of the painting is the picture plane. Sometimes correctly constructed perspective can lead to unsatisfactory visual appearances and has to be modified accordingly. Large surfaces may contain areas that are outside the cone of vision and visually distorted. This could be overcome by the use of a traveling vanishing point.

Aerial, or atmospheric, perspective, is based not on a geometrical system, but on the handling of tone and color. Paler and cooler colors are placed in the distance, increasing in richness and warmth through the middle distance to the foreground.

Linear perspective occurs in a rudimentary form in Greek and Roman painting. After the Renaissance it is accepted in European art until the mid-19th century; Courbet, the Impressionists, and Cézanne rejected it to varying degrees; in the 20th century, Renaissance perspective is used only in academic works. Traditional Oriental art did not generally make use of linear or aerial perspective.

piazza
Italian: "city square; place." In Italy, a formal, open space, not necessarily square in shape, which is surrounded by buildings. The French *place* is synonymous.

pictograph
A pictorial representation that symbolizes an object or idea. Pictographic writing, the oldest form known, is composed of a succession of pictures.

picture plane
The plane formed by the actual surface of a picture. Some artists, particularly in 17th-century Baroque painting, sought deliberately to bridge the gap between the artificial representation of space on the two-dimensional picture plane and the real world around it by strategically placed figures or objects. Abstract art, on the whole, re-asserts the importance of the picture plane.

pietà
Italian: "compassion; pity." A picture or sculpture of the Virgin holding the dead Christ. The form first appeared in 14th-century Germany and became popular throughout Europe.

pigment
Prepared coloring matter which, when used with a binding agent such as oil or egg yolk, forms a paint.

Pittura Metafisica
Italian: "metaphysical painting." A style in painting that was an important factor in the formation of Surrealist art. Giorgio de' Chirico had been working for some time in this direction, but it was after his meeting with Carlo

Carrà at Ferrara in 1917 that the style finally emerged. The paintings are characterized by deserted settings, lonely people without faces, and ordinary, even despised, objects endowed with strange power and personality of their own. As in dreams, forms are remarkably clear-cut and direct, but always imply the mysterious and inexplicable. Colors are flat and usually vivid.

plasticity
In painting or drawing a use of tonal contrasts and spatial organization to achieve the illusion of three-dimensional forms. In sculpture and similar three-dimensional art, it implies a flexible, pliant quality.

Plateresque
From Spanish *platero*: "silversmith." A style of architecture and ornament found in Spain that developed in the first half of the 16th century. Basic structures were simple, but smothered with decorative motifs taken from Moorish, Gothic, and Renaissance sources. The results were more reminiscent of the intricacies of silversmiths' work than of architecture. At the end of the 17th century there appeared a revival of the style, often termed Neo-Plateresque.

plein air
French: "open air." The capture of the actual feeling of the outdoor world, rather than the mere, physical fact of the artist having executed his painting there. Artists as diverse as Constable, Corot, van Gogh, for example, all achieved this quality in their work. See also **outdoor painting.**

pochade
A small sketch usually made in oils in the open air, and often used later as a basis for a large, formal landscape. Almost all of Constable's paintings were prepared in this way.

Pointillism
The technique favored by the Neo-Impressionists, consisting of small dots or strokes of pure color whose position on the canvas was so calculated that the final fusion of color and form took place in the eye of the spectator. The technique is also known as Divisionism. See also **Neo-Impressionism, optical mixtures.**

polychrome sculpture
Sculpture, usually of wood or stone, which is painted in naturalistic colors after being carved. This practice, which to modern eyes is somewhat garish, was usual before the 16th century in Europe. It continued in some countries, such as Spain, well into the 17th century and even later.

polyptych
Paintings or relief sculpture, most commonly used as altarpieces, that consist of more that three panels.

Pop art
One of the recent trends in painting. In its attempt to produce an art that expresses the spirit of the world of today, it does not hesitate to use some of its ugliest and most sterile objects as models: electric light bulbs, beer cans, or plaster hamburgers, for example. Its contact with the spectator is immediate, and its aim physical rather than intellectual. Its name is an abbreviation of the word "popular." Pop artists, who include Robert Rauschenberg, Peter Blake, David Hockney, Jasper Johns, and Joe Tilson, display no homogeneity of style, but bright colors, an over-all two-dimensional, decorative effect broken up by three-dimensional rendering of certain individual objects, and a sense of the expendable, are tendencies commonly found. Pop art cannot be regarded as an established school or as an end in itself. Rather it is a phase through which art is passing, comparable, for example, to Dadaism of some forty years ago.

Post-Impressionism
A term used generally of the development away from Impressionism by such painters as van Gogh, Gauguin, and Seurat. In Post-Impressionist work, subject matter regained its importance, and greater stress was placed on formal values. The term was introduced by Roger Fry and Clive Bell and became established after Fry had arranged an important exhibition in London in the winter of 1910 entitled "Manet and the Post-Impressionists."

Poussinistes
In French Academy circles of the 17th and 18th centuries, controversy arose concerning the use of color in painting. The official view adhered to the concept that drawing and design were the more important, and that color should be used merely to clarify these. Those who upheld this view were inspired by Nicolas Poussin and were therefore called Poussinistes. Their opponents, who stressed the importance of color for naturalistic reasons, took as their hero Rubens, and were known as Rubénistes.

predella paintings
The series of small paintings on the predella or base of a large altarpiece. They commonly depict scenes from the lives of the saints featured in the large panels above, or of the Holy Family. The painting of the predella panels was often entrusted to an assistant.

Pre-Raphaelite Brotherhood (P.R.B.)
A group of English artists working together in imitation of the conditions of medieval fraternities. The Pre-Raphaelite Brotherhood was formed after discussion between Holman Hunt and John Everett Millais in 1848. Engravings representing the frescoes in the Campo Santo in Pisa, by Orcagna and others, inspired the P.R.B. to return to a "purer" form of art,

(C) POP ART

(D) PRE-RAPHAELITE BROTHERHOOD

(C) PETER BLAKE
On the Balcony, 1955-57
London, Tate Gallery

(D) SIR JOHN EVERETT MILLAIS
Christ in the House of His Parents, 1850
London, Tate Gallery

such as that existing before the Renaissance. Dante Gabriel Rossetti used the initials P.R.B. on a painting he exhibited in 1849. When he revealed the meaning of the initials the following year, a storm of criticism and hysteria broke. Ruskin became the Brotherhood's spokesman and defender.

The original members were Hunt, Millais, D. G. Rossetti, William Rossetti, James Collinson, Thomas Woolner, and F. G. Stephens. The number was kept deliberately to seven, which was considered to have mystical associations. They did not remain together very long, but its mystical aspects were continued in the work of Rossetti. He, together with Morris and Burne-Jones, emphasized the influence of medieval art and subject matter.

primary colors
The basic colors — red, yellow, and blue — which can be mixed in varying combinations to produce all other colors.

priming
The preparation with which a sized panel or canvas is coated to form a smooth surface for painting. For panels, the usual priming was gesso; for canvases, white lead is employed.

primitive
An epithet that is applied to the art of peoples without a fully developed civilization. It is also used of painting—mainly Italian and Flemish—produced before about 1500. "Primitive" is applied without much discrimination to later painters of a seemingly naive and unsophisticated style, whether skilled artists such as Rousseau, or untutored Sunday painters. See **Sunday painters.**

proportion
The relation of one part to another or to the whole. The subject held a particular fascination for artists of the Early and High Renaissance in Italy. Purporting to be based on classical authority, many elaborate mathematical formulas and systems were devised and applied in the quest for ideal beauty and harmonic proportion. Alberti, Piero della Francesca, Pollaiuolo, Leonardo, and Bramante, are a few of the great artists who consciously sought to embody these theories in their work.

Purism
Considering that Cubism had become too decorative and lacking in discipline, Amédée Ozenfant and Édouard Jeanneret (Le Corbusier) issued a manifesto in 1918 entitled "After Cubism," in which they sought to re-establish art in a purified form. In this new art all fantasy, individuality, and unnecessary detail would be eliminated. In its place would appear the precision, clarity, and impersonality of the machine which became the Purists' symbol. These views were further enhanced by articles in "Élan," 1915, and "L'Esprit Nouveau," 1920-25. In practice, Purism bore a marked resemblance to Cubism, although recognizable objects were more apparent in it, and it tended to be more mechanical than dynamic. The theories bore most fruit in the later architectural work of Le Corbusier.

putto (pl. putti)
Italian: "boy." The dimpled infant that appears in many paintings and sculptures of the Renaissance and Baroque.

quadratura
A type of decoration of walls and ceilings with painted architecture and other details that gives an illusion of recession into space. The earliest example is Peruzzi's Sala delle Colonne, Villa Farnesina, Rome, of about 1516. It was popular in Bologna during the second half of the 16th century. With the Bolognese Pope Gregory XIII (1572-85), quadratura became fashionable in Rome, and from there it spread to most European countries. The most fantastic achievements of quadratura can be seen in the 18th-century Baroque buildings of Germany and Austria.

quatrefoil
From Old French: "four-leaved." A Gothic sculptural and architectural motif. It can take many forms, and can be inscribed within other shapes (circle, square, or diamond) but it must have four leaves, petals, or lobes.

QUATREFOIL

quoin
From French: *coin*: "corner." The corner of a building; the large cornerstone used in forming angles; a decorative cornerstone used in brick structures.

Rayonism
One of the earliest movements in abstract painting. It was founded by Michel Larionov in Russia in 1911-12, and appears to have links with Futurism. By the use of crossed, parallel, and diagonal lines of bright colors, like rays, it attempted to capture a fourth dimension in painting. It was seen at its most effective, however, in the brilliant décors which Larionov and his wife, Gontcharova, created for Diaghilev's "Ballets Russes."

Realism
The antithesis of idealism in art. A determination to represent objects, scenes, or figures as they are in reality, uncolored by imagination or philosophical concepts. See also **Kitchen Sink School, Social Realism.**

refectory
In monastic or collegiate buildings, the communal dining hall.

regionalism
A feeling rather than an art movement. Although not necessarily confined to any one country, it is particularly associated with the United States in the 1930's. Writers as well as artists began again to express in their works a national rather than an international or cosmopolitan spirit and pride was once more felt in portraying scenes of local character which, because of the diverse nature of the American scene, were varied and individual. Artists mainly associated with regionalism are Thomas Hart Benton, John Steuart Curry, and Grant Wood.

relief
Sculpture which is not free-standing. Reliefs have varying designations and depths of carving, such as *relievo stiacciato*, amounting to little more than a design scratched into the surface, or *alto rilievo*, in which the carving is so deep as to make the sculpture almost detached and free-standing. See also **bas-relief.**

Renaissance
The cultural revival, especially in literature and art, that took place in Italy from the 14th to the 16th centuries and spread all over Europe. This revival took as its inspiration the example of Classical Antiquity.

In the late 13th and early 14th centuries, the atmosphere favorable to the emergence of Humanism had brought about the Tuscan proto-Renaissance, in which artists such as Giotto and Nicola Pisano laid the foundations for Renaissance art. With the 15th century, the ideas crystallized and became more widely accepted. The new importance given to man and the desire to make him the focal center gave impetus to secular art, and was also responsible for the creation of centrally planned churches. Brunelleschi, Alberti, Donatello, Masaccio — the outstanding artists of the Early Renaissance — all interpreted Classical forms, ideals, and techniques and used them as a basis for their work. The High Renaissance, lasting from about 1490 to 1520, is dominated by Leonardo, Raphael, and Michelangelo. In their work art reached a zenith of balance, harmony, symmetry, and stability. A faithful representation of nature was combined with a rejection of unnecessary detail.

In Northern Europe, the Renaissance produced a new vocabulary of forms and decorative motifs taken from Italian art, at first without an understanding or real interest in its inherent principles; it is not until the 17th century, in the work of men such as François Mansart, Poussin, or Inigo Jones, that a true sense of Classic art is seen. See also **Humanism, Mannerism.**

retable
The frame enclosing carved or painted panels, placed above the back of an altar; the ledge above an altar on which the cross, candlesticks, or other furnishings are placed.

Rococo
Probably from French *rocaille*: "rock-work" or "grotto-work." An artistic style that first appeared about 1720 and gradually merged into Neoclassicism during the 1770's. Originating in France, the style was taken up by many other European countries, notably Germany and Austria. Rococo tendencies can be detected in all branches of the arts as, for example, in the painting of Fragonard, Boucher, Tiepolo; the sculpture of Günther or Falconet, the architecture of Boffrand; in metalware of the period; and in Meissen porcelain. The style is, however, at its most impressive in interior decoration. Here the fusion of architecture, sculpture, and painting presents a highly sophisticated and often frivolous abundance of gay pastel colors, curvilinear forms, grotesque motifs, stucco-work, gilding, and a marked taste for the asymmetrical. Much Rococo work can still be found in 18th-century Parisian houses.

Romanesque
A term applied to the art of Western Europe from about 1000 A.D. to 1200. Each European country had its own version of Romanesque, such as the Lombard of Italy and the Norman of England. To a certain extent, individual features and motifs are a heritage from Roman art. In Romanesque architecture is seen a new massivity of forms in the great pillars, heavy rounded arches, and geometrically patterned moldings and capitals. Sculpture was widely varied both in style and accomplishment, but on the whole, it tended to be anti-naturalistic, and often abstract. Romanesque painting tended to be crude, executed in bright, sometimes garish coloring. There is a marked linearism and flatness of forms well suited to mural decoration.

Romanticism
An attitude of mind or a style that rejects Classical ideals of reason, order, symmetry, and harmony in favor of emotion, imagination, and asymmetry. Although these tendencies found their fullest expression in the Romantic movement of the late 18th and the 19th centuries, almost all periods have produced art in which are manifested "romantic" leanings, such as an emphasis on feeling, an emotional reaction to natural phenomena, a naive hankering after a bygone age or remote culture, a sense of mystery, and a negation of realism. See also **Neo-Romanticism.**

Romantic movement
The Romantic movement, which first found expression in literature, was a force in art from about 1780 until the middle of the 19th century. Its earliest manifestation was in Germany, the greatest exponent there being the landscape painter Caspar David Friedrich. In England, the atmospheric effects of Turner and the pioneer work of Constable in capturing the ever-changing, transitory aspects of nature, put them among the greatest Romantics of Europe. In France, the effect of the movement is seen in the work of Gros, Géricault, Delacroix, Rousseau, for example. The most marked contrast to Classicist ideals is the substitution, by the Romantic painter, of feeling for reason, and this breaking through unnatural boundaries imposed by theories and tradition is expressed in a new approach to nature, seen no longer as a static background but as a living protagonist. In painting, the Romantic movement produced a new freedom of composition, open brush strokes, and a new and subtly graded color range.

rood, rood loft, rood screen
In medieval churches, the rood, or crucifix, was placed at the junction of chancel and nave, often being flanked by free-standing figures of the Virgin and St. John. It could be suspended, but more often rested on the rood loft, a gallery stretching across the width of the chancel, which itself was supported by the rood beam. Between the rood beam and the floor was an open, often elaborately carved screen, the rood screen, which served to divide the east and west parts of the church. In Roman Catholic Spain, the rood structures are at their most elaborate, but very few remained in England after their denunciation by Queen Elizabeth I in 1561.

rotulus
An early type of manuscript in the form of a long roll. It was usually illuminated by pictures in continuous succession and, when opened, gave a panoramic effect.

Rubénistes
See **Poussinistes.**

sacra conversazione
Italian: "sacred conversation." A type of religious picture that appeared about the middle of the 15th century in Florence. In it, the Madonna and Child are placed in the center of a group of angels and saints. Whereas formerly the dividing frames of the polyptych altarpiece had separated the sacred personages, in the sacra conversazione they are on one large panel, related to one another by action, gesture, or emotion. Thus the human attributes of the figures are stressed. Fra Angelico's altarpiece for the Convent of S. Marco, Florence, 1438-40, is one of the earliest examples of the type.

salon
An exhibition of paintings and sculpture held annually in Paris by the Société des Artistes

(A) PUTTO

(B) ROCOCO

(A) ANDREA DEL VEROCCHIO
Putto with a Dolphin, about 1480
Florence, Palazzo della Signoria

(B) JEAN HONORÉ FRAGONARD
The Swing, about 1766
London, Wallace Collection

(A) SARCOPHAGUS

(B) SFUMATO

(C) SOCIAL REALISM

(A) Sarcophagus, 3rd century A.D.
Rome, Lateran Museum

(B) LEONARDO DA VINCI
Detail from: St. John the Baptist, 1503-13
Paris, Louvre

(C) DIEGO RIVERA
Detail from: The Workers' Revolution 1929-35
Mexico City, Palacio Nacional

Français. Its origins go back to 1667 when the first exhibition of this kind, organized under the auspices of Louis XIV's finance minister Colbert, was held in the Louvre to display the work of living artists who were members of the Royal Academy of Painting and Sculpture. A number of other salons are also held in Paris as, for example, the Salon d'Automne.

sanguine
A reddish, soft-textured chalk used as a drawing material, especially popular in the 18th century.

sarcophagus
From Greek: "flesh-eater." A stone coffin ornamented with reliefs, paintings, or inscriptions. The name was derived from the use of a particular kind of limestone that was said to consume flesh. In ancient Egypt mummies cased in a series of coffins, one within the other, were finally placed in sarcophagi.

school
The country of origin of a work of art, regardless of period or artist, for example, French School. More specifically it refers to a limited area in a particular country, for example, Sienese School, or to a style that covers a certain epoch, for example, School of Fontainebleau. It can also be applied to the assistants or pupils of a particular painter, for example, School of Raphael.

scumbling
The working of an opaque layer of oil color over a previous layer, usually lighter in color, in such a way that the lower layer remains partially visible. This gives an uneven textural effect. The technique was much favored by Rembrandt.

Scuola Metafisica
See **Pittura Metafisica.**

secondary colors
The colors purple, green, and orange. Each is obtained by mixing two of the primary colors (red, blue, and yellow).

Section d'Or Group
The name adopted by a group of artists for an exhibition in 1912 at La Boétie Gallery, Paris, which featured the work of all important Cubists except Braque and Picasso. Jacques Villon was the prime mover in organizing the exhibition which had a marked avant-garde success. The name is also extended to the group itself.

sepia
A brownish pigment extracted from the dark liquid secreted by the cuttlefish. It can be used for wash drawings or for pen and ink sketches.

Sezession
German: "Secession." The name given to groups of artists in different cities in Germany and Austria who renounced and withdrew from the official academic societies or exhibitions in order to associate themselves with more advanced movements and stylistic innovations. Their work was linked with Impressionism and Art Nouveau. The Munich Sezession took place in 1892, the Vienna in 1897, and the Berlin in 1899.

sfregazzi
From Italian *sfregare*: "to rub." A method used by painters of rubbing a glaze shadow over flesh colors with the finger.

sfumato
From Italian *sfumare*: "to tone down; to disappear; evaporate; blend." Sfumato relates to a concept of Leonardo in which he advocated the gradual dissolution of outline of objects by a subtle series of color changes or graduations of shading. Thus the edges appeared slightly hazy and blurred or "smoky," enhancing the plastic, three-dimensional qualities of the object or figure.

sgraffito (pl. sgraffiti)
See **graffito.**

silk screen printing
A method of printing widely used for works that are not too finely detailed and for which comparatively few copies are required, such as posters or show cards. It is cheap and requires very little outlay in equipment. A stencil is placed on a piece of silk stretched over a wooden frame. Ink, of a thick, paint-like consistency, is forced through the silk and passes through the cut-out design of the stencil onto the surface to be printed. Separate stencils are used for different colors. Sometimes photography is utilized to transfer more detailed designs onto the screen.

silverpoint
A drawing technique frequently used during the 15th and early 16th centuries in Italy, Germany, and the Netherlands. The drawing was made with a metal point on paper that had been specially prepared with a white opaque ground, which was usually tinted. The line drawn with a silver point is a delicate gray in color and is indelible. Gold and lead points were also sometimes used. White highlights could be applied to the finished drawing with a brush for greater effect.

simultaneous representation
A basically primitive approach to pictorial representation in which several views of an object or person are shown at the same time. It must, of necessity, be a flattening-out, two-dimensional process. Its history extends from ancient Egyptian painting to some aspects of Cubism.

size
A composition of glue and water, used for sealing canvases before they are primed.

Paper can also be coated with size in order to obtain a particular kind of ground.

sketch
A preparatory drawing, painting, or model for sculpture, usually of a schematic nature, used by the artist in order to determine the intended scale, composition, or lighting effects of the final work. A landscape painter frequently makes rapid sketches out of doors in the lighting conditions he wishes to depict. These may then be worked up to scale in the studio. Preliminary sketches are also employed in portrait painting.

Sketches may be used for reference by students or assistants collaborating with the artist, as, for example, in the workshops of masters like Raphael or Rubens.

Social Realism
An art that portrays subjects taken from the everyday working life of ordinary people. It came very much into prominence in French painting about the middle of the 19th century. Although its existence has continued spasmodically since that time, the impact of this type of subject matter has been lessened by familiarity. In the work of the Kitchen Sink School, for example, the pathos of a situation is often exploited for its own sake. A notable exception to the diminishing potency and force of this art is the work produced in Mexico by the Social Realist painters Diego Rivera and José Orozco. Renato Guttuso's *Sulfur Miners in Sicily*, 1949, in the Tate Gallery, London, is a fine modern example of Social Realist art.

Soft Style
A form of the International Gothic style in painting that appeared in Germany, especially in the Cologne area, at the end of the 14th century. The style is characterized by its flowing linear rhythms, rich decorative motifs, and soft, gentle mood. The most common subject was the Virgin and Child seated in a garden in full flower. Stefan Lochner was its leading exponent.

spandrel
The triangular space between the outer curve of an arch and the right angle formed by a line drawn horizontally from its apex and vertically through its springing.

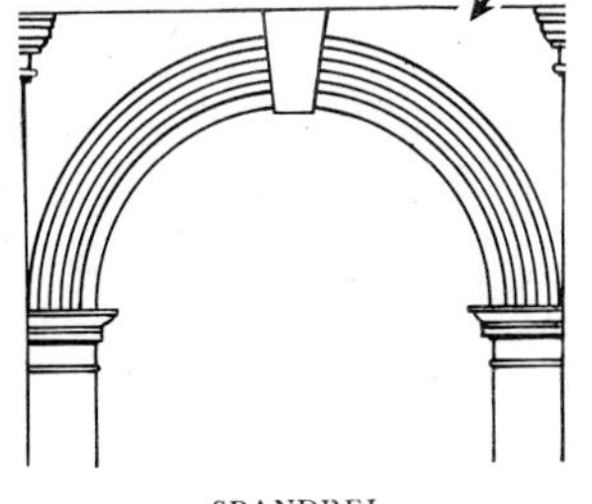

SPANDREL

stained glass
Glass colored by fusion with metallic oxides, generally used decoratively in windows, especially in churches. The pieces of colored glass are joined by strips of lead which form an important element in the design. The origins of stained glass are obscure, and its use for storiated windows dates only from about the mid-11th century A.D. The peak in this art was reached between 1150 and 1250, as can be seen, for example, in Chartres Cathedral, France. In the 16th century a new method of producing stained glass was developed: enamel colors were painted onto the glass which was then fired. In the following centuries, a debased form of the art was practiced. Traditional methods were revived in the 19th century, but the colors were generally less rich and clear than in the Middle Ages. Examples of modern stained-glass design are in the new Coventry Cathedral, England.

stanza (pl. stanze)
Italian: "room." In art, "stanze" normally refers to the series of rooms in the Vatican, Rome, decorated with frescoes by Raphael and his school between 1509 to 1520 for Popes Julius II and Leo X.

Stijl, De
Dutch: "The Style." An art movement of painters, architects, and sculptors formed in Holland in 1917 by Mondrian, van Doesburg, van der Leck, Oud, van 't Off, and Vantongerloo. In October of that year, the review "De Stijl" was instituted to give expression to the new ideas that, starting from Cubism, reduced natural forms, rhythms, and relationships to geometrical patterns in order to achieve works of fundamental harmonies and universal elements. The theories and practice of De Stijl, called Neo-Plasticism after 1920, had a profound effect on modern painting and architecture everywhere. See also **Neo-Plasticism.**

Stile Liberty
One name under which Art Nouveau was known in Italy. The name was derived from Liberty's, a store in London which made a point of stocking and displaying materials and colors for Art Nouveau decorative schemes. See also **Art Nouveau.**

still-life
Painting which has as its subject inanimate objects. Of very ancient origins, still-life is found, for example, in ancient Egyptian tomb paintings, in the depiction of food used as offerings in ancient Greece, and in Roman mural and panel paintings. It emerged as a subject in its own right during the 16th century, but even then was endowed with much religious and moral symbolism, as in the memento mori reminding the beholder emphatic-

(D) SOFT STYLE

(E) DE STIJL

(D) STEFAN LOCHNER
The Madonna of the Rose Bower
Cologne, Wallraf-Richartz-Museum

(E) Cover of De Stijl catalog No. 81

(A) STUCCO

(B) STUDY

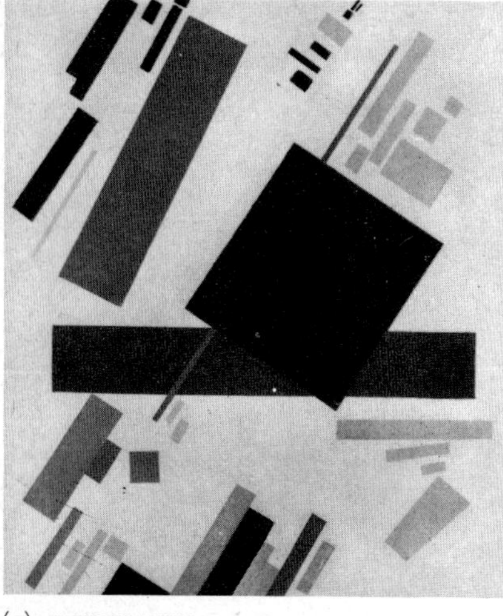

(C) SUPREMATISM

ally of his mortal state. Artists of Northern Europe, particularly the Netherlands, have always shown a great flair for the depiction of objects based on meticulous observation, and it is in these countries during the 17th century that still-life painting moved forward appreciably, both in naturalism and in attractiveness. It reached new aesthetic levels in the work of Chardin in the 18th and Cézanne in the 19th century. In modern art it has not only provided the most popular basis for experiments in abstraction, as in the work of Braque, but has also been continued representationally in the work of the Kitchen Sink School. See also **vanitas, memento mori, Kitchen Sink School.**

stipple
To build up and model a drawing by means of many strokes or dots.

stretcher
The adjustable wooden frame, on which the painter stretches his canvas; in architecture, a brick set lengthwise into the surface of a wall.

stucco
A fine plaster, usually composed of gypsum and pulverized marble, frequently used in interior architectural and sculptural decorations, and sometimes as a ground for relief modeling and fresco decoration. Stucco of a coarser composition is also used externally for architectural decoration and to simulate stone. Stucco was in use in antique Rome. It was revived during the Renaissance period, and has been used widely since, especially during the 17th and 18th centuries.

study
Careful drawings of details such as drapery, foliage, or parts of the body, made for reference or for integrating into a large finished composition.

stump
A tightly rolled piece of chamois leather or paper, pointed at one end, with which drawings in pastel, chalk, pencil, or charcoal are rubbed to soften or blend tones.

Stürm, Der
German: "The Storm." A magazine in newspaper format founded in 1910 by Herwarth Walden. Although originally intended for literary criticism, it soon became a vital influence in art. The young Kokoschka, the artists of Die Brücke and Der Blaue Reiter, Kandinsky, and Klee made contributions to the magazine. From March, 1912, it sponsored the Stürm-Galerie, where a series of exhibitions were held that helped to spread knowledge of contemporary German painting centered in Berlin. In the years preceding World War I, Der Stürm made contact with most of the great exponents of modern art. After the war, although its activities were extended by the Stürm school, theater, and bookstore, it was no longer in the avant garde.

Style Guimard
The name under which Art Nouveau was known in France. It derives from Hector Guimard (1867-1942), the French architect, whose best work was a block of flats at 16 Rue de la Fontaine, in the Passy section of Paris, built between 1894 and 1898, and his Paris Métro stations of about 1900. See also **Art Nouveau.**

stylization
In art, the execution of a work in accordance with a given convention.

Sunday painter
A modern term used to describe the non-professional and largely untutored artist who paints purely as a hobby.

Suprematism
A movement, founded by Kasimir Malevich in Moscow in 1913, that lasted until the 1920's. It advocated a purely abstract art based on the simple elements of the circle, rectangle, triangle, and cross. The first example produced was a perfect black square on a white background. All later art based on geometrical abstraction is indebted to Suprematism. Its adherents included Rodchenko, Puni Rosanova, and Lissitzky.

Surrealism
The name given by Guillaume Apollinaire in 1924 to the type of 20th-century art that is virtually the pictorial expression of the subconscious mind. The Dadaists prepared much of the way for the Surrealists who, with their seemingly irrational juxtaposition of unrelated objects, or their placing of an ordinary object in the sphere of the extraordinary, attempted to intimate in their art a world beyond perceptible reality. Because of the supreme importance of the artist's own vision, Surrealist art is probably more individual than any other, so that homogeneity of style is not very evident in the work of such exponents as Picasso, Tanguy, Dali, Arp, Ernst, or Duchamp. See also **found object.**

Symbolist Painters
In France, a movement formed in 1889 by Émile Bernard and Paul Sérusier, in reaction against both the Impressionist and Realist schools of painting. Taking their orientation from contemporary poets such as Baudelaire, Mallarmé, and Verlaine, they sought to express ideas, emotions, and states of mind by symbolic objects, figures, patterns, and color. Gauguin disassociated himself from the group, while Gustave Moreau and Puvis de Chavannes, although close in feeling, never actually belonged to it. Odilon Redon, with his highly personal and fantastic vision, is probably the truest Symbolist of all.

Synchromists
Two American painters, Morgan Russel (1886-1953) and Stanton Macdonald-Wright (born 1890), who exhibited in Paris and Munich in 1913 and in New York a year later. Their concepts, deriving from Orphism, advocated the use of pure color in geometrical shapes to evoke rhythm, expression, and spatial dynamism. See also **Orphism.**

Synthetic Cubism
The last phase in the Cubist movement, lasting from about 1912 to 1914. It is marked by a return to the use of color, a richness of pattern and design, and a further move toward abstraction in order to capture the essence rather than the visual aspect of objects. Gris and Léger were particularly active in this phase. See also **Cubism.**

tabernacle
A place of worship of temporary character; in certain sects, a church for regular worship; a type of cupboard with doors, or a recess, in Roman Catholic churches for conserving the Host; a decorative recess containing a religious statue. In medieval architecture, the highly decorated niches, canopies, or similar embellishments of church furniture or plate, are known as tabernacle work.

TABERNACLE

tachisme
See **action painting.**

tactile values
The qualities whereby a painting or drawing evokes a sense of touch, as would the represented object itself if handled. This quality was first identified and named by Bernard Berenson.

tan-ye
Japanese paintings characterized by red lead pigment.

tanzaku
Japanese term for a relatively narrow vertical print, generally about 14×6 in., embellished with verses of poetry.

t'a p'ien
A Chinese method of taking inked impressions from inscriptions on stone or bronze statuary. It may have been a first step toward the invention of printing.

Tatlinism
See **Constructivism**

tempera
A painting medium made by mixing ground-up pigment with a binding agent and diluting with water. The binder can be varied —beeswax, gum arabic, or casein— for example, but the most common is egg yolk or egg yolk and white together. Egg tempera, the general medium of panel painting in medieval Europe, was superseded during the 15th century by one utilizing an oil glaze, and from this developed oil painting. Tempera painting is firm and durable, but it requires special handling since it dries so rapidly that re-touching is almost impossible. Also, the colors become several shades lighter when dry.

temple
A building used as a place of worship for any religious creed, but not normally those serving the Christian or Muslim faiths. Exceptions are the Christian churches of the Knights Templar and the Utah temples of the Mormons in America. The most common usage is in connection with the pagan temples of ancient Greece and Rome.

Ten, The
A group of painters from New York and Boston who first exhibited together in 1895. They were Thomas Dewing, Frank Benson, J. Alder Weir, Willard Metcalf, Childe Hassam, Edmund Tarbell, Joseph de Camp, John Twatchman, E. E. Simmons, and Robert Reid. During the closing years of the 19th century, they represented an anti-academic force with their Impressionist style derived from Monet. By refinement they evolved their own palette of quiet, pale tones.

Tenebrists
Italian *tenebroso*: "dark; murky; gloomy." A term applied to certain 17th-century painters, mostly from Spain, Naples, and the Netherlands, who took Caravaggio as their model. They adopted and intensified his marked chiaroscuro and specialized in interior night scenes, such as of taverns, in which light emanates from a candle, fire, or single lamp, casting mysterious shadows and spot-lighting parts of the bodies and faces of the figures. The tenebrists were never an organized group and rarely reached a high aesthetic standard, but they were extremely popular throughout the first third of the 17th century.

terracotta
Italian: "cooked earth." A material, obtained by baking fine earth, which varies in color from pale pink to deep red-brown. Because it is easy to handle and lasting when set, it is favored for much modeling, ceramic work, and architectural decoration. Terracotta was widely used on architecture in Northern Italy and Northern Europe during the late 16th and early 17th centuries.

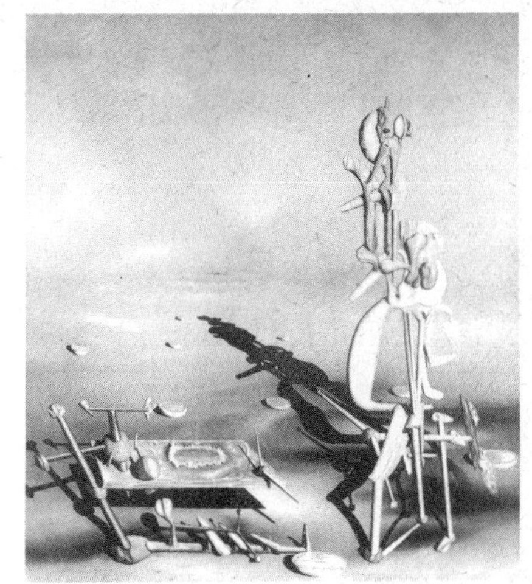

(D) SURREALISM

(E) SYMBOLIST PAINTERS

(A) PRIMATICCIO
Chimneypiece
Fontainebleau, Palace, Francis I Salon

(B) RAPHAEL
Detail from: Venus and Psyche, about 1516
Paris, Louvre

(C) KASIMIR MALEVICH
Blue Rectangle over Purple Bar, 1915
Amsterdam, Stedelijk Museum

(D) YVES TANGUY
Divisibilité Indéfinie, 1942
Buffalo, N. Y., Albright-Knox Art Gallery

(E) ODILON REDON
Le Regard
London, Private Collection

(A) TONDO

(B) UKIYO-E

(A) MICHELANGELO
The Holy Family, 1504
Florence, Uffizi

(B) SUZUKI HARUNOBU
Courtesan with Attendants, about 1770
Tokyo, National Museum, et al.

terre verte
French: "green earth." A clay containing iron and manganese, used as a pigment, particularly in mural painting, and also as a glaze for ceramics. One of the most ancient of pigments, its facility in handling and permanency has made it popular at least since Classical Antiquity. Several names, such as Cyprian, Bohemian, Verona, Tyrolean, are applied to describe its various forms which, in color, range from yellow-green to pure green, blue-green, or gray-green.

tessera (pl. tesserae)
The small cubes of stone, glass, or marble, of which a mosaic is composed.

theater
A place set apart for the presentation of dramatic, musical, or other performances. The history of the theater can be traced back at least as far as the classical Greek era. Although the theater need be little more than an open space with rising terraces about a central platform, it is usually a building constructed specifically for performances. Theatrical scenery has often influenced taste and fashion in art, as for example, in the Baroque and Rococo periods. In modern times Diaghilev, in his "Ballets Russes," 1909-29, created an inseparable fusion of the elements of painting, movement, and form.

tondo
Italian: "round." A circular picture or relief. The tondo was at its most popular in Florence during the late 15th and early 16th centuries.

tone
The general effect of a painting in terms of gradation from light to dark; the various gradations within a single color.

topography
The description of a particular place or locality. In art, an exact representation of an identifiable place is not necessarily aesthetically sound. In 15th-century Flemish art, a certain pleasure was derived from recognizable details in landscape and background. Great artists, however, mostly prefer to approach landscape intellectually and to select visually and aesthetically satisfying features from it to construct their pictures.

tracery
The type of patterning in Gothic window architecture that arises from the decorative treatment of the stone mullions and ribs. Window tracery developed out of "plate tracery" which virtually amounts to the punching out of a pattern in the solid stonework of the upper part of a window, a development first seen in France toward the middle of the 13th century. Tracery also indicates patterned framework and paneling on vaults, screens, or walls.

TRACERY

transept
The part of a cruciform church that corresponds to the transverse part of the cross. Some churches have double transepts.

trascoro
In a Spanish church the space sometimes left behind the high altar or choir.

trefoil
A form of decorative motif found in medieval architecture and sculpture. Though widely varied, it always has three lobes, heads, petals, or cusps.

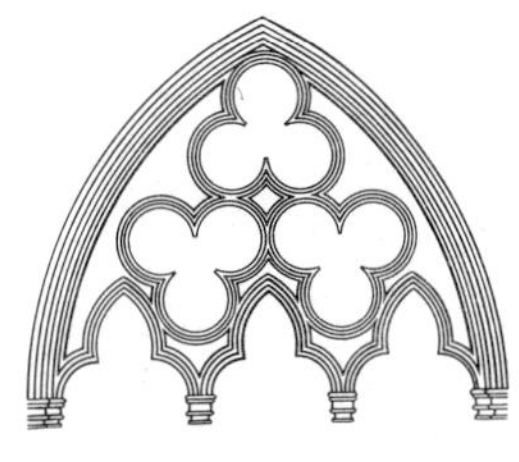

TREFOIL

tribune
In a basilican church or similar secular structure, the semi-circular or polygonal apse; a raised platform, pulpit, or dais; an elevated area with seats in a gallery of a church.

triforium
In a Gothic church, the gallery above the side aisles of the nave, opening onto the nave through an arcade between the nave arcade and the clerestory. The term was for many years used exclusively in connection with Canterbury Cathedral, England. The triforium is a decorative rather than a functional part of the structure.

triptych
A panel painting or relief, usually an altarpiece, in three parts. The center panel is often twice the width of the wings, which can be folded over it. For this reason, the backs as well as the fronts of the wings are painted.

trompe l'œil
French: "deceives the eye." Painting in which still-life objects are so realistically rendered that they appear three-dimensional and tangible. Netherlandish artists were particularly skillful at this and usually achieved it by empirical means rather than by the application of scientific theories of perspective. In modern art, *trompe l'œil* is used in collage works, where an actual piece of material,

such as fabric or wood, may be stuck onto the picture surface.

tympanum
The feature above a doorway occupying the space between the lintel and the enclosing arch. The term is also applied to the triangular area of a pediment above the frieze and below the apex. A less common meaning is the die or cubic portion of a pedestal.

uchiwa-ye
Japanese pictures shaped as fans.

uki-ye
Japanese prints that utilize the Western type of perspective to give an effect of three-dimensionality.

ukiyo-e
Japanese: "mirror of the transient world." Japanese prints showing everyday scenes of people at work or at their leisure. This form of popular art emerged in the 17th century. The prints, made from wood blocks, were at first in black and white. Printing in a range of colors was developed in the 18th century. Utamaro, Hokusai, and Hiroshige were the most famous artists associated with this form that lasted into the 19th century.

ultramarine
A pigment for painting obtained by grinding the blue stone lapis lazuli and removing from it the gray rock. The pigment is of a very rich blue and permanent in use. From the 12th century it was highly prized by artists. More costly than gold leaf, it was usually reserved for very special parts of a painting, such as the Madonna's robe. Nowadays the color is manufactured from other ingredients. During the process a deviation, green ultramarine, can also be obtained.

umber
A pigment widely used in painting that derives from earth containing manganese dioxide as well as the normal iron oxides. When raw, its color range is from dark to greenish brown. When roasted (burnt umber) it takes on reddish tints. The best known type, Turkey umber, comes from Cyprus.

underpainting
The layer of paint on a picture in which details of composition, tone, and modeling of the finished work are set. These details are almost always painted in grisaille and are covered by the final application of color.

Utrecht School
The name given to a group of painters led by Honthorst, Terbrugghen, and Baburen, who settled in Utrecht, Holland, about 1620 after spending some years in Rome. They took back with them the more obvious aspects of Caravaggio's art, his marked chiaroscuro effects of artificial lighting and localized colors, and added it to their own repertoire and taste for genre scenes. Their fondness for indoor scenes spotlit by candlelight earned them the name of the "Candlelight Painters." They were popular with Dutch bourgeois patrons, and although sometimes their work tends to be repetitive, it is usually endowed with a lusty, vigorous quality all its own. The school also produced religious works and was responsible for the spread of Caravaggio's influence throughout Holland. Many of the extraneous aspects of Rembrandt's art relate to the Utrecht School.

values
In painting, values of tone are established in the relationship of one part of the work to the other, regardless of the actual color of the object involved. Color values, on the other hand, depend on the significance of each area of color to the whole work, and a combination of the two must be considered in the appraisal of a picture.

vanishing point
The point at which parallel lines appear to meet on the horizon. Artists who experimented with perspective in the 15th century came to use a single vanishing point. Later artists came to the conclusion that several vanishing points were necessary in a single work in order to capture the reality of the natural world. See also **perspective.**

vanitas
Latin: "emptiness; deception; nothingness." A form of still-life painting very popular in the 17th century, representing objects symbolic of human mortality, such as a skull, book, candle, or hour-glass. The type no doubt derived from the earlier memento mori subjects and symbols. See also **memento mori, still-life.**

varnish
A protective film applied to paintings, sculpture, and other works. It is normally composed of a resinous substance mixed with oil.

vault
The self-supporting structure covering a building, usually constructed of stone or brick; a room covered by a vault; often, by extension, subterranean structures such as catacombs.

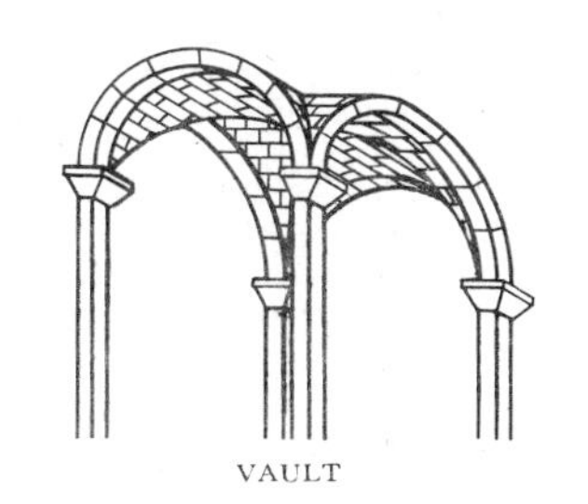

VAULT

veduta (pl. vedute)
Italian: "view; sight; prospect." The pictorial representation of a particular place, much

(C) UTRECHT SCHOOL

(D) VEDUTA

(E) VEDUTA

(C) HENDRICK TERBRUGGHEN
The Calling of St. Matthew, 1621
Utrecht, Holland, Centraal Museum der Gemeente

(D) FRANCESCO GUARDI
Venice, the Punta della Dogana with S. Maria della Salute
London, National Gallery

(E) HUBERT ROBERT
Le Pont du Gard, 1787
Paris, Louvre

applied in the 18th century to views of Venice and Rome, as for example in the works of Canaletto.

vellum
A very fine leather obtained from the skin of lambs, calves, and goats. It is reserved mainly for book-binding. The same type of skin, when treated differently, can be used for writing. In this form it is commonly known as parchment. Sheets of vellum dusted with chalk are also used in the process of making gold leaf.

Venetian red
An orange-red pigment obtained from earth containing up to 40 per cent iron oxide. Since the mid-19th century it has been produced by chemical means. It is permanent, forms a very firm surface, and is much used for oil painting.

Verism
An objective, anti-Expressionistic movement in German painting that arose during the 1920's. Its members included Otto Dix, Georg Grosz, and Georg Scholz. Radical in feeling, and bearing unmistakable implications of social criticism, it provided a contrast to the contemporary, more romantic aspect of realism seen in the work of Kanoldt, Schrimpf, and Mense.

view finder
A device for ascertaining the field of vision that is to be shown in a picture. A simple example is a board from which has been cut a piece corresponding proportionately to the canvas to be painted. When held to the eye, the form and composition of the proposed work can be calculated.

vignette
A small, decorative device used to fill in blank spaces in book design, as, for example, at the end of a chapter; small pictures, book illustrations, or photographs whose edges gradually shade away.

villa
Originally a country residence, usually with a farm or farm buildings attached. It was a common type of Roman dwelling, of which many important examples remain. During the Renaissance, the word came to mean a house surrounded by its own gardens, used mainly for pleasure; many of Palladio's villas, however, were provided with farm buildings. The modern sense of the word is a medium-sized house within reach of a town, or a summer residence.

Vingt, Les
See **Les XX.**

Vorticism
An English art movement led by Wyndham Lewis which lasted from about 1912 to 1915. In feeling, it was anti-Impressionist, taking its orientation from Cubism and, particularly, Futurism with its dedication to the rhythms and forms of the machine. The works of the movement show flat, geometric lines and arcs radiating from one salient point, the vortex, giving the effect of rotary and often vertiginous motion. Participants in Vorticism included the writer Ezra Pound, Epstein, Gaudier-Brzeska, William Roberts, Edward Wadsworth, and C. R. Nevinson. It was associated with the review "Blast," which had only two issues, in 1914 and 1915. The sole Vorticist exhibition was held at the Dore Gallery in 1916. World War I virtually brought the movement to an end, but it holds an important place in the establishment of abstract painting in England.

wall painting
See **mural.**

warm colors
Colors such as yellow, red, reddish browns, orange, or purple, which strike a warm note in a painting, as opposed to the cool effect of blues.

wash drawing
A drawing in which washes of color are used either alone or in conjunction with other media.

wax painting
See **encaustic painting.**

white lead
One of the most ancient of artificially produced paint pigments, derived from lead carbonate. It mixes easily with oils and is reasonably stable. White lead often darkens due to contact with the hydrogen sulfide found in air. For this reason, many Renaissance paintings and drawings in which it was used have deteriorated.

woodcut
See **engraving.**

wood engraving
See **engraving.**

workshop production
The method of picture production formerly used in the workshops of master painters. A number of assistants and apprentices would participate on a work, each being assigned a particular part. One might specialize in the landscape parts, another in draperies, and so on, the master adding finishing touches and signing the work as proof of its authenticity. Rubens and van Dyck, for example, were able to achieve their tremendous output by methods of this sort.

W.P.A. Project
Works Progress Administration Federal Arts Project. An organization which was set up by the United States government in 1935 to provide relief for unemployed artists during the Depression. By 1936, 5000 artists and sculptors were engaged on producing works of art to decorate government buildings in return for a regular salary. The first exhibition was held at the Museum of Modern Art, New York, in that year. Although all types of art were included, the project was particularly the means of bringing about a new interest in mural painting. Ben Shahn, Frank Mecaan, Arshile Gorky, and Jackson Pollock are among the many artists having some association with the project.

wrinkling
Damage to the surface of an oil painting caused most commonly by shrinkage in one of the layers of the underpainting. Wrinkling is often due to faulty paint-mixing technique, or to atmospheric conditions.

yellow ocher
An earth color. It gives a permanent yellow in a wide range of shades. See also **earth colors, ocher.**

yoko-ye
A type of Japanese print.

Index

HOW TO LOOK AT ART

Names in italics indicate titles
Numbers in italics indicate reproductions
Names in parenthesis indicate locations

7209 28